Dear Nancy —

You are so amazing!

Acting Teachers of America: A Vital Tradition
Ronald Rand & Luigi Scorcia

Thank you —
Thank you —
I can't begin to tell
you how wonderful
you are —
Wishing you so much joy
& lots of love!!
Warmly, Ron
Ronald Rand
2009   June 15th

Acting Teachers of America: A Vital Tradition
Ronald Rand & Luigi Scorcia

11   10   09   08   07   5   4   3   2   1

Published by Allworth Press
An imprint of Allworth Communications, Inc.
10 East 23rd Street, New York, NY 10010

Cover design by Derek Bacchus
Interior design by Mary Belibasakis
Page composition/typography by SR Desktop Services, Ridge, NY
Cover photos by Luigi Scorcia

Library of Congress Cataloging-in-Publication Data
    Rand, Ronald.
    Acting teachers of America: a vital tradition / Ronald Rand & Luigi Scorcia.
        p.   cm.
    Includes index.
    ISBN-13: 978-1-58115-473-3 (pbk.)
    ISBN-10: 1-58115-473-9 (pbk.)
        1. Acting—Study and teaching—United States.   2. Acting teachers—
United States—Interviews.   I. Scorcia, Luigi.   II. Title.

PN2078.U6R36   2007
792.02'807073—dc22

                                                        2006035277

Printed in Canada

*Dedicated to
every acting teacher who has shaped another's life,
including my own teachers, Stella Adler and Harold Clurman;
to my loving parents, Jay and Marilyn;
and to the theater—which sustains our life.*

CONTENTS

40
MAGGIE FLANIGAN
Kadee Strickland

44
JULIE GARFIELD
Jill Bianchini

48
KATHRYN GATELY
James Gandolfini

52
MICHAEL HOWARD
Boyd Gaines

57
ZINA JASPER
Betsy Aidem

62
MILTON KATSELAS
Doris Roberts

67
ED KOVENS
Bethany Butler

71
BARBARA MACKENZIE-WOOD
Megan Hilty

75
JOANNA MERLIN
Dawn Arnold

80
ROBERT X. MODICA
John Turturro

84
ERIC MORRIS
Joan Hotchkis

89
GEORGE MORRISON
Gene Hackman

94
LARRY MOSS
Pamela Gien

100
ELIZABETH PARRISH
Robbie Sublett

104
ROBERT PATTERSON
Jo Beth Williams

108
CAROL FOX PRESCOTT
Libby Skala

114
JOANNA ROTTÉ
Saxon Trainor

118
TERRY SCHREIBER
Edward Norton

123
SANDE SHURIN
Jicky Schnee

128
MELISSA SMITH
Daniel Beaty

133
ROBIN LYNN SMITH
Kate Wisniewski

138
ALICE SPIVAK
James Dale

ACKNOWLEDGMENTS

This book rose out of the many conversations Luigi Scorcia and I had together. His unquenchable drive, sense of humor, and unending enthusiasm made our collaboration a blessing and a joy. I know you will agree the beautiful photographs captured by this gifted artist provide a moving and visual record for all time.

There are also very special individuals whose support, guidance, passion, and love contributed to make this book possible.

Tad Crawford, the founder of Allworth Press, and Nicole Potter-Talling recognized the value of *Acting Teachers of America*, and its potential to touch lives and open minds. Nicole especially always guided me forward with a firm eye and a very warm heart.

Katie Ellison was a blessing who shared with me her rich editorial skills and abundant advice; Cynthia Rivelli, Michael Madole, and Nana Greller's care and expertise lead this book forward toward further recognition.

Jay and Marilyn, my parents, and Janice, my sister, have showered me with their unwavering love, support, and encouragement.

J. Michael Miller's enduring vision of what we're truly capable of, his rich generosity of spirit, and the beautiful foreword he has written to this book are a huge inspiration to me.

Gregory Abels' deep well of understanding and his beautiful embrace of my work has meant so much to my continuing growth and creativity.

Steven and Alida Brill Scheuer's embracing love continues to enrich me as a human being.

Lauren Bond's gentleness of spirit, warmth, and insight have been invaluable assets to the heart and soul of this book; I remain endlessly grateful.

Joanna Rotte and Libby Skala's artistry and 'light' is inspiring.

Joan Micklin Silver's vision and her faith in me touches my soul every day.

Gwen Bucci, Marilise Tronto, Wendy Neuss, and Karen De Mauro's encouragement and insights have been exceedingly important.

Nora and Emily, in a time known.

For their rich gifts of art and sharing; for their time and energies—thank you to the featured teachers, actors, and actresses. They see that this book can be an important contributing force for our culture. For feeding the soul of the world, Luigi and I remain eternally grateful.

—Ronald Rand

This book was a path of learning for me—about myself. I believe that all you have to do in life is take action; it's that simple. What you do defines who you are. The journey with Ron was one of integrity.

While doing this book, I became more appreciative of the art of acting; it's a skill, a craft. It's beautiful to see a teacher trying to get through to a student. The teacher cares so much, like a surrogate parent.

As a photographer, capturing the art of acting being taught, I saw that sometimes no words had to be said. The hands told the story.

—Luigi Scorcia

AUTHOR'S NOTE

What is a vital tradition? How do we describe it?

Is it something that sustains us from one generation to the next? Does it serve as an invaluable part of who we are?

The fifty unique individuals in this book have, each in his or her own way, significantly contributed to the tradition of actor training in America and many different areas in the performing arts throughout the world.

Their impact cannot be measured merely by the fame or success achieved by their students. One must also appreciate how these mentors helped their students grow into active members of our community, who serve our society by telling us the truth about who we are.

It is my hope and desire that this collection of interviews will make us more aware of this incredibly important tradition of actor training in this country (and a second volume containing another fifty teachers, as it was impossible to include everyone I wanted to in this book).

When I first began to act at six years old, it was fun—and continues to be today as I travel and perform across the country and around the world in my own solo play. Acting is make-believe. It's play—as well as an art form—as old as the cave drawings that line the walls deep underground in France, and no doubt even older.

Of course, "role-playing" isn't an activity reserved for children or performers. We all find ourselves in life having to "act" at times; we play different roles. Roles we may not always be aware of. Roles we may not desire or, at other times, choose. We wear "masks" in life to protect ourselves. Sometimes we even shut ourselves off from feeling. But actors must be vulnerable, reveal their innermost feelings and thoughts, and produce them on demand for hours at a time or in a single instant. This requires craft.

While there are those who are born with a gift to be "natural" in front of others, if it is an actor's desire to assay a great role, transform himself into someone else, or understand the intricacies of a writer's creation and truly touch an audience, being "natural" is not enough. Training becomes necessary—because the actor's body, voice, and speech, his or her entire heart and soul, are all meanings of expression.

I was fortunate to have had teachers who inspired me with their unique perception and vision of what it means to be human. You could never wish for two more inspiring teachers than Stella Adler and Harold Clurman. I was nourished in ways that are almost impossible to describe; these teachers imparted to me a larger vista of what is possible in the theater.

Like Adler and Clurman, the teachers in this book provide their students with artistic sustenance. Although the opinions and beliefs expressed in these interviews are diverse, all of these teachers have devoted themselves to passing on the vital tradition of the art of acting.

I am very excited about the extraordinary photographs by Luigi Scorcia within the pages of this book, which provide us with a unique glimpse of each teacher caught in action.

Following each teacher interview is a brief interview with a former or current student that the teacher personally chose for me to talk with. The students add a unique perspective, speaking about what they learned, what the teacher's technique meant to their development as actors, and how they have actually applied it in their own work.

Every day the ground shifts; every day we're presented with new challenges. But we each, in our own way, have the capacity to grow—to learn more about ourselves and, through our talents, make this world a better place to live in.

These teachers continue to inspire—through their love and knowledge—the vital tradition of actor training, and—through their humanity and passion—the art of acting.

—Ronald Rand

FOREWORD BY J. MICHAEL MILLER

The storyteller, impersonator, shaman, priest—roles that have been intertwined for thousands of years—were an essential presence in every culture. The continuing revelation of the possibilities of our own humanity, the seeming miracle of our own survival in a world controlled by the forces of nature, led not only to an understanding of ourselves, but to a reoccurring need to give credence to those things one could not explain.

Over two thousand years ago, in that seminal, nearly Eastern civilization called Greece, the actor was separated from his priestly role and began to be recognized as a professional artist for hire. While those actors continued to be celebrated as priests, conduits to the blessings of the gods, at the same time they were recognized as significant artists in service of their people. In that way, actors began to be freed, to whatever extent, from the orthodoxy of their particular tribal traditions of performance, into a more secular world. After the Greek civilization fell, that perception of the actor became tarnished, and in the Western world, rather than being identified as a priest, the actor was seen as a vagabond, hustler, and whore, as actors became regarded as gifted entertainers at best, and as profane charlatans by most.

Our veneration of "acting teachers" can be traced back to how those more "primitive" civilizations passed on a tradition of revelatory performances that exposed the daily challenges of human nature and reflected a timeless respect for the inexplicable. Those who taught others how to present these traditional rituals and stories were masters themselves and their students apprentices, devoted acolytes to the practices and mysteries of their calling. Students today may also be devoted acolytes; however, present-day acting teachers may enjoy esteem because they supposedly represent a conduit to fame and fortune, rather than to a spiritual calling.

What I trust you will find in this book is a range of acting teachers who believe in the possibility of actor as artist. Most of you who read this foreword will understand that few actors in this country are afforded the opportunity to work as artists. The conditions of professional production onstage or in film work against those aspirations. However, if young actors are only to be fed the "you are being prepared for the real world" line, our theater will be deprived of generations of talent that could mean so much to maintaining the substance of this society. The sad fact is that so much of the teaching in this country ignores the natural aspirations of our young and focuses on secondhand strategies for getting the job in television.

I founded The Actors Center with the goal of supporting the continued development of our most accomplished actors in pursuit of artistry and the development of the next generation of acting teachers who can truly support that mission. My own life's work has been to support and encourage our very best actors, not just in their performances, but in their continuing searches for personal discovery. That is where I see their very best work, because that is where they are given the freedom and permission to reach beyond what they think they know. For the last forty years, I have had the good fortune to work with leading acting teachers from America and wide-ranging parts of this world. Every time I sit in a class with a great master teacher, I begin to understand another dimension within myself, as well as within an actor I may have known for years.

Look for that experience in this book. You will find it affirming of your own beliefs, and reaffirming that there are a number of us out there trying to make this world and this profession a better place. Remember, Stanislavsky accomplished his groundbreaking work under a censorious, oppressive dictatorship. We only have to struggle with a society that tends to use creativity and artistic achievement for more materialistic purposes. When you read this book, I suggest you start with the questions, "Why do we teach acting? How can we help aspiring actors do the work they really can and want to do?" My guess is that you will find it supportive of your own personal calling and a ray of hope for this society.

—J. Michael Miller
The Actors Center

INTRODUCTION
A SHORT HISTORY: ACTOR TRAINING IN AMERICA

The development of actor training in America really began, I believe, soon after this country was cultivated. Native Americans had been performing rituals here for thousands of years, handing down what they knew from one generation to the next in order to live upon the land, enacting the colorful stories of their lives—to teach, to remember, and to contemplate.

Before its founding in 1776, as this country grew and developed, various acting companies and bands of players came from abroad, bringing with them a distinctive way of performing which served the audiences of the day and the plays of the period.

Actor development at that time consisted of on-the-job training—performing over and over, imitating what others had done before, and learning the tricks of the trade. This could mean simply turning away from the audience during a dramatic moment, applying a substance similar to Vaseline under the eyes, and then turning back with "tears" in one's eyes, able to actuate fear or immense sorrow. Of course, there were particular performers who gave "memorable" performances owing to their natural gifts, and that elusive ingredient—inspiration. Still, as time passed, a distinct "American style of acting" was born.

Although formal academies were slow to arrive in this country while they existed abroad, recognizable giants in the acting profession rose to prominence here. Actors of size and significance such as Edwin Booth, Edwin Forrest, Charles MacCready, Charlotte Cushman, Ira Aldridge, Junius Brutus Booth, and Joseph Jefferson ushered in a new age of vitality and genuineness on the stage.

Inspiring performers impressed theater audiences and the country at large with their "high art"—notably Eleanora Duse, Sarah Bernhardt, Jacob Adler, Julia Marlowe, Jacob Ben-Ami, Giovanni Grasso, and Tommaso Salvini.

By the turn of the twentieth century, a new generation of actors and actresses—E. H. Southern, Minnie Madern Fiske, Charles Mansfield, Pauline Lord,

Jeanne Eagels, William Gillette, Otis Skinner, John Drew, Charles S. Gilpin, Ethel Barrymore—and soon her brother, John Barrymore—were among those who brought a gallery of unforgettable performances to the stage. And soon other artists surfaced: Laurette Taylor, Pauline Lord, Jeanne Eagels, Alfred Lunt and Lynn Fontanne, Helen Hayes, and Eva Le Gallienne.

Across America, in every major city and town, dramatic clubs, schools, and academies sprang up to train those with hopes of pursuing a career on the stage, including the American Academy of Dramatic Art, the Neighborhood Playhouse, and the Clare Tree Major School. Concentrating on the basics, the teachers gave training in acting, elocution, singing, ballet, and other various disciplines.

New plays by Anton Chekhov, Henrik Ibsen, August Strindberg, and Eugene O'Neill, were forcing the actor to reveal more of himself than ever before. New tools were used to release "the life of the human spirit," as Stanislavsky referred to it.

In the Broadway theater season of 1923–24, something occurred that would change the face of the American theater and acting training forever. The Moscow Art Theatre, led by Constantin Stanislavsky and Vladimir Nemirovitch-Dantchenko, arrived from Russia, performing plays by Chekhov, Tolstoy, and Gorky. Though reports noted that their makeup was overly exaggerated, the productions poorly lit, and their costumes almost in tatters, what occurred onstage was a theatrical truth and reality not before seen in this country.

While there were American performers whose singular performances were revelatory, here for the first time, each actor in the entire ensemble of the Moscow Art Theatre created a seamless reality and truth. Stanislavsky's relentless probing and testing of his theories with the actors in his company, discovered a means by which an actor could work on himself and on a role. This would have a dramatic impact on all those who witnessed their performances. These discoveries would become known as the Stanislavsky System.

When the company returned to Russia, two members of the Moscow Art Theatre, Richard Boleslavsky and Maria Ouspenskaya, stayed in this country, opening the American Laboratory Theatre in New York City on MacDougal Street, right next to the Provincetown Playhouse. Those who studied there included Stella Adler, George Auerbach, Harold Clurman, Francis Fergusson, John Martin, and Lee Strasberg.

Boleslavsky and Ouspenskaya taught a concentrated period of study on the actor's body, voice, and speech, as well as exercises to affect actors' souls, by developing their emotion, imagination, and inspiration.

In 1931, Harold Clurman, Cheryl Crawford, and Lee Strasberg founded the Group Theatre, creating, arguably, America's greatest ensemble acting company. In a mere ten years, this socially relevant ensemble company had a dramatic and long-lasting influence on actors, playwrights, directors, scenic designers, and other acting teachers in America and abroad. In their work on the new American plays they chose to produce, great time and effort was given over to the actor's development and to training the actor. The life values that the Group Theatre espoused breathed life into the discovery process in this country. Out of this company came Stella Adler, Harold Clurman, Sandy Meisner, Robert Lewis, and Lee Strasberg—some of the foremost acting teachers of the twentieth century.

Since 1949, The Actors Studio in New York City continues to be a major force in the growth of the actors' training in this country, as are the burgeoning regional theatre acting programs. University and college theater departments, acting schools and centers, as well as private acting instructors flourish today across this country.

There are acting teachers whose high ideals, deep commitment, and dedication to the art and craft of the actor must be recognized as part of the continuing tradition of actor training in America: Joseph Anthony, William Ball, Herbert Berghof, Joseph Chaikin, Jeff Corey, Jasper Deeter, Robert Elston, Peggy Feury, Gene Frankel, Uta Hagen, Wynn Handman, Bill Hickey, Charles Jehlinger, Peter Kass, Alvina Kraus, Roy London, Paul Mann, Sonia Moore, Pearl Pearson, Harryetta Pertrka, Warren Robertson, Diane Shalet, Rose Schulman, Viola Spolin, Clay Stevenson, Constance Welch, and Jeremy Whalen.

Certain extraordinary theater artists, actors, directors, choreographers, and producers who have or who continue to inspire through their teaching and through their courageous example as theater artists must also be recognized: Jane Alexander, Antonin Artaud, Eugenio Barba, Jean-Louis Barrault, Julian Beck, Augusto Boal, Phoebe Brand, Marlon Brando, Peter Brook, Robert Brustein, Ellen Burstyn, Zoe Caldwell, Morris Carnovsky, Michael Chekhov, Ossie Davis, Ruby Dee, Michel Saint-Denis, Eva Le Gallienne, John Gielgud, Carlin Glynn, Martha Graham, Lee Grant, Jerzy Grotowski, Julie Harris, John Houseman, Robert Edmond Jones, Elia Kazan, Harvey Keitel, Martin Landau, Stephen Lang, Judith Malina, Marcel Marceau, Arthur Miller, Ruth Nelson, Laurence Olivier, Al Pacino, Geraldine Page, Joseph Papp, Estelle Parsons, Dorothy Patten, Arthur Penn, Harold Prince, Charles Nelson Reilly, Andrei Serban, Anna Sokolow, Ellen Stewart, John Stix, Tadashi Suzuki, Tamaris, Barbara Ann Teer, Stuart Vaughan, Dr. Douglas Turner Ward & the Negro Ensemble Theatre, Orson Welles, Robert Whitehead, Shelley Winters, and Joanne Woodward.

I have discovered, as I've shared what I learned from my teachers, our responsibility to communicate our humanity. The craft of acting continues to be a shared authentic experience. It is up to each one of us dedicated to this art form to nourish its growth and ignite the inspiration necessary to enrich our fellow man.

Acting Teachers of America: A Vital Tradition
Ronald Rand & Luigi Scorcia

PART I
ACTING TEACHERS

GREGORY ABELS

Revered by his students and highly respected as a director and actor, Gregory Abels began as a student of Stella Adler from 1961 to 1963 at the Stella Adler Studio of Acting. Trained as a classical actor, he performed on Broadway, in Off-Broadway's experimental theaters, and on daytime television dramas. Mr. Abels has been a master teacher at New York University, Circle in the Square Theatre School, National Theatre Institute, Stella Adler Studio of Acting, National Shakespeare Conservatory, Warsaw State Academy, and the National Academy of Prague. From 1996 to 2004, he ran his own New York acting conservatory, GATE (Gregory Abels Training Ensemble). He is the leading

American director in the Czech Republic, including a highly acclaimed production of *Roman Nights* by Franco D'Alessandro, starring Simona Stasova as Anna Magnani. In 2001 he first directed Ronald Rand in his solo play, *Let It Be Art: Harold Clurman's Life of Passion*, which continues to be performed by Mr. Rand around the world. Mr. Abels is a master in the White Plum lineage of Soto Zen.

RR: Who has been most influential in how you teach?

GA: Stella Adler's passion for communication and detail and the pursuit of those elements affected me deeply.

Ingmar Bergman once said that the most crucial ingredient for success was creating a positive atmosphere in rehearsal. I've never forgotten that.

That I was an actor for thirty years has certainly given me compassion and directness.

RR: Have you changed the way in which you teach acting?

GA: The basics haven't changed. I've always taught from the inside out and the outside in. To inspire connection with instincts and fertilize what is organic and to instill trust in pure external stagecraft.

My growth in Zen (I am also a Zen teacher) has certainly brought an equilibrium to my nature and outlook over the years. Identifying and getting rid of bad acting habits and channeling the actor's energy is something I've become more skilled at. Chief among the obstacles for the young actor are: faulty breathing, misinformed concepts of acting (often based on TV and film viewing), and ignorance of their role as storyteller. Most of the exercises I've developed are aimed at these problems.

RR: Why should an actor study the craft of acting?

GA: Precisely because it is a craft. That art is ephemeral and instinctive should not obscure the fact that it is made, fashioned—like a meal that will be eaten by others. Craft ensures that the actor will be an effective communicator.

I want to develop actors who are not afraid of size—who understand that bigness and truth are not mutually exclusive. As I've become a better director, I've become a better teacher.

I work to make it clear that there is no one who does not have weaknesses to be corrected.

RR: Do you place an emphasis on the actor understanding the playwright and the world of the play?

GA: Yes, you have to wonder: How does this playwright's mind work? I encourage my students to look at everything they have written, to hear how a playwright speaks. It holds great value. How did Tennessee Williams and Arthur Miller speak, or Harold Pinter or Sam Shepard? Listen to their rhythms, their textures and spirit. Those dynamics show up in their characters. Fortunately, we have recordings of many playwrights.

RR: How important is imagination in the actor's work?

GA: I advise my students to "fall in love with the make-believe." When both the actor and the audience enter into a state of make-believe and use their imagination, theater is at its best.

Imagination is a dynamic, a force, a process electrified by the body and brain. Therefore, the body and brain should be exercised daily. Young actors are so eager to run before they can walk. But their imaginations should be allowed to run only after they understand the milieu of the play and are guided by the wisdom of solid stagecraft. The actor must respect the playwright. Then the actor's imagination will be on fire within the words. This is why an avid voice, speech, and breathing training are mothers to freedom.

RR: How valuable is your unique presence to the work that is actually occurring in the classroom?

GA: Actors are, and always will be, hungry to hear someone speak about acting with real authority and congruity and to hear someone go directly to heart of the matter.

MICHAL SINNOTT

Michal Sinnott completed her first feature-length screenplay, *Born That Way*. She can be seen in Spike Lee's *Inside Man* and the film *Quid Pro Quo* opposite Nick Stahl and Vera Farmiga.

RR: What drew you to study with Gregory Abels and how long did you study with him?

MS: I met Mr. Abels at the New England Theatre Conference as a senior in college at Catholic University, where I was finishing up a B.A. in drama. After seeing me audition, he approached me about studying at GATE. I was really impressed with what his program offered but I just wasn't ready to go back to school. Then, after a year and a half as an international flight attendant, I felt I was too far away from acting. So I wrote him and asked if he would reinstate the scholarship he had offered me, which he did. It was a beautiful thing to be given the opportunity to study at GATE for nine months. There were only eight students and we had six teachers. I went roughly forty hours a week, roughly nine A.M. to five P.M. The other teachers taught movement, voice and speech, yoga, Alexander technique, mask, tai chi, and stage combat.

RR: How would you describe what you learned?

MS: Mr. Abels talked a lot about "meeting the part." Great roles are bigger than our everyday selves, and we'd work on the classics to challenge ourselves. Every class started with a conversation about what performances we had seen that week, and we'd talk about dance, music, opera. One exercise we did was "conducting" an orchestra while it played on a tape. We had to know all the instruments and be able to break down all the parts of the orchestra. It really gave me a sense of timing, and an ability to be really present in the moment, to not anticipate. It also filled me with grace.

RR: How have you been able to apply what you learned in your work?

MS: Any beautiful thing requires a degree of work and planning, but elevating it to art also requires a certain weightlessness, an unplanned poetry of sorts. I've always been a perfectionist, but I've learned to be more Zen in my approach. To work hard but to not get stressed out—to have faith in my abilities. Mr. Abels gave me a confident base and the opportunity to trust myself.

GARY AUSTIN

Gary Austin performed with the famed improv company the Committee Theatre in San Francisco, and he founded and was the original director of the Groundlings, the Los Angeles theater company, which recently celebrated its thirtieth-anniversary season. Many of *Saturday Night Live*'s actors and writers have come from the Groundlings. He conducts workshops in Los Angeles, New York, Seattle, and Washington, D.C. He co-teaches with Carol Fox Prescott, Lindsay Crouse, and his wife, Wendy MacKenzie. Mr. Austin has formed an alliance with the Deaf West Theatre in North Hollywood, California. He also directs *Works in Progress* for Artistic New Directions in

New York City. He has performed his solo show, *Church and Oil*, in New York, Los Angeles, Santa Fe, Seattle, D.C., Woodstock, and Colorado. Mr. Austin's students include: Lindsay Crouse, Jennifer Grey, Helen Hunt, Lisa Kudrow, Pat Morita, Helen Slater, and Lillias White.

RR: Who has been most influential in how you teach?

GA: Carol Fox Prescott, Wendy MacKenzie, and Tom Tyrrell. Tom Tyrrell was my favorite teacher at San Francisco State University. It was an exciting theater department. Jules Irving and Herbert Blau taught there. I was terrified by Jules Irving. His work was amazing; he painted pictures onstage. He and Blau ran The Actors Workshop, probably the best regional theater in America at the time.

Tom Tyrrell was a real hands-off director. He allowed those in his productions to do what they did best. He thought I was better than I thought I was. In rehearsing for *The Cherry Orchard*, I had decided that everything I was doing was wrong, so I stayed up all night one night and reworked everything. At rehearsal the next day, Tom said, "Everyone take five." Then he said to me, "Gary, it couldn't be more wrong." I was devastated. He said, "I cast you because your first reading was already the performance. You just have to show up." I had gone into my head.

After moving to Los Angeles, I worked as a social worker in Watts and did theater at night. I happened to drive by a theater marquee: "The Committee Opening Tonight." I had never seen or done improvisation. I went to see the show because a friend, Christopher Ross, was in the show. Rob Reiner, Jessica Myerson, Peter Bonerz, John Brent, and others were in the cast. I had never seen this kind of work; I wanted to be a part of it. I was told that for one dollar I could participate in a Saturday-afternoon workshop. Ellen Burstyn was also a student, among about fifty others every Saturday.

One day Del Close from Second City flew in from Chicago and ran the workshop. He said to us, "I'm establishing the rules. If you break a rule and it works, I will applaud you. If you break a rule and it doesn't work, I will castigate you. Let's begin." My first improv got huge laughs, and I hadn't done a twenty-eight-page analysis of my character, as I was wont to do. I had entertained without preparation. I realized this was what I wanted to do.

Del chose me to do shows and workshops, and that's when we created the long-form improv. I didn't realize we were creating something that would be performed all over the world.

RR: Have you changed the way in which you teach acting?

GA: Constantly, especially during the last eight or nine years. Since I met Carol Fox Prescott. I've been very much influenced by her. I co-teach with her, and she has been my acting teacher. I have found I can improve people's work. My job is to help actors solve problems, to expand their work. Viola Spolin worked in the same way, creating exercises to solve problems.

I have also learned about teaching from my wife, Wendy MacKenzie, who is one of the top vocal coaches in the country. Since she teaches in the house, I overhear lessons day and night. I'm her student as well.

RR: Why should an actor study the craft of acting?

GA: We get stuck in habits and have conditioned responses. When that happens, the work suffers. We need to be constantly working to create new responses, new ways of working, breaking habits, because onstage we must always make compelling choices, being alive and present for the audience.

One of the exercises I give my students is an exercise called Solo Exploration. It came about several years ago, just before a workshop in a New York apartment. I was sitting and looking down the length of the living room. And I thought: What can I do in this space? Suddenly an image flashed in my mind—an image from old film farces (i.e., the Marx Brothers) in which we're looking down a long hotel hallway, and lots of characters are crossing the hallway, running out one door and into another. Wouldn't it be interesting to see an actor entering and exiting, back and forth across the living room, and every time the actor, he's a different character?

The exercise began with that action, and then other steps followed, as I created the Solo Exploration exercise, which I do to this day. In Solo Exploration, the actor changes physicality often, which compels new voices to emerge, which in turn creates new characters, text, creative freedom, emotional depth, subtext, situations, points of view, actions, and behaviors. As in all my work as an artist, there is no planned result in Solo Exploration. Process is everything. Results are a surprise.

RR: Do you stress the importance of voice/speech and body work of the actor's instrument?

GA: Voice and physicality are just about everything. I get frustrated when actors don't know what a diphthong is. I'm constantly working with actors on their speech, having them sometimes emphasize consonants, elongate vowels, play with pitch and rhythm and speak at various volumes with differing amounts of air over the vocal chords. Sometimes I say to the class, "Everyone freeze." And I look around, and I see that all or most of the actors in their seats are asymmetrical. And my question to the class is, "What does this tell you about human beings?" I direct actors to listen to their bodies.

It's important to me that the actor is always physically alive in the present moment. Breathing brings the actor into the present moment. Committing to purposeful physical tasks brings the actor into the present moment.

RR: How should an actor begin to work on a role?

GA: Read the text a hundred ways while doing physical things, with no concern for what the character would or would not do. Do accents, play with sound, move your body and face in arbitrary and outrageous ways.

The actor plays the character, and feels like the character, but she's always aware she's an actor and she is in fact herself.

If the actor is really in the moment, he's only aware of the moment he's in. Whereas the audience retains everything that's happened, is happening, and is expected to happen—past, present, and future. The only truth in the theater is what's happening with and between the people who are present.

RR: Do you place an emphasis on the actor understanding the playwright and the world of the play?

GA: It's very important to find out as much as you can and then forget it. You won't actually forget most of it. It gets filed away in your brain. You let the information about the play and the playwright influence you and then you let it go. If you've done the research, the play will be there for you.

RR: How important is imagination in the actor's work?

GA: Imagination is actually happening more in the mind of the audience than the actor. When the actor imagines, it's a result of playing actions in the physical world, not because she sets out to imagine. If the actor is standing on an empty stage, and tells the audience it's his living room, the audience imagines the room.

When I perform my autobiographical solo shows, I remember a physical place that actually existed, but since the audience members weren't with me when I lived in that place, they each imagine a different physical place that corresponds with similar places they've known.

RR: How valuable is your unique presence to the work that is actually occurring in the classroom?

GA: It's immeasurable. The environment that I create in the classroom and in the theater is the most important aspect of my work. And that comes from who I am. I do what I do because I must. The problem for the actor is to keep learning how to be an actor. I can see when an actor denies an impulse. I teach people to follow their impulses. And that's what it's all about, isn't it?

LILLIAS WHITE

Her Broadway appearances include *Chicago*, *The Life* (Tony, Drama Desk, Outer Critics, Friends of New York Awards), *How to Succeed in Business without Really Trying*, *Dreamgirls*, *Cats* as Grizabella, *Once on this Island*, and *Barnum*. Off-Broadway, she appeared in *Crowns* (Audelco Award), *Dinah Was*, and *The Vagina Monologues*. Her television and film work includes *Law & Order*, *Sesame Street* (Emmy Award), *Pieces of April*, *Hercules*, *Game Fix*, and a concert version of *South Pacific* aired on PBS. Ms. White has performed at Lincoln Center, Carnegie Hall with the New York Pops, Boston Pops, at Feinstein's, and at Joe's Pub in New York City.

RR: What drew you to study with Gary Austin, and do you continue to study with him?

LW: When I met him, I really didn't know his reputation as the founder of the Groundlings; I didn't know about his technique with improvisational acting. Gary is married to my vocal coach, Wendy Mackenzie.

One time I was visiting with them in California and he said to me, "Why don't you come to class tonight?" At that point I was working on *The Life* (before I had won the Tony Award).

So I went to his class and I was astounded by the work.

I had been acting for over twenty years, but when I got up onstage and he had me do something, I realized that maybe my chops were a little rusty, because I found him telling me I was thinking too much. I had gotten away from being spontaneous as an actor, of going with the flow.

When you're doing a Broadway show night after night, month after month, you can get into a pattern. But there has to be a different motivation each time you perform. Certainly there's a different audience, plus there are all these different components happening in your life every day, things you experience, and they should flavor what you do onstage.

I realized in that one hour in his class that I had gotten out of touch. It's what I've been working on with Gary for at least ten years. I continue to study with him at every chance.

RR: What were you hoping to discover about yourself and the craft?

LW: I was hoping I would get looser and more creative, more uninhibited in terms of reacting. Acting is reacting in the moment, hopefully in good taste. It has to do with spontaneity, with letting go of the mind, the gut.

RR: How have you been able to apply what you learned in your work?

LW: Working with him, he's made me aware of everything in my daily life; it's made me freer as a performer to take more chances.

I had a part in *Chicago* on Broadway as a supporting character opposite Rita Wilson, and working with Gary allowed me to be unpredictable onstage—to "up the ante" with the other actors onstage.

I've been working with him on my own solo play, finding all these different characters in myself for the show. He's able to bring out all these components in the actor's personality—to surface, to flourish and develop.

He's totally honest with me; he "gets" me as a creator. There's a real sense of encouragement, to take the time to breathe, but to get the information, process it, digest it, and let it go so the creative process can happen.

There are a lot of people inside me, and he draws them out. It's an amazing process. He allows me the freedom and ease for them to emerge. It's definitely his patience with me as an artist, and he's taught me to trust myself. I love him as a teacher and as a human being.

HAROLD BALDRIDGE

Harold G. Baldridge was the artistic director of Theatre Calgary (Canada) from 1972 to 1978. He was an acting instructor at the Neighborhood Playhouse from 1960 to 1963 and at the Woodstock Playhouse in Woodstock, New York, from 1963 to 1972.

RR: Who has been most influential in how you teach?

HB: Sandy Meisner. I was a student here at the Neighborhood Playhouse and went through the two-year program, graduating in 1960. I stayed on as assistant to learn how to teach acting. I also studied here with David Pressman, who had been Mr. Meisner's assistant and was the head of acting at the Neighborhood Playhouse when Sandy was in California. I was honored to sit in both their classes as a teacher-in-training, and subsequently became a teacher with a class of my own. In the mid-sixties, I returned to the Neighborhood Playhouse whenever I could assist Paul Morrison with the end-of-the-year productions. In 1981, Robert Whitehead, the Broadway producer and then-president of the board of the Neighborhood Playhouse, asked me to become the director of the school.

RR: Have you changed the way in which you teach acting?

HB: In a sense. I did some studying with Stella Adler, Lee Strasberg, and Harold Clurman. They all influenced me, but the Meisner work remained the most important influence. There's no one right way to teach, just as there's no one right way to act. You use what works for you as a creative artist and sometimes this is an amalgam of many mentors' input and a lot of self-discovery. You discover what feels right for you.

RR: Why should an actor study the craft of acting?

HB: Unless you want to be limited to one-of-a-kind roles, you need to stretch the possibilities of your acting instrument. To make self-discoveries. To learn how to build a character and develop a performance. Good training enables you to do that. It puts the actor in the driver's seat of his career. It gives the actor the confidence needed to face the showbiz marketplace.

Sandy always worked to help actors get at what was buried inside themselves. He found that if the actor could get the attention off himself and live off the behavior of the other person in a scene, discoveries could be made about your own instrument. The other person's behavior would "trick" you into revealing something about yourself to yourself. This, of course, all goes back to some of the ideas Stanislavsky had come up with in Russia.

RR: Do you stress the importance of voice/speech and body work of the actor's instrument?

HB: Sandy [Meisner] said, "In no sense is the Stanislavsky-trained actor limited to naturalism. What more does he need now? A body as flexible as a gymnast's, a voice as malleable and responsive as a singer's, and a director who understands and can communicate the way of life which gave birth to the play."

The students here work on all the elements of their instrument in order to become aware of all the technical ability at their command in order to eventually master highly complicated theatrical demands.

RR: How should an actor begin to work on a role?

HB: The credo of the Neighborhood Playhouse is "to do real things in the imaginary circumstance." The actor has to ask: What am I doing? It is the actor's job to investigate and find out as much as he can about who he is and who he isn't. To eliminate superfluous traits and discover the ones you need for the character.

RR: Do you place an emphasis on the actor understanding the playwright and the world of the play?

HB: The world of the play is dealt with in the second year of the program, along with character and style work. The actor has to find where he fits into the mosaic of the play.

The director finds the shape of the play, and you need to know where you fit into the world the playwright has written.

Acting is always about taking and giving between you and the other characters. It helps the actor to know that Tennessee Williams's relationship with his mother affected how he created the character of Amanda in *The Glass Menagerie*. The actress has to translate this information into how she does things for the character. Doing real physical things often helps you go in the direction of finding the theatrical reality of the play.

Sandy Meisner suggested that a big step toward playing a cold winter scene on the stage would be to turn your collar up, hunch your shoulders, and rub your hands together—real things that you do when you are out in the cold.

RR: How important is imagination in the actor's work?

HB: I think this is where Sanford Meisner differed from Lee Strasberg. Lee put a great deal of emphasis on emotional memory—remembering the day your little puppy *really* died. Meisner felt it might be better to *imagine* what it might be to lose your little puppy. If an actor is able to draw from his or her rich imagination, then a larger emotion that may exist in the actor is possible. It's a way of pulling it out of themselves. When the actor investigates why he does that, he is investigating the emotional life of the scene. What does it mean to me to ask my sister for money?—and your imagination will start to affect you emotionally as a result of what it means to you if you don't get the money needed. This feeds the actor's emotional base. Robert Edmond Jones' book *On Dramatic Imagination* also expressed the idea that the imagination can carry you anyplace.

RR: How valuable is your unique presence to the work that is actually occurring in the classroom?

HB: I think what I do is try to teach in such a way that what's occurring also happens on a subconscious level. I may try and make a certain point, but the student will still take away what it means most to him.

My background as an educator, a professional director with many years of real, practical experience out there in the professional theater, has given me much to share with students. It is that sharing and passing on of techniques that makes teaching so rewarding.

AMOS CRAWLEY

Mr. Crawley has performed coast to coast in Canada, from Halifax's Shakespeare by the Sea Festival to Vancouver's Orpheum Theatre. He has been seen frequently Off- and Off-Off-Broadway in New York City. He has appeared in dozens of films and television shows and created many voices for Saturday-morning cartoons.

RR: What drew you to study with Harold Baldridge and how long did you study with him?

AC: After a relatively successful career in my native Canada, I felt that were I to continue pursuing the life of the actor, I needed further training. My mother, an accomplished actor in her own right, had been a student of the Playhouse, and so I decided to have an interview with Harold. He did most of the talking, and I realize now that he was sizing me up, making sure that I would be able to fulfill the prime requisite of the Meisner-trained actor: a willingness and ability to listen. I studied with Harold (and had the pleasure of being directed by him) for two years at the Neighborhood Playhouse.

RR: What were you hoping to discover about yourself and the craft?

AC: I was attempting to enter the room an empty vessel, and one of the first things I learned was how truly difficult that can be. I was hoping to discover virtually everything about myself and the craft of acting.

Harold had warned me at the beginning that I might well be entering a boot camp, and truer words were never spoken. What I learned at the Playhouse has influenced everything in my life, both as an actor and as a person. Harold, along with his excellent staff, particularly my first-year acting teacher, C.C. Courtney, was at the forefront of that remarkable journey.

RR: How would you describe what you learned?

AC: I like to think that I learned how to employ the right kind of ego for my work. When I began studying with Harold and the other teachers, there was less of a concentration on self-discovery and more focus placed on the actual fundamentals of being an actor in the professional world. Harold was a wellspring of information and a great source of confidence that comes from a true knowledge of the subject he was discussing. I am very grateful for his honesty and have found it a source of strength ever since.

RR: How have you been able to apply what you learned in your work?

AC: I can say that everything I know about harnessing one's talent comes from the lessons I learned from Harold and the rest of the staff at the Playhouse. I would not be able to walk onstage with the confidence that I do without them. Harold's generosity as a man, and his many small daily kindnesses as a teacher, were fundamental to my education.

BUD BEYER

Bud Beyer is a tenured full professor at Northwestern University. Mr. Beyer received his B.S. from Northwestern and had studied acting with Alvina Krause and mime with Etienne DeCroux. He was head of the acting program from 1972 until 1989, when he was chosen to chair the Department of Theatre, a position he filled until 2002. He is the founder and director of the Northwestern University Mime Company, which has toured throughout the United States and Europe. During the past twenty-five years, Mr. Beyer presented lectures and workshops on gesture and movement for orchestral and band conductors throughout the country. Mr. Beyer has conducted workshops in mime and acting at colleges, universities, and festivals across the United States, and published, with Charlotte Lee, *Speaking of . . . Theatre*.

RR: Who has been most influential in how you teach?

BB: My first teacher was my father. He was an Olympic gymnastics coach, so my childhood was spent watching him teach and coach. He formed a theatrical unit around the gymnastics team and called it Acrotheatre.

The second major influence was Robert Edmund Jones and his vision of the theater.

Another great influence was Alvina Krause and her concept of the actor and of the artist's responsibility. She was a harsh disciplinarian and, during the time I studied with her, either you delivered or you got off the stage. When a student would complete a scene, Kraus was famous for saying, "Cut! Flunk! Next!" She was a very creative acting teacher, with the ability to pull phenomenal moments out of actors. What she taught kept you from becoming an "in-your-head" actor. What she created was vibrant theater, and she had the ability to enliven the text. For Ms. Krause, that was the foundation of acting.

Another great influence was Michael Chekhov. His method of approach through imagination and transformation answered many of my questions as an actor and later as a teacher. When I was twenty-one years of age, I was in Los Angeles, and close to Francine Fitch, an actress and one of his devoted students. (Mr. Chekhov had recently passed away). And because she was a close friend of the family, she took me to visit Chekhov's house and sit with Madame Chekhov and have Russian tea. After a while, Madame Chekhov would go to the closet and pull out a large box of audiotapes of Michael Chekhov lecturing, and together, we would listen to each tape. When Madame Chekhov was too overcome with emotion, she would stop and put the tapes away.

It took several months to hear all the recordings, but for me, at that young age, to hear Mr. Chekhov codify his way of working created a very deep impression within me and upon my future work. What he taught exemplified the active approach. It was based on the actor's image of himself, on his whole sense of transformation, on the ability to believe yourself as the role, and finally, on the ability to communicate that to the viewer. Those in Russia who had seen Michael Chekhov in his performances as an actor swore that he could change, without device, the color of his eyes for the characters he played. He was a brilliant teacher.

Finally, my teacher—Etienne Decroux, and his creation of a new geometry of the body in motion, and my sensei in Chinese gung fu—for teaching me discipline, the power of the mind and body, and showing me how to incorporate those elements into my own work in the theater.

RR: Have you changed the way in which you teach acting?

BB: Yes. I better have, as I have been teaching for forty years! My teaching has simplified to what I consider to be the basic elements of acting: the ability to believe the given circumstance, a personal connection to the human truth of the character, the capacity to imagine, and the lack of punitive judgment as one examines human motivations within the context of the drama.

RR: Why should an actor study the craft of acting?

BB: We study the craft of acting to lessen the distance between brilliant and terrible acting. When we act, there are always moments of brilliance when we are struck by the muse. But when the muse does not arrive, the result should not be a terrible performance. In those times, it is craft that allows us to give a performance of quality. Without craft, our performances are more a result of mood and accident than the result of ability. It is difficult to reconcile this dilemma because it feels so spectacular when we give performances driven by the accident of the muse. But our audiences also arrive on those nights when we are less in tune and they also deserve a performance of quality.

RR: Do you stress the importance of voice/speech and body work of the actor's instrument?

BB: It's huge! The emphasis is always targeted in the realm of the relationship between voice and body, both as the students are being taught and as the skills are being utilized. All voice and body work is dependent on the style, the tradition, and the historical context of the plays being studied. The first test of a student's self-discipline is his ability to spend the required hours in the drill of voice and body work.

RR: How should an actor begin to work on a role?

BB: I do not have recipes and I do not believe in them. Every role is different for every actor in every production. The actor works from the text, from self, and from imagination, in whatever proportions are dictated by the problem at hand.

I try to teach actors a method to join themselves to every role they play. I ask them to work first from the text, and then from themselves and their imagination. Sometimes an actor dreams a dream, falls out of bed, and the role is complete. It is so close to who they are and to what they know. And then there are those roles that trouble actors for their entire creative lives. We must have a method of working that allows for both occurrences.

RR: Do you place an emphasis on the actor understanding the playwright and the world of the play?

BB: Our entire program in acting is driven by, and revolves around, the text, what the text reveals, and understanding the driving force of the writer's ideas. When actors read a play, they have to ask: What is the historical base for this play, and what is the universal human truth that is revealed? That balance point between historical context and what is essential truth becomes our search.

For instance, in the play *Hedda Gabler* by Ibsen, at the beginning of the play, Hedda is standing at the French windows wondering why the leaves are so yellow. Her husband, Tesman, tells her that it is September, and she says quietly, "September . . . September already . . ." The line alone means nothing unless the actors understand the historical, national, and emotional context of the characters' world. In Norway, the word "September" means that the harsh six months of winter are just around the corner, travel will be mostly impossible, and everyone will be staying at home. Additionally, Hedda is pregnant, by a husband she has found boring during her six-month honeymoon, and the decorum of the period demands she stay out of public. She is facing six months of isolation, a birth in midwinter, and the constant companionship of only Tesman and Julia. "September already . . ." takes on a fuller meaning in that context.

RR: How valuable is your unique presence to the work that is actually occurring in the classroom?

BB: Any teacher or director is the catalyst and stimulus for what happens in the room. We are there to serve the actors, the students. I am simply the person opening a door so that the students, the actors, may move themselves to places that are difficult for them to reach alone.

KATE VANDEVENDER

Kate VanDevender graduated from Northwestern University's theater program, and her storytelling abilities have led to multiple careers in film editing and directing. Her Manhattan-based company, Imagine Edit, specializes in short films, documentaries, and demo reels for artists. Ms. VanDevender has spent the last few years in New York City honing her craft.

RR: What drew you to study with Bud Beyer and how long did you study with him?

KVD: I wanted to study with Bud because I was awed by the fact that he treated his students as artists. Bud made it clear from the start that art was something much bigger than ourselves, something worth the discipline and personal risk required to understand it. During the three years of his class, I came to see acting not only as a way to engage with the world, but as a way to change it.

RR: What were you hoping to discover about yourself and the craft?

KVD: I had hoped I would discover how to work with my own talent. I didn't really understand how to get my body and instincts and intelligence to work together at the same time. If I had had a great moment onstage, it seemed more like coincidence than skill.

Bud gave us creative tools: how to create characters, how to work with text, how to deal with personal obstacles. I could now take my creativity and work with it, so that a great moment onstage was not only something I could enjoy on a deeper level, but something I could repeat.

His classes were very hard. The first hour of class everyday was an eight A.M. workout in tights and leotards, which, for a college student, was like asking someone to run a marathon after three nights of no sleep. It got us to understand discipline and to think about our bodies as an integral part of our jobs as actors. The second hour was scene work and exercises.

RR: How would you describe what you learned as an actor?

KVD: I never felt that Bud imposed any certain method on his students. We covered a lot of territory: from Meisner work to mime. From the Greeks, Shakespeare, and Chekhov to Williams, Mamet, and Shanley. You could also see flexibility in his teaching style. There would be times when he'd critique one performance ruthlessly, and in the next moment he would gently nurse an actor through an emotional moment. What we got from that was that we are unique, and the more we regarded ourselves as individuals, the more we would come to understand our own artistry.

We would talk about why Buster Keaton was such a theatrical revolutionary, or what made Katharine Hepburn's performance so electric in *Long Day's Journey into Night*. He presented acting history as something palpable and alive, open to both critique and wonderment, so that we would learn to think of ourselves a part of a long and rich timeline.

I started to learn what it meant to be an actor in the real world. His attitude was, "Listen, working as an artist is one of the most difficult things you could do, and your main job will almost always be looking for more work. It's scary and unpredictable, and that can keep you from being creative, so you've got to figure out what you're willing to tolerate and how you're going to make this work. Because part of being an artist is being able to embrace change."

RR: How have you been able to apply what you learned in your work?

KVD: I think I have a good grasp of story structure, which has been invaluable in my acting work. I can look at a script and say, "Okay. This has to happen in the first moment of the scene; otherwise the rest of it won't make sense." And I can break down a script into beats that my creative brain can understand and take over. That's a process that began in Bud's class and will probably continue to evolve over the rest of my artistic life.

RON BURRUS

Originally trained as an actor, Ron Burrus evolved into a teacher through mentoring and apprenticeship with Stella Adler in the mid-1970s. After ten years alongside Ms. Adler in the classroom, Mr. Burrus opened his own acting studio in Los Angeles for film and TV actors. Presently, his teaching, directing, and coaching work is divided between L.A., New York City, and international seminars. In 2007, Mr. Burrus will mark thirty-four years of working with learning actors.

RR: Who has been most influential in how you teach?

RB: My mentor, Stella Adler, and the students I teach.

I was with Stella Adler ten years, every day. She was impeccable with the principles of acting. First—that every time is *as if* it's the first time. Then, for realism, supplying the life underneath the dialogue. Next, the flame of the actor's talent is justification. And the most moving for me is the ability to live a private life onstage or in film, as a created character.

RR: Have you changed the way in which you teach acting?

RB: Stella used to ask me, "Why do they keep coming back?"

I told her, "Because you do what you say." Therefore, as a teacher, you reshape what you teach according to the current students.

Stella is often quoted as saying, "Talent lies in your choice." But she meant a *stimulated* choice. It must come from you. The actor has to experience that choice, and it must be doable. All exercises are focused toward that goal.

When I moved to California, I adjusted the technique I teach for working in film. And boy, does it work in film! When the camera moves in close, it's all about what's moving *inside you* before you speak. You have to make slight adjustments, but the essence of what you have to be able to do is the same, regardless of medium.

It's vital for the actor to not just hear and memorize a technique, but evolve his own process. To learn more than just what it takes to get a part—to have a technique that will serve him for the rest of his life. The key is to get an actor to slow down inside.

RR: Do you stress the importance of voice/speech and body work of the actor's instrument?

RB: If an actor isn't physically or vocally connected, he's unable to connect emotionally. Vibrations will not get through if there is a tightness. Technique leads an actor to physical and mental relaxation. The actor's job is to "vibrate" under pressure. It's a skill to have a tone full of feeling and life. Language is a partner to the body and the voice. "Playing" in the present is the "key" to the reality of repetition.

RR: How should an actor begin to work on a role?

RB: The first time an actor reads a script is the freshest it will ever be. An actor has to allow the script to speak to him. Allow it to move him and then begin to work with it. Be able to sum it up in two words. Find the theme, or you won't know where to put the pieces. Especially in film. All the pieces are shot out of order. It's the actor's job to reassemble the pieces.

RR: Do you place an emphasis on the actor understanding the playwright and the world of the play?

RB: Not as much as to why the playwright wrote the play, but the play itself. I'm looking for what's universal—what the writer is saying to the world. If you work on a period play, it takes place at a different time; it could be a different country, its best you do research. And if you're interested in playing character, (not just your own character), it's up to the actor to rise to the material, instead of bringing the material down to your size.

Actors can only play a projection of themselves for so long in TV and film, and even 'personality actors' have edited their persona so that we see a selected side of them. There are exceptions—those actors who fight for the chance to show a very different side of themselves. It's matter of finding a 'key' into your character's world. The understanding of the human condition is the actor's responsibility.

When I watched Bertolucci's "The Last Emperor," there is a scene when the emperor is at the train station, with his guards nearby. And he couldn't tie his shoe. He didn't know how to. This was the genius of Bertolucci and the writer to allow us this understanding of his character. Of course, he was raised that he never had to tie his shoes. He was dressed everyday. That's a key to showing what the actor has to look for, to get in. Once you do, then you can run.

RR: How important is imagination in the actor's work?

RB: So much of the preparatory work is in the imagination. Probably 85 percent. Imagination has powerful, ironclad rules that you must adhere to. If you're tense, it shuts off. Imagination can be very ethereal. But it's the actor's job to make it doable. Your technique is there to help you release it.

I use an exercise: The actor has a tennis ball in his hand and in front of him is a wastebasket. I say, "For one second, let the ball and the basket tell you how to throw the ball into the basket. Trust yourself enough to slow down inside and allow it to happen."

RR: How valuable is your unique presence to the work that is actually occurring in the classroom?

RB: It's a matter of plugging into the students' energy—they always tell me what has to be said. It's paramount to me to give the actor tools he can use to bring to life the words on the page and practice those tools once he leaves the classroom.

MICHAEL LANDES

Michael Landes started his career on the television series *The Wonder Years*. He has appeared in 100 hours of television, including *Lois & Clark: The New Adventures of Superman* and the upcoming BBC miniseries *Love Soup*. He also starred in the West End production of *When Harry Met Sally*. He has appeared in ten films, including *Final Destination 2* and *Hart's War* opposite Bruce Willis.

RR: What drew you to study with Ron Burrus and how long did you study with him?

ML: I started acting at sixteen, and I did an independent film two years later. There was an incredible group of actors in the film—Fisher Stevens was among them. I loved the way Fisher worked, and he had taken classes with Stella Adler. I went into Ron's class, so I was working and learning at the same time. I was in his classes for about six years on and off, and I also have been working with Ron as a coach.

RR: How would you describe what you learned?

ML: Ron's work gave me the freedom to use my imagination, to build on what the writer had come up with. Working on a script, I allow the first impressions to come; they're so important. I try and get as much information as I can, to find all the clues I can. Then I work on finding the actions to play.

RR: How have you been able to apply what you learned in your work?

ML: I take a lot from the physical circumstances and I apply it to the script. It's about making a contribution; that's rewarding to me.

I'm always in a state of learning. Ron helped me to look at my life without judgment, to be present. I'm able to articulate what I want to do with the material. I can have a discussion with the director, whether I do a play on the West End in London and rehearse for six weeks, or a *CSI* in Miami. I always keep an open mind.

What I love about his way of working is that it has to do with the universal. Ron also said that a script is skeletal, and it's our job to add the heart, the soul.

Ron gave me a discipline for a lifetime, and when I'm able to step back sometimes, I can see a lot of the things he talked about and understand how to use them.

IVANA CHUBBUCK

Ivana Chubbuck is the founder and director of the Ivana Chubbuck Studio, one of the foremost acting schools in the world and creator of the Chubbuck technique. Some of the actors Ivana has taught during her twenty-five-plus-year career include Halle Berry, Brad Pitt, Charlize Theron, Terrence Howard, Elisabeth Shue, Jim Carrey, Jake Gyllenhaal, Katherine Keener, Djimon Hounsou, Hank Azaria, Eriq La Salle, Matthew Perry, Damon Wayans, Kate Bosworth, Beyoncé, and Jon Voight. She has also been a guest master teacher at The Juilliard School. Penguin Books published her best-selling book, *The Power of the Actor*. Currently her book is being adopted for use as a text-book in many colleges and universities across America and Canada, as well as being translated and published in a number of other countries. Ms. Chubbuck was honored by the Russian International Film Festival with a special award for her contributions to the film industry. She has been featured in the *New York Times*, *Vanity Fair*, *People*, *USA Today*, *Cosmopolitan*, *GQ*, *Premiere*, *Spin*, the *London Times*, the *London Guardian*, and *Movieline*, as well as in periodicals around the world. Ms. Chubbuck has also appeared on *Entertainment Tonight*, *Today Show Australia*, the CBC, and the BBC.

RR: Who has been most influential in how you teach?

IC: Due to the fact that I grew up with a physically and emotionally abusive mother and a distant, workaholic, dysfunctional father, I spent my childhood and young adulthood making choices that were based in fear. Fear-based choices result in a weak person. Out of necessity for survival, I came to know that the only way to accomplish anything was to use my angst and trauma to fuel my way to overcome and achieve. It became clear to me at that time in my life that a character's journey could also become more dynamic if the actor (as the character) were to do the same thing. This then becomes a path that would ultimately be more enjoyable to play as well as to watch. Utilizing "empowerment" as the main key to the actor and the character that the actor is playing is what and how I teach. This is the foundation of my technique. You could say that the most influential people in the way I teach are my mother and father . . . unintentionally . . . but nevertheless, significant.

Additionally, most of my life experiences have allowed me to better understand the human need that exposes itself through behavior. Our past establishes a way that we presently negotiate life—a "map" that informs the way we operate. Being married, watching my child grow up, seeing my father die, have all helped me more profoundly appreciate life's absolutes. Understanding it on a deep level has allowed me to more accurately and effectively apply it to an actor's performance.

I could also add everyone who has crossed my path in an essential way.

RR: Have you changed the way in which you teach acting?

IC: It always continues to change. Art is malleable; it never stops evolving. If I don't explore and discover new ways, thoughts, and ideas, then I shouldn't be a teacher. I will continually grow, through life experiences and through a symbiotic relationship with my students. They educate me as much as I educate them.

RR: Why should an actor study the craft of acting?

IC: I think anybody who thinks they can do it without studying is not doing it for the right reasons. The years when Oscar winner Charlize Theron was in class, she rehearsed all the time, often asking for double the workload by doing two scenes at the same time. She also always asked for challenging scenes and would show up doing her scene work by making the boldest and riskiest choices. The other students would watch her from week to week, anticipating what new and unpredictable choices Charlize would make.

When she was working on one of her movies that happened to be shooting at a studio half a mile away, she would come to my class during her lunch hour—skipping lunch. Wanting to be fed educationally instead of nutritionally. When she was on the final days of a movie shoot, she'd call me to ask for a scene partner so she could start working on a scene for class. And to back up her bets, she would call one of her friends from class and ask if she wanted to do a scene with her during her brief two- or three-week downtime between movies.

Brad Pitt worked so hard in rehearsal for class scene work that he'd often get complaints from his scene partners that he wanted to work too often. Halle Berry and I worked thirty hours on *Monster's Ball*, a part she was only in one-quarter of the movie. It could all be broken down into a mathematical equation: Study and hard work + risky, bold choices = success.

I work at understanding the reasons why one actor gets hired and the other two actors do not. I go through the choices that were made and I decipher systematically what makes someone a working actor and what simply gets good feedback. You can't take a callback to the bank. Students come to me because, as they say, "I'm tired of being the second choice." Through the over twenty-five years I've been teaching, I've continued to discover ways of teaching that will inspire the most effective actor.

RR: Do you stress the importance of voice/speech and body work of the actor's instrument?

IC: Acting is about characters creating relationships within the context of the script. Dynamic acting is about being the one who drives the relationship, and thereby drives the scene. When you truly and desperately want something from another person, you are heard and seen. Say you're in a foreign country, and you are trying to communicate in the local language, a language you have a pidgin acquaintanceship with. You speak slowly and loudly and gesticulate every thought and idea wildly in order to be understood. Essentially, voice and behavior is produced by need.

Furthermore, when you examine your character from a psychological and behavioral point of view, you feel compelled to move and speak differently. The actor must ask himself: What is the neurosis/psychosis of the character? How does that apply personally to me? How does that info realize itself in the bigger, "What-do-I-want-from-life-and-from-you?" picture? Mannerisms and affectations will emerge that will surprise the actor. I believe that voice and body in acting should be motivated from the inside, like it is in life. However, that being said, it never hurts to study anything and everything that will exercise the actor's instrument.

RR: How should an actor begin to work on a role?

IC: By starting with the psyche of the character. See how the character negotiates life, and how the character overcomes obstacles. Then you explore how that is duplicated from your own life, turning the fraction of that information into a whole. We, as human beings, are an accumulation of experiences, our reactions to those experiences, and how others respond to our experiences and reactions. There's a lot of detail and texture to being human. An actor has to find that detail, first from the point of view of the character; then he needs to see how that information is emotionally replicated from within. This allows the actor to truly behave in a role as opposed to just acting it out. Sure, it takes a lot of time and effort. But the end result is much more satisfying and cathartic.

RR: Do you place an emphasis on the actor understanding the playwright and the world of the play?

IC: It's important to respect the writer's words. Keeping that in mind, an actor also needs to know how the author's words are true to him or her—to match the character's journey to that of his own. To personalize. That's what a great writer does—

he writes from what he knows. A great actor needs to do the same. We can't read the writer's mind. We can't possibly begin to know everything of why he wrote it. The actor has to do script analysis from the base of his own world, while at the same time respecting the writer's words. An actor has to feel he is the character.

RR: How important is imagination in the actor's work?

IC: One hundred percent—and nothing. Every person's mind is filled with imagination. On the other hand, there are historical absolutes of our lives that trigger love, hate, sexual feelings, sadness, anger, and guilt. The actor needs to be aware of what precisely are those *real* events, moments, experiences that will personally activate the *imagination* part of our minds. This comes from skill and practice. What works and doesn't work can only be found through trial and error. There's no such thing in the arts as "right" or "wrong." Essentially, if it works, it's right. If it doesn't, it's wrong. It's really just a matter of what's least effective and most effective when making specific choices in creating a living, breathing character.

RR: How valuable is your unique presence to the work that is actually occurring in the classroom?

IC: I gave up my ego long ago. My accomplishment is measured in my students' accomplishments. My posterity is in the book I wrote.

ERIQ LA SALLE

Eriq La Salle is best known for his portrayal of Dr. Peter Benton on *ER* (three Emmy nominations, several Golden Globe, SAG, NAACP Image Award nominations, and three NAACP Image Awards for best actor). He made his feature-film directorial debut with *Crazy as Hell*, which he produced and starred in. Under his Humble Journey banner, Mr. La Salle produced *The Salton Sea* and *Mind Prey*, which Mr. La Salle starred in. He also directed the acclaimed short *Psalms from the Underground* and directed and appeared in *Rebound*. His film credits include *One Hour Photo*, *D.R.O.P. Squad*, *Jacob's Ladder*, *Coming to America*, and *Five Corners*.

RR: What drew you to study with Ivana Chubbuck and how long did you study with her?

EL: I moved out to California from New York City, where I had attended Juilliard for two years, and New York University grad school for two more years. I studied with the late Clay Stevenson; he was an amazing teacher, and he instilled a strong work ethic. When I moved out here, I wanted to continue to learn. I heard about Roy London and it was one of the strongest classes. But they told me I had to study with Ivana first, who was Roy's protégé. So I studied with her for about two years.

I had already started directing short films. My interest was moving into directing and Ivana recognized it and encouraged me.

RR: What were you hoping to discover about yourself and the craft?

EL: Ivana's teaching comes from the gut, the groin. She talks about human behavior, the things that motivate us. When she talked about what a character needs in a scene, those were things that were very relatable to what we're going through in our own lives.

RR: How would you describe what you learned?

EL: Actors are the only artists that feel they don't need to continue to practice every day. If you play an instrument, you're practicing every day. I come from strict training, and Ivana encouraged and appreciated that discipline. She made it clear: The more you do your art, the better you'll become. I saw enormous progress in class in the work I did. She gave me a consistency, a consistent playground, a consistent gym, a library; it gave me a place where I could grow and push myself. She'd push me further—it's so important when a teacher does that.

Ivana comes from the school of thought: "Don't give them fish, teach them how to fish." She made me feel safe to go places, and she made it attractive, sexy, scary, and interesting.

Ivana and I teach using similar language with the goal being to get actors to make "hot" choices. That's the phrase we always use.

When I was her student, that's what it became about—making "hot" choices. At an audition I would continually ask myself: Am I making the hottest choice? And instead of giving myself permission to go from A to B, I could go from A to M or Z.

RR: How have you been able to apply what you learned in your work?

EL: Once I've set a bar for myself, and I realize what that bar is, I don't think I'm ever satisfied with less. It's always about being the best artist I can be and being in it for the right reasons.

SUSAN GRACE COHEN

A graduate of The Juilliard School, Ms. Cohen is currently a faculty member at NYU/Tisch School of the Arts, Film and TV Division. For seven years, she owned and operated a private acting studio in New York City. Ms. Cohen coaches principals for Broadway and Off-Broadway, film, and television. She is author of *Bridging the Gap: Student to Professional Actor* and is a contributing essayist to the newspaper *The Soul of the American Actor*. Ms. Cohen received the James L. Hearst Guest Lecturer Award in the Arts and Humanities at the University of Northern Iowa. She has led workshops with Pace University and the Bank Street College of Education. Ms. Cohen's former students include James Gandolfini, Linda Hamilton, Karen Allen, James Spader, Melora Walters, Mel Harris, Justin Chambers, and Heather Juergensen. Ms. Cohen has been a faculty member at the Lee Strasberg Theatre Institute for twenty years.

RR: Who has been most influential in how you teach?

SGC: Lee Strasberg. I studied with him in his classes at Carnegie Hall for nine months. Toward the end of my training, he approached me and said, "Darling, would you like to teach?" (He had reviewed my resume and noticed that, as a senior at The Juilliard School, I was teaching freshmen.) Prior to studying with Lee, I worked with George Morrison, who suggested that I apply for Lee's classes. I was accepted.

The more I watched Lee and listened, I realized I understood his teaching formula. I saw the route, the journey. I understood how he was guiding students in employing the Method—sense memory work—in scenes and monologues.

This is exactly what I teach—Lee's work. I believe this work opens up the actor's instrument. Actors learn to start and stop emotion at will. Their work becomes original, creative, spontaneous, and sometimes truly emotional. There is no right or wrong in acting—I learned from Lee how to nurture talent and inspire creativity. I try to make the actor's journey clear, easy, and logical.

RR: Have you changed the way in which you teach acting?

SGC: I've never changed it—I only use Lee's work. It's what I learned and have trusted. Because people are different and come from many diverse backgrounds in my classes, I give specific exercises to my students, according to their needs. A lot of actors today don't know how to put it all together when they rehearse. I want my students to love acting and be stimulated by the process.

RR: Why should an actor study the craft of acting?

SGC: For an actor to have an exciting career he needs to consider training as ongoing. I constantly remind students to work on their own. An actor needs to be able to tell a story and communicate it to an audience; it's not about how the actor feels.

I train actors to use the sense memory work in scenes, in monologues, at auditions, even at cold readings. By encouraging this, I see the actor thinking real thoughts. My work encourages them to release themselves—to go beyond their expectations and to use their intelligence to fight harder for their art.

In the period we're living in, we need to collaborate and inspire happiness within ourselves and in the world. In Stanislavsky's *My Life in Art*, he states that technique is the backbone of creativity.

RR: How should an actor begin to work on a role?

SGC: Reading the play or script, privately, is most important. This allows creative thinking about a role and the play. An actor should prepare with sensory choices, alone, and add behavior (with objects). Costumes help tremendously and should be worn in rehearsal. The use of imagination plus technique creates work that is both spontaneous and joyous.

RR: How valuable is your unique presence to the work that is actually occurring in the classroom?

SGC: I have devoted my years of training to encouraging disciplines within actors' work, while developing their talent and allowing creativity, confidence, and inspiration with literature. By demanding ongoing, serious training of these disciplines, I have developed many fine actors and major stars of today's stage and screen.

KAREN ALLEN

Ms. Allen is an adjunct professor in the theater department at Simon's Rock College of Bard. Her work began as a member of the Washington Theatre Laboratory in Washington, D.C., as an actress and director. She starred in over thirty films, including *Raiders of the Lost Ark, Starman, Malcolm X, The Glass Menagerie, Scrooged,* and *The Perfect Storm.* On Broadway she performed in *The Monday after the Miracle,* Off-Broadway in *Extremities, The Country Girl, The Miracle Worker, Speaking in Tongues,* and regionally at the Long Wharf Theatre, Berkshire Theatre Festival, Williamstown Theatre Festival, and with Shakespeare & Company in *As You Like It.* Ms. Allen is a member of The Actors Studio.

RR: What drew you to study with Susan Grace Cohen and how long did you study with her?

KA: Susan was one of the teachers at the Strasberg Institute when I auditioned for Susan Strasberg. I was coming from having spent four years working with an experimental theater. The company's artistic director had studied with Jerzy Grotowski and the Polish Laboratory Theatre for six years and based the work we did on Grotowski's work, his books, and his teachings.

When I came to New York City in 1976, I felt I needed to get a more traditional approach to acting, since the company's process of working was very unusual. I decided I'd study at the Stella Adler Studio of Acting, and at the Strasberg Institute to study both techniques and get some training in sensory and emotional work. Susan Grace Cohen was one of the teachers at the Strasberg Institute that Susan Strasberg put me in touch with.

Susan was very supportive and solid in her teaching, and we've developed a relationship that has lasted thirty years.

RR: What were you hoping to discover about yourself and the craft?

KA: I knew a little about the Strasberg Method from reading about it. Anthony Abeson, who had directed me in the company, told me he had studied at the Strasberg Institute before he went to Poland.

I was aware that relaxation was a challenge for me and was hoping to learn how to work with my energy. I feel it's good to work in a lot of different ways, to have a lot of different approaches to use, to find out what works for me. I feel I need every approach possible.

RR: When you left the class, how would you describe what you learned as an actor?

KA: The sensory work was very important. I'm now teaching sensory work to my students. For me, it's never been about the Method as a way of working, but as a way of honing one's own ability to concentrate. To really send your senses into your own interior and kind of touch those parts of yourself. We all have an internal, emotional life—at times we're more aware of something that elicits it. Those "wells of emotion" are so important for an actor—where the deeper, emotional life resides. Sensory work has always created a channel into those places for me. When I have a sense of it, I'm able to access it, and then I'm able to sustain it in incredibly emotional and devastating scenes for four to six hours at a time on a set.

When I'm working on a film and there's a break for lunch or I'm waiting for lighting setups, people are constantly hovering around me, putting powder on me, and I have found this work extremely valuable in helping to sustain a very volatile scene, in keeping things emotionally strong for my character. When I have to keep going back to the beginning of the scene over and over again, I have to keep making new discoveries to keep it fresh and alive. It's about being able to do it with a certain amount of resilience again and again.

RR: How have you been able to apply what you learned in your work?

KA: If I have to audition for a woman casting director and I'm doing a romantic scene, I have to know how to do my best work for her, to bring out what's needed in the scene, especially if she says to use her as my partner. Having a technique allows you to sustain a performance in the theater for months—or handle the complexity of doing a role in a film, where everything is shot out of order.

In the mid 1980s I studied with Ryszard Cieslak. It was a luminous experience. He really made me want to be an actor. I had no interest then in acting, but when I walked into a church to see a performance of *Acropolis* by Jerzy Grotowski's Polish Laboratory Theatre, I had a kind of an epiphany. I had never heard of them before. Maybe I had seen two plays in my life.

After I watched the performance of *Acropolis*, when I walked out I was a different person. Richard was responsible, from what I had seen him do onstage, in a huge way. I had never seen anything remotely like it; it was profound. It had to do with creating the greatest freedom possible to create in. In regard to the ability to communicate one's deepest feelings in performance. I couldn't even put into words what I had seen. He was an enormous source of great inspiration.

I now teach at Simon's Rock College of Bard for gifted students, mainly with juniors and seniors. The students are very serious minded and usually have had some traditional training at their high school. They're so full of the desire to learn, to discover who they are.

What I believe in doing is stretching the concept of self that we develop in the course of being in a culture that encourages us to define ourselves from a very early age. For an actor that can be an obstacle. I believe we decide who we are— the way in which we choose our journey. It's a matter of instantly knowing something you know.

WILLIAM ESPER

William Esper has been teaching acting in New York for over forty years. He is a graduate of Western Reserve University and the Neighborhood Playhouse School of the Theatre, where he trained as an actor with Sanford Meisner, with whom he subsequently worked in close association as a teacher and director for fifteen years. Mr. Esper was on the staff of the Playhouse for twelve years. From 1973 to 1976, he was associate director of the Playhouse acting department. In 1977, he founded the MFA and BFA Professional Actor Training Programs at Rutgers University, where he remained as program head until 2003. In 1965, he established the William Esper Studio, where he continues to teach today. He has been a guest artist/teacher at Canada's Banff Summer Arts Festival, the National Theatre School of Canada, Vancouver's Workshop for the Performing Arts, Chicago's St. Nicholas Theater Company, and Schauspiel München (in Munich). He has directed both Off-Broadway and regionally and is a member of the Ensemble Studio Theatre in New York City. The professional actors Mr. Esper has worked with include: Kim Bassinger, Kathy Bates, Jennifer Beals, Kristen Davis, Aaron Eckhart, Calista Flockhart, Jeff Goldblum, Dule Hill, William Hurt, Christine Lahti, John Malkovich, David Morse, Sam Rockwell, and Paul Sorvino.

RR: Who has been the most influential in how you teach?

WE: Sanford Meisner was without question the most important influence in my work. Martha Graham was a powerful teacher and an extraordinary artist.

But Sandy was, of course, the most important. He was my mentor and "artistic father." After getting out of the army, I studied with him at the Neighborhood Playhouse. Right after I graduated, Sandy left the Playhouse and went to Los Angeles to run a school for contract players for Twentieth Century Fox. When he came back in the early sixties, he became involved as head of acting at a new school that was meant to train actors legitimately as well as for musical theater.

I went to Sandy and told him that I wanted to learn to teach. He said, "Wonderful," and put me into teacher training. My timing could not have been better because Sandy was at the very peak of his career. After two years of training, I was rewarded with my own class to teach under Sandy's supervision. In 1965, Sandy returned to the Neighborhood Playhouse and asked me to join the staff there. I stayed for twelve years, co-teaching both first- and second-year classes and directing many productions. It was there that I first began to explore my interest in language and style work. Sandy himself loved theatricality and encouraged me in my own experiments. Having those years of work with him was an incredible blessing for me. In 1977, I left to found the BFA and MFA Professional Actor Training Programs at Mason Gross School of the Arts at Rutgers University. Today my teaching is totally focused on the work at my studio.

RR: Have you changed the way in which you teach acting?

WE: I hope that over the years I have grown as an artist and as a teacher. My teaching has evolved as I have evolved. I am by nature a searcher.

But my work has always remained grounded in the precepts of Sanford Meisner's teaching. The cornerstone of his work is the reality of doing. I have never wavered in my belief in the importance of that principle. Like Sandy, I put tremendous concentration on enabling the actor to make genuine contact with his fellow actor and to let that fill his conscious awareness. But as Sandy said to me one day, "It's dangerous because anyone can teach it and anyone can do it." The exercise is deceptive in its simplicity because it can be egregiously mistaught. I believe that it's important to teach an actor to work directly off of what the other person's behavior means to him.

I hope my teaching has always been responsive to the realities of the profession.

One way in which I have not changed is that I am still just as demanding regarding a student's professionalism and work ethic.

RR: Why should an actor study the craft of acting?

WE: My goal has always been to help actors develop genuine virtuosity, to give them a foundation that rests firmly on the dependable craft that will serve them in weathering the vicissitudes of a professional career. When we speak about craft we are speaking about a set of ingrained habits. It is only when the actor cannot help doing certain things in a certain way that it becomes a part of what we may call "craft." My work is all about identifying those habits and continuously drilling the actor until they become second nature. I am talking about fundamentals like listening, leaving one's self alone, working off the behavior and subtext of one's fellow actors—things like this.

The second year focuses on the use of that instrument for interpretive purposes, to the complete realization of characters. Beyond the two years, I do advanced work in Shakespeare and other classical texts, as well as the intensive on-camera work. I cannot emphasize too much the need for real expertise in today's profession; this means you had better really know what you are doing.

RR: Do you stress the importance of voice/speech and body work of the actor's instrument?

WE: I am fanatical about the importance of voice and speech and physical training. You must have an instrument that is capable of processing and experiencing every aspect of the actor's experience and rivets the audience's ear to all he has to say. He also requires a physical instrument that can experience deep and profound emotional experiences without a trace of strain or blockage, or he will not be free to be totally in the moment when he acts, and it will seriously limit the parts he is able to play. After all, you cannot play Beethoven on a kazoo.

RR: How should an actor begin to work on a role?

WE: By reading the script with great care. A script is like a road map: It has lots of little signposts along the way. You approach it like a detective—until it begins to form some sort of pattern. Sometimes an actor may have an instant response—he immediately knows who the character is—and sometimes it takes longer. Important plays are dense. Good questions to ask are: What is the theme of this play? What is the idea that the author is trying to communicate? How does my character dramatize that theme?

Degas said, "I never paint what is; I paint what might be." You can't stay in your own life; it's too narrow if you're going to tackle important roles. Great artists understand this. It's all about living authentically in an imaginary world and freeing your imagination in service to a part.

SAM ROCKWELL

Sam Rockwell has appeared in such television shows as *The Equalizer, NYPD Blue,* and *Law & Order.* His films include *Last Exit to Brooklyn, Teenage Mutant Ninja Turtles, Box of Moon Light, Lawn Dogs* (best actor honors— Montreal World Film Festival, Catalonian International Film Festival); *The Green Mile, Galaxy Quest, Confessions of a Dangerous Mind, Matchstick Men,* and *The Hitchhiker's Guide to the Galaxy.*

RR: What drew you to study with Bill Esper and how long did you study with him?

SR: I was only twenty and took a summer session with Bill and then for two years. He had been recommended to me as *the* teacher to study with. At the end of the six weeks, he wanted me to do the two-year program. "I don't know," I told him, "I'm beginning to get work."

"It will go by *like that,*" he said, "and if you get a job, I'll let you go and do it."

I was like a sponge in class and soaked up everything.

RR: What were you hoping to discover about yourself and the craft?

SR: I was hoping to learn more about how to be more consistent as an actor. To have more of an idea what I was doing, to respect myself to create true moments. Bill stands for truth and honesty and wants your acting to be full and vibrant. I worked on *The Dumbwaiter* in class and then I ended up doing the play at the Williamstown Theatre Festival. A lot of the work in class really made an impression on me. What Bill said made a big difference for me. He taught me how to listen to what was really going on in a scene; to truly respect acting; to have my own standard, and to know what makes something good.

RR: How have you been able to apply what you learned in your work?

SR: While I was still in the class I was auditioning, so I was using what I was learning.

One of the projects I did soon after I had studied with Bill was an HBO film about drunk driving. My character kills a girl in an accident, and as punishment, her parents made my character write a check every week for a dollar. (It's actually based on a true story.)

Well, when I had the scene where I had to write these checks, the character got very upset, and I, as the character, stopped writing the checks because it brought back horrible memories. And it's exactly what the parents wanted.

So right at that moment in the scene when we're shooting it, there are all these activities I have to do in the scene. In class, Bill had taught us how to work in the circumstances, about preparation, the structure of a scene, what has to be working for that moment. And I had been terrible at these activities in class. But when I had to do the scene, it all clicked in. I wrote the checks, I had a very strong emotional reason for everything I did, and it was all there for me.

If you really know why you're doing what you're doing, it comes to life, but only if you're really doing it. That's always been true for me, and a lot of the credit goes to Bill. It's really an ongoing lesson you can never stop learning.

MAGGIE FLANIGAN

Maggie Flanigan has been teaching professional acting classes in New York City since 1981. She is the artistic director and master teacher for the Maggie Flanigan Studio. Ms. Flanigan trained as an actor and teacher of Meisner's work with William Esper and quickly became one of the most revered teachers at his studio. She also served on the faculty of the Mason Gross School of the Arts Professional Actor Training Program at Rutgers University for eighteen years. Ms. Flanigan is currently working on a manual based on her writings and teaching experience.

RR: Who has been most influential in how you teach?

MF: Over the years, there have been many artists from across the creative spectrum who have influenced me both as an artist and as a teacher. I consider many writers, painters, sculptors, dancers, choreographers, and directors to be mentors:

Stanley Kunitz, Rainer Maria Rilke, Henry Miller, William Faulkner, Cézanne, Richard Diebenkorn, Jasper Johns, Louise Bourgeois, Giacometti, Martha Graham, Louis Horst, Anna Sokolow, Jerome Robbins, Harold Clurman, Stella Adler, Elia Kazan—all mentors to me. Of the actors who have inspired me I will name five: Robert Duvall, Marlon Brando, Kim Stanley, Geraldine Page, and Montgomery Clift. They have been a profound inspiration to me and their work continues to teach me about the process of creating art.

William Esper, with whom I trained as an actress and as a teacher, has been a steady, true, deep, and inspirational guide.

RR: Have you changed the way you teach?

MF: Changes in my teaching have been the natural result of my growth as an artist over the past twenty-five years. My main focus as a teacher has always been clarity, as well as instilling in my students a great respect and passion for the art of acting. I have strived to make the technique my own, always working to make it as clear as possible. This, I believe, is the cornerstone of good teaching. How the student receives and relates to the information is very important. Passion, simplicity, and clarity in teaching are everything.

RR: Why should an actor study the craft of acting?

MF: Do you realize that acting is probably the only performing art around which this question ever arises? People never watch a ballet and think they can become a ballet dancer without years of training, just as no one listens to a great pianist and goes home thinking he can be a great musician without years of training and practice. Acting requires the same dedication and discipline. If an actor is very serious about becoming the best possible actor he can be, he needs to be clear about what this means to him. Martha Graham said, "Technique can set you free." The actor's technique must be second nature; only then can the actor live through an experience fully, freely, and truthfully.

Craft and skill are how the actor closes the gap between what he envisions in his imagination and what he can create. Without passion, all the skill in the world cannot lift the actor above his craft; and without the skill, all the passion in the world will leave the actor eager but floundering. They really go hand in hand.

I want my students to be able to solve the problems they will encounter in a creative, organic, and truthful way. This is the struggle of any creative artist.

They should be able to come to their first reading of a script in what I refer to as the "creative state"—completely open and available to receive the author's words and their connotations; to let the unconscious do its work.

RR: How important is imagination in the actor's work?

MF: It is part of the actor's talent and the soul of the actor's work. An actor must have a vivid imagination to center himself in the world of the script. The magic "what if" is a key to the actor's imagination. It is very important for the actor to fully imagine himself in the world of the character, which may be entirely different from his own life. An actor can begin to wed himself to a part by making an empathetic identification with the character's problems and issues, then beginning to truthfully do what the character does, in order to create the world of the character. The imagination is the bridge that closes the gap between the character and the actor so that he is living and breathing the part.

RR: How valuable is your unique presence to the work that is actually occurring in the classroom?

MF: I offer my students a passionate commitment in their training in the art of acting. I expect the same commitment from my students in return. I set a high bar of excellence that my students must strive to meet. I love the creative process and try to support my students in their struggle to make the work their own, to build a craft and develop a skill. My responsibility is to aid them in acquiring clarity, simplicity, truth, and grace. This takes skill and craft—twenty years to be really good at it. It's an art, which you work on until the day you die.

Twyla Tharp has a wonderful phrase: "the habit of creativity." So hopefully my students will have learned to develop this "habit of creativity."

KADEE STRICKLAND

KaDee Strickland appeared in such films as Woody Allen's *Anything Else*, *Anacondas: The Hunt for the Blood Orchid*, *The Grudge*, *Fever Pitch*, *Walker Payne*, and *The Flock*.

RR: What drew you to study with Maggie Flanigan and how long did you study with her?

KS: I studied with her from 2001 to 2003 in the two-year program. This was during the time she started the Maggie Flanigan Studio. I had a degree from a conservatory program, and after completing my studies, I moved to New York City and put up plays around town. I came across actors with a more cohesive base, and Maggie's name kept coming up. One of the actors suggested I interview with her about entering her program.

RR: What were you hoping to discover about yourself and the craft?

KS: I really didn't have an articulate approach to the work. I had a strong will to do good work but wasn't satisfied with where I was as an actor or with my craft. I wanted one that was founded on nothing but truth, playing full out, never wavering from the world of the character and the script. This is the foundation for Maggie's teaching.

When I met Maggie, she had such reverence. Everything she expressed made me want to be the best version of myself in the work. She is one of one of the most truthful individuals I've come across, and that has had a tremendous impact on me. She forced me to look into a mirror. It was scary, but I found it personally enlightening. There were times when she reduced me to the size of a thimble. It never made me doubt myself or my desire; it challenged me. It still encourages me in the process.

RR: When you left the class, how would you describe what you learned as an actor?

KS: I can't live without acting. I realize that I've been spoiled with great material and a safe environment to work in. Maggie would tell us to stop "acting," that we are enough, and encouraged us to leave ourselves alone.

When I'm in New York City, I still sit in on her class. It is easy to forget how hard it is to just fold a piece of laundry, live and build on the circumstance, and truthfully stay in contact with the other person. You have to always be "truthfully doing" in the given circumstance. That you can never take for granted.

RR: How have you been able to apply what you learned in your work?

KS: Maggie teaches a cold-reading class in the second year that is invaluable in the professional world. I have found myself in audition situations with directors throwing a new scene at me or even asking me to read a completely different character on the spot. Without that class, I would have fallen apart. The fundamentals I learned have allowed me to trust my homework and my instincts. I don't think it's ever going to be simple, but that's part of the beauty of growing in the work. Maggie reminded me to never be satisfied.

JULIE GARFIELD

Julie Garfield began teaching in 1984 at the American Academy of Dramatic Arts, then at the Lee Strasberg Theatre Institute, Ensemble Studio Theatre, UCLA Extension, and The Actors Studio. She currently teaches acting and coaches privately in New York City. Ms. Garfield graduated from the Neighborhood Playhouse School of the Theatre, training with Sanford Meisner and William Esper. She also studied with Robert Lewis, Stella Adler, Allan Miller, Warren Robertson, and Jack Waltzer and became a member of

The Actors Studio, where she worked with Lee Strasberg. She has performed on Broadway, Off-Broadway, and at regional theaters and portrayed Sonya in *Uncle Vanya* at the Roundabout Theatre (Theatre World and Variety Drama Critics Awards). She appeared in numerous films and played Robert De Niro's wife in *Goodfellas*. Ms. Garfield narrated *The John Garfield Story*, a documentary about the life and career of her father, John Garfield.

RR: Who has been most influential in how you teach?

JG: First and foremost, my father, John Garfield—the honesty, depth, and spontaneity of his work. He brought such a rich inner life to his characters on the screen. In fact, he revolutionized film acting.

Then, my wonderful teacher Sandy Meisner. He taught me what it means to be spontaneous in a moment—the importance of listening and being specific. That acting is an active experience. My favorite lesson from Sandy: "Acting is the reality of doing moment to moment under imaginary circumstances," and "The single most important element in anything you do is the reason why." His "repetition" exercise is about intercommunication—picking up on the behavior of another person.

Lee Strasberg was a great influence. His relaxation and sense memory exercises enabled me to make better physical choices, to break through my own physical and emotional blocks.

RR: Have you changed the way in which you teach acting?

JG: Of course I have. I started teaching in 1984. Time and living have made me a better teacher. I'm a better human being now, more patient and compassionate—which makes me capable of giving more of myself.

RR: Why should an actor study the craft of acting?

JG: Because there's so much to learn about acting. The craft of acting requires the actor to have great discipline, to transform himself in his body and voice, to understand the human soul. It takes a lifetime. You are constantly learning, discovering about behavior.

It's my job to help the actor trust his impulses and be in the moment. I use activity exercises to teach the actor how to ask the right questions—what, why, where, how. I combine the exercises with repetition and sense memory exercises, asking actors to apply them to activities. They're introduced to improvisation, emotional preparation, and more complicated objectives, to begin to experience the conflict of needs. Then they're ready for scene work. As scene work becomes more sophisticated, the actor begins work on character. I use "animal work," "paintings and photographs," "private moments," "moments before and after."

I teach them how to use real thoughts and fears, instead of allowing them to be obstacles—those thoughts become a part of the process. Dreams and fantasies are very useful. I have to be flexible and address the problems that arise in the actors' work.

RR: Do you stress the importance of voice/speech and body work of the actor's instrument?

JG: It's absolutely imperative. Students should be obligated to study and work on these tools. I tell actors to study with a private dialect and vocal coach, or they can use the great educational recordings out there.

If you look at Philip Seymour Hoffman's performance in *Capote*, you see an actor who has completely transformed himself both vocally and physically. That requires great skill to carry off.

RR: How valuable is your unique presence to the work that is actually occurring in the classroom?

JG: I feel my students bond with me. They feel safe so that they can fall on their face and take chances. A teacher has to know when to set the actor free. I try and inspire people; that's always been my goal. It's the journey I take with each student, so they gain a deeper understanding to their own life.

JILL BIANCHINI

Jill Bianchini is a graduate of New York University, where she studied at Circle in the Square, Tisch School of the Arts. She continues to study and perform at the T. Schreiber Studio, where she was Lee in their production of *Marvin's Room*. Jill was also seen in the Palm Beach Playhouse production of *The Vagina Monologues*.

RR: What drew you to study with Julie Garfield and how long did you study with her?

JB: A friend told me about a teacher she liked at the T. Schreiber Studio. So I went to an Open Night, where the teachers tell you about themselves, and the second I heard Julie speak, I just loved her immediately. I hadn't studied for ten years, but studying with her, I remembered what acting was about all over again. I was with her for two years.

RR: How would you describe what you learned?

JB: As far as auditioning, I now approach what I do in a completely different way. There were things I had forgotten, and that I improved immensely. What had been missing was the "heightening of the stakes" involved in the scene. Julie's so articulate in how you should approach the work. She changed my life.

RR: How have you been able to apply what you learned in your work?

JB: I used to have enormous stage fright; it was horrible. When I started in class, I just couldn't go first. I was petrified. But after a couple of months, Julie put me so much at ease with the relaxation work that I don't struggle with it as much.

The change in the confidence in myself has been enormous. She gave me the confidence I needed that I started believing it. I was really lucky to have found her.

KATHRYN GATELY

Ms. Gately serves as head of the MFA University/Resident Theatre Association (URTA) National Association of Schools of Theatre (NAST) acting program at Northern Illinois University (NIU) and is director of an international student production program in Dublin, Ireland. She studied with Sanford Meisner at the Neighborhood Playhouse and has taught in Ireland at the Abbey Theatre and the Gaiety School. She received her MFA in acting from Mason Gross School of the Arts, under William Esper, with whom she eventually co-taught the BFA and MFA acting candidates. Ms. Gately co-founded the Gately/Poole Studio on Theatre Row in New York City, which grew into one of the country's leading conservatory training programs. During the summers she teaches in New York City, Los Angeles,

Boston, and Chicago. She was artistic advisor for the film *Wild Iris*, starring Gena Rowlands and Laura Linney, and coached NIU's production of *The Birds* (performed in Russia at the Moscow Art Theatre School). Ms. Gately was on the board of directors and headed the undergraduate division of the Illinois Theatre Association.

RR: Who has been most influential in how you teach?

KG: Sandy Meisner and William Esper. They taught with clarity, with integrity, and with a sequential through line.

Martin Waldron—I loved his sense of fun and joie de vivre.

My father, a successful Boston politician, taught me how to reach out to people and motivate them. My mother had very high standards and believed if you did something, you had a responsibility to do it to your highest capability.

RR: Have you changed the way in which you teach acting?

KG: No, I don't think so. My methods have remained constant, but some have adapted to the needs and attitudes of each generation. As I've grown, I feel I've become more versatile, experimental, and specific. I have developed a greater need to have this generation of students take more responsibility for their work.

RR: Why should an actor study the craft of acting?

KG: Because it's a craft, it's an absolute necessity.

Actors like Spencer Tracy or Humphrey Bogart in the 1920s and before—leading stars like the Lunts, or family troupes such as the Barrymores and the Adlers (led by Jacob Adler, and his daughter, Stella Adler, who was the ingénue in the company) would tour the country. I heard Stella say, "In my day, you didn't play Juliet. You either had a Juliet in the company, or you didn't. If you wanted to play Hamlet, they taught you how to hold a spear, and you moved up in the company."

It takes time, hard work, and a great deal of honesty for a young actor to achieve depth and richness in his work.

I try to challenge the students to get specific about their responses; to find the nuance, color, and vividness rather than just playing the obvious; to develop greater theatricality, characterization, spirituality, and mystery.

RR: Do you stress the importance of voice/speech and body work of the actor's instrument?

KG: I struggled with Martha Graham's work, so it's quite amazing that I've been such a proponent of movement and voice. As a young teacher, I brought Loyd Williamson into my classes at Rutgers and then at the Gately/Poole Studio, to find ways to process deeper emotional behavior. Loyd's hands-on work was extraordinary and fresh and very much in the forefront of its time.

At NIU, voice and movement training is constantly integrated into the actor training in the classroom and productions to help the students develop fuller, richer responses. I insist on daily voice and movement lessons in the acting class during every session. It's absolutely essential.

RR: How valuable is your unique presence to the work that is actually occurring in the classroom?

KG: I'm able to bring a body of expertise, experience, and stature that is motivating and inspiring—a grace and dignity. I'm tremendously demanding on my students. I'm passionately dedicated and devoted to an actor understanding the nobility of what he's involved in. Being an artist is like being a priest: It's a calling. Acting is about serving something greater than yourself. Artists need to provoke, to illuminate. I continually challenged my students to have great hearts, to be givers. I'm certainly proud of what a number of my students have accomplished; it's very moving to me. I still need to do more.

JAMES GANDOLFINI

James Gandolfini appeared on Broadway in *A Streetcar Named Desire* with Alec Baldwin and Jessica Lange. His most acclaimed role is that of Tony Soprano, the Mafia boss and family man in the HBO series *The Sopranos*, which debuted in 1999. He has won three Emmys for best actor in a drama. Mr. Gandolfini has also starred in several films, including *True Romance, A Stranger among Us, Get Shorty, The Man Who Wasn't There, Mr. Wonderful, Crimson Tide, The Juror, Night Falls on Manhattan, Twelve Angry Men, Fallen, The Mighty, A Civil Action, The Last Castle, 8MM, The Mexican, Romance and Cigarettes,* and *All the King's Men.*

RR: What drew you to study with Kathryn Gately and how long did you study with her?

JG: I was referred by my friend Roger Bart. (He went on to star in *The Producers*.) I was managing a nightclub at the time. I had taken some classes before, but I had never really committed to a long process.

RR: What were you hoping to discover about yourself and the craft?

JG: For some reason, I thought I could do it. I thought I'd try it, but I was petrified by some of the exercises she'd have us do in class. It would make me angry that I couldn't do them. I could tell from the beginning that she was good teacher. She was tough; she didn't take a lot of nonsense. And I got along with the other people in class.

RR: How would you describe what you learned as an actor?

JG: I learned a lot. Most of the time, at the beginning, you're trying to make a fool of yourself. I started to get a point of view about things. She knew when you were faking it; she had an eye for truth. She had a very professional approach. She'd tell us, "You need to work on yourself if you want to succeed." She'd try to get me to go certain places. I didn't want to lose my temper, but she'd push me. When I did, I broke a few things. She said, "Okay, see, everyone's alive, it's all right, a few things are broken, but that's what they pay for, that's what they want to see." After that, I realized I could make a lot of things happen.

RR: How have you been able to apply what you learned in your work?

JG: What I learned mostly was that your emotions are kind of your fingertips, and that they have to be fluid. When you're working in film, and especially in television, you don't have any time to prepare. Kathryn would tell us, "You don't need more than five or ten minutes to prepare in film work, especially since they don't give you more than five minutes." It's true—you have to shift gears and get going.

MICHAEL HOWARD

Michael Howard has been in the theater since 1940, the year of his first professional acting job. Teaching has been a major part of his life since 1953, the beginning of the Michael Howard Studios. Mr. Howard taught for five years at The Juilliard School, Drama Division, served as an adjunct professor at the Yale School of Drama, and was a visiting associate professor at Boston University. He also taught in the inaugural season of the American Conservatory Theater with William Ball (who studied with him), serving as a teacher-director. While at ACT, he directed *Misalliance* for public television. A pioneer in the Off-Broadway movement, he directed the American premieres of *The Waltz of the Dogs*, *Time of Storm*, and *Land Beyond the River*. On Broadway, he directed *The Trouble Makers* and the Theatre Guild's *Third Best Sport*, with Celeste Holm. Mr. Howard was the founding artistic director of Atlanta's Alliance Theatre, where he directed the landmark production of John Dryden and Henry Purcell's opera-masque *King Arthur*, as well as fifteen other productions.

RR: Who has been most influential in how you teach?

MH: The most profound and truest answer is Constantin Sergejevitch Stanislavsky. Not simply because of his system, which changed the world of the theater, but for his questions, even more than his answers. His passion for the theater, his love of actors—their bravery and generosity—and his awe of the actor's intuitive process. That said, I suppose I am a great-great-grandchild of Stanislavsky: Michael Chekhov, Yevgeni Vakhtangov, and Richard Boleslavsky are his children; and then his grandchildren here in America: Sanford Meisner, Stella Adler, and Lee Strasberg. I am one of the many grateful great-great-grandchildren.

As a teenager, I studied at the New Theatre League School, an offshoot of The Group Theatre, and then with Madelyne O'Shea (Boleslavsky's "creature," to whom he referred in his book, *Acting: The First Six Lessons*) and then Sanford Meisner, Martha Graham, et al., at the Neighborhood Playhouse. After serving in World War II, I began a long period of study with Strasberg in his private classes, and then as a member of The Actors Studio. Soon after that, Sidney Lumet, who taught seniors at the High School of Performing Arts, bequeathed his job to me when he left. That was the beginning of my teaching.

RR: Have you changed the way in which you teach acting?

MH: Yes, of course. It happened in slow increments. When I taught at Juilliard, I learned about Jacques Lecoq's work; about clown work, which is extremely useful in developing one's "clown," one's "foolish self," a sense of humor in one's work. Kelsey Grammer, who studied with me at Juilliard, once reported that I told him to "stop making a joke of everything." Fortunately, he didn't listen to me. No question, "to clown" is very important. Strasberg knew that. He enjoyed actors who had a sense of their own foolishness. Although it isn't generally reported, Strasberg also emphasized work on one's voice, the use of one's breath, in addition to the enormous importance of muscular relaxation—all of these things are absolutely essential. I changed as I was exposed to new influences; and, of course, as playwrights change, as the theater changes, teachers must change.

RR: Why should an actor study the craft of acting?

MH: Well, probably, some actors shouldn't. We've all seen some child actors at six, seven, eight years old who are so astonishingly truthful, present, emotionally responsive—their intuitive involvement is so pure, immediate, uncontaminated—

that we are awestruck. There is no block to the intuition. No ego, no fear, no doubt. So, as an adult, one reason to study is to find ways to get rid of those blocks to the intuition.

Most of us need to learn how to concentrate, how to achieve a state of active relaxation, how to live in imaginary circumstances. We need to learn how to read a play, how to break down a play into its various events. Finally, in our world, we need to learn how to recapture the inspired moment eight times a week or in fifteen takes.

I didn't want to have a studio where one method is taught, even though most of the things that are introduced here at the Michael Howard Studios come from the Stanislavsky tradition. The studio brings teachers from many disciplines and many approaches; for example, Patsy Rodenburg, the head of the voice department at the Royal National Theatre, and Isabelle Anderson, whose teaching is based on the work of Jacques Lecoq.

RR: Do you stress the importance of voice/speech and body work of the actor's instrument?

MH: It's essential. Teaching at Yale and Juilliard, it was a joy to work with and learn from other teachers who taught voice, speech, Alexander, mask. I saw the enormous value to those actors who developed a voice and body at least as expressive as their internal emotional instrument. What matters is that the actor integrates these skills; that's what we work on.

RR: Do you place an emphasis on the actor understanding the playwright and the world of the play?

MH: First and most important, all the work should be an understanding of the event of the play. Reading the play is about raising questions. The answers come during the rehearsal. Great playwrights do not only write good stories (not in itself an easy thing to do); they construct stories, narratives in order to illuminate elements of the human condition that concern them. O'Neill, Miller, and Williams reveal themselves in the core of their plays. The worlds of *Long Day's Journey*, *Salesman*, and *Streetcar* are so specific, so detailed, so personally experienced that the writer cannot help but reveal himself.

RR: How valuable is your unique presence to the work that is actually occurring in the classroom?

MH: Those giants who came before us were enormously creative, stimulating mentors. They shared themselves unreservedly. You didn't get a little bit of Meisner or Stella Adler. When they worked, you had all of them. They were fully present. When I teach, you get all of me—what I think, my point of view toward the theater, my life as an actor. Horace Mann said, "Teaching without inspiration is like hitting cold iron with a hammer." If the iron is hot you can mold it—inspiration is the heat. There is no greater gift than what the actor gives us. He or she stands up and changes us. I believe in the theater. Why? Because the audience needs us.

They've needed us for 5,000 years, to stand in front of them and help them understand themselves and their dilemmas more clearly.

BOYD GAINES

Boyd Gaines has appeared on Broadway in *The Heidi Chronicles* (Tony Award), *The Show-Off, She Loves Me* (Tony, Drama Desk, Outer Critics Circle Awards), *Company, Cabaret, Contact* (Tony and Lucille Lortel Awards), and *Twelve Angry Men*. Off-Broadway credits include work at the Public Theater, Roundabout, Lincoln Center Theater, Manhattan Theatre Club, Playwrights Horizons, New York Theatre Workshop, Irish Rep, and BAM. Regional appearances include the Williamstown Theatre Festival, Westport Country Playhouse, Yale Rep, Baltimore's Center Stage, Long Wharf Theatre, Guthrie Theater, and the Kennedy Center. His films and TV include: *Second Best, I'm Not Rappaport, Heartbreak Ridge, Fame,* and *Ray's Male Heterosexual Dance Hall* (Oscar-winning short), *One Day at a Time, Law & Order,* and *Angela's Eyes.*

RR: What drew you to study with Michael Howard and how long did you study with him?

BG: I studied with Michael at Juilliard. He was my first-year acting teacher and he and Michael Kahn remained my mentors there. He focused on basic technique, how the instrument works, and improvisation. In my first year, he directed me in *Look Homeward, Angel,* where I played the father. And in my second year, he directed me as Trigorin in *The Seagull.* That was a great gift. It was a very direct way of putting class work into practice. They weren't finished productions; they were studio productions, with more of a teaching element involved.

RR: What were you hoping to discover about yourself and the craft?

BG: I didn't really know anything more about Michael than what was printed in the Juilliard catalogue. My only concern was that the school's focus on external technique might take precedence over its focus on internal technique, and I have always thought that internal technique was most important.

At Juilliard, I was taught along the lines of what Michel Saint-Denis had talked about in his book *Theatre: The Rediscovery of Style.* He described American acting as "reality in all styles." Every country has a natural style. The English theater has theirs, the French theirs. He thought the American style had been influenced by The Group Theatre and those who had come out of it. He believed that even in the most extended farce, American actors must find the reality in the world of the play, grounded in a strong internal life.

I found Michael incredibly intimidating, although he was warm and friendly. I do remember that I was seeking a stronger inner technique—that was very important to me. As I got past feeling intimidated, I found I had a strong personal simpatico with Michael.

One day in Michael's class I told him about seeing my very first play when I was a high school student in Atlanta. My English class had gone to see a production of *Long Day's Journey into Night* at the Alliance Theatre with Jo Van Fleet, Robert Foxworth, and Armand Assante. At that point, I really had no interest in the theater; I was in a rock band. We went to a matinee and I was transported. Not only was the play spectacular, but I was transfixed by the acting, by the life created onstage. It's the reason I wanted to become an actor. When I told Michael about that experience, he asked me, "Oh really, when was this?" I told him, and he said, "I directed it."

RR: How would you describe what you learned?

BG: One thing I credit Michael with was helping me develop my own aesthetic and a technique that supported it. In a sense: "To thine own self be true."

Michael had an extraordinary overview; it allowed me to develop a strong point of view—to be more flexible and more rounded. He would ask, "What do you know about this?" Not intellectually—he was asking for something deeper, more personal, more intuitive. It gave me a place of truth to start from. And all the questions that were raised along the way came back to it as I rehearsed. As I performed, what I knew about the character allowed the play to continue to grow and deepen.

I remember him asking, "What do you do if you're working with a director and he's asking you to jump to results?" He told us, "You have to know more about your process and your character than anyone else, because that will give you a position of strength, and enable you to convince a director who either disagrees with you or pushes you to results before you're ready to slow down and allow you to work organically."

If I'm in trouble, I still hear Michael's voice saying, "Take a breath; move to the next object of concentration."

RR: How have you been able to apply what you learned in your work?

BG: Right out of school, I got a phone call as I walked in the door with my Juilliard diploma in hand, saying I had a supporting part in the film *Fame*. It turned out to be a struggle for me because it was the first time I was in front of a camera, and I didn't know anything about film acting. I had terrible performance anxiety, terrible camera fright. I went to Michael and we worked it through. He reminded me of ways to relax, things to concentrate on, how to prepare myself. I have, because of Michael, a technique that allows me to get through the hardest moments.

ZINA JASPER

Zina Jasper has been an acting teacher and private coach for twenty-two years. As a director, some credits include: *Starting Monday* (WPA Theatre), *The Lover* and *27 Wagons Full of Cotton*, and *Waiting for the Parade*. She co-wrote and directed *I'm Here*, presented at the Passage Theatre. She was awarded the Outer Circle Critics Award for her performance as Rochelle in *Saturday Night*. Off-Broadway credits include *House of Blue Leaves*, directed by James Nicola; *Quail Southwest* and *Artichoke* (MTC); and *A Different Moon* (WPA). She originated Strawberry in *Raven Rock* (La Mama, E.T.C.), and Chelsea in *On Golden Pond* (Hudson Guild). Regional credits include

Regina in both *The Little Foxes* and *Another Part of the Forest*, played in rotating repertory at Trinity Square and directed by Adrian Hall; Marsha in *The Three Sisters* (Stage West); and Olivia in *Twelfth Night* (Washington, D.C.'s Arena Stage). She also appeared in *Crimes and Misdemeanors*, in many TV shows, and on Broadway.

RR: Who has been most influential in how you teach?

ZJ: Harold Clurman and Stella Adler. Harold and Stella had such resonance for me as a young actor. Harold taught me to always look at the play in terms of the totality. He demanded it of you. His passion for the theater was unquenchable. Stella taught me to trust my instincts but encouraged me to delve into my intellectual understanding. When I included the intellect, acting became this wonderful search to uncover the truth of the play, however elusive it might be. I learned that acting was like detective work, searching for clues within the text. Why did the character do this? Why did she do that? The process goes on and on and is never-ending.

Brian Shaw, a wonderful teacher who was an actor from the Michael Chekhov Acting Company, created a supportive atmosphere in his class. As a result, I understood the need for a nurturing environment, and I have embraced this concept in my own classroom.

My first acting teacher, Wendell Phillips, taught me to see duality in life. I came to realize that it is essential to bring this understanding to the creative process in interpreting the text. I look for the duality within the characters, and as an actor I always included duality in my interpretations. As a teacher, I emphasize this search for the contradictions.

RR: Why should an actor study the craft of acting?

ZJ: "Craft" is a mighty word and leaves so much to be considered. Without a way to work, you are left only with your instincts, which can fail you. When that happens, what do you do? Performing at the highest level eight times a week with passion and instinct can only take you so far. Craft allows you to communicate your interpretation of the play under every possible condition. This is your responsibility to the playwright, your fellow actors, and the audience.

RR: Do you stress the importance of voice/speech and body work of the actor's instrument?

ZJ: These things are absolutely necessary. I encourage my students to go to speech teachers, to work on voice production, to work on movement, as well as working with Alexander Technique teachers so that they can meet their emotions with a flexible physical instrument. I keep my classes affordable, so my students can do this kind of work in conjunction with my class.

RR: Do you place an emphasis on the actor understanding the playwright and the world of the play?

ZJ: Absolutely. The actor needs to think about what the author wishes to communicate. I encourage my class to be "political." Plays chronicle particular times. Actors have to know about the world. I encourage my students to go to museums, see films, and read books, and we discuss them in class.

I know I was hired as an actress because of the choices I made. But they can't be general. I ask the actor, "Can you use the choice you've made, can you see it? If not, get rid of it."

RR: How valuable is your unique presence to the work that is actually occurring in the classroom?

ZJ: I would like to think that my particular energy, passion for the work, and ability to have a good time does inspire my students to work hard in the way Harold Clurman inspired me.

I've devoted my life to the art of acting. I chose to be not only an actor, but also an artist; it's everything to me. I couldn't sustain my life without it.

BETSY AIDEM

She has performed in plays at the Atlantic Theater, The New Group, Playwrights Horizons, Lincoln Center Repertory Theater, Ensemble Studio Theatre, Circle Rep, Edge Theater, Second Stage, McGinnis Castle, Lucille Lortel, Orpheum, Minetta Lane, Promenade, WPA, Naked Angels, MCC, Williamstown, George Street Playhouse, Hartford Stage, Long Wharf Theater, Portland Stage, New York Stage and Film, and in nineteen cities across Europe. Ms. Aidem has appeared on many television shows, and in films by Kenneth Lonergan, Julie Taymor, and Adam Rapp.

RR: What drew you to study with Zina Jasper and how long did you study with her?

BA: I was in a play, *A Different Moon,* at the WPA Theatre in New York City in 1983, costarring Chris Cooper—Zina was our mother in the play. The director was leading me in a direction I wasn't entirely understanding. I took the bus home with Zina one day after rehearsal and asked her, "What do you think about what he's asking me to do?" She said to me, "You're playing a teenager. If you act like a child, we'll catch you acting, but if you insist on being a grownup and try to have all the answers, you'll actually seem younger." It immediately made sense for my performance.

We started working together, and she coached me. When she started her first class in 1983, there were only three students, but people joined quickly.

When I was doing *Steel Magnolias* (the original production at the Lucille Lortel Theatre), I still went to her class every week on my night off. It gave me the opportunity to work on Shakespeare, Ibsen, Strindberg, Chekhov, Jacobean tragedy, thirties comedies. It was a place to work on my craft.

Zina doesn't encourage sentimental choices; she favors human choices. She respects the intelligence of an audience.

RR: What were you hoping to discover about yourself and the craft?

BA: I wanted to strengthen the areas I was insecure about. Early on, I had studied the Method, and I was fairly secure playing naturalistic things, but I had a fear about "style." Zina has an intuitive gift; she's brilliant about script interpretation. My training at Circle in the Square wasn't focused so much on the script, but more on working toward emotional truth. We worked on a lot of Chekhov, Williams, Ibsen, Miller, but I didn't really have a handle on how to "arc a part" or how to meet language plays with an inner life.

She's given me a lot of confidence by believing in me, rooting for me, and supporting my progress so I can work on my own to serve the writer. To this day, when she'll coach me, she'll catch me and say, "You're commenting a little too much. Play it straight, don't judge the character."

When she came to a preview, that little note improved my performance. I tend to overwork and she catches me at it. "Don't put so much spin on the ball," she'll say, and she is forever reminding me to slow down. I've done several monologue plays by David Henry Hwang (*1,000 Airplanes on the Roof*) and Craig Lucas' work, and sometimes I'm rhythmically too facile at moving a mountain of language. She'll help me find the places when I get lost and stumble, where I cover myself and I have to back up.

RR: How would you describe what you had learned?

BA: My own sense of being able to interpret a script. After going to class, I'll work on a script and it comes more easily.

We discussed how to talk on the phone onstage. Zina reminded me of Greta Garbo's work in *Grand Hotel*: "The way she holds the phone tells us how much she loves him." Her "antenna" is always up; she's a great observer of human behavior.

RR: How have you been able to apply what you learned in your work?

BA: I apply what I've learned to every character I work on. I never thought I could play style or a privileged character. Zina encouraged me to notice what distinguishes the needs of a rich Southern girl (as I played in *Steel Magnolias*) and "cheap white trash," which I recently played. There's a degree in knowing how to "throw things away."

When I did *Celebration* at the Atlantic Theater, Zina noticed I had tension in my face, which indicated that I was overcompensating instead of just being. She asked me, "How do you cover your feelings without getting tense?"

When we worked on *Jolson Sings Again*, she asked me, "In the scene when you're drinking, have you had one glass of liquor, or did you have two or three? It makes a difference in how you behave."

The foundation of her work is to free you to be a better actor, to find truth, and to take flight. She does it firmly, devotedly, with great passion and kindness. To Zina, failing is a big part of the learning curve and taking risks will always ignite your creativity. She's like the perfect flight instructor.

MILTON KATSELAS

Milton Katselas' directing career began in the 1960s with the original Off-Broadway production of Edward Albee's *The Zoo Story*. He was nominated for a Tony Award for his direction of *Butterflies Are Free*. He has directed over sixty plays, eight feature films, and is a renowned teacher of actors. His school, the Beverly Hills Playhouse, is one of Los Angeles' oldest and most respected ongoing acting workshops. Under his direction, Blythe Danner won the Tony Award, Eileen Heckert the Academy Award, and Bette Davis her only Emmy Award. The actors Mr. Katselas has directed include Al Pacino, Gene Hackman, Goldie Hawn, Christopher Walken, Burt Reynolds, George C. Scott, Elizabeth Taylor, and Richard Burton. He studied with Lee Strasberg at The Actors Studio and was mentored by Elia Kazan and Joshua Logan. As an author, he has penned two books: *Acting Class*, his renowned book on acting technique, and *Dreams into Action.*

RR: Who has been most influential in how you teach?

MK: When I studied at Carnegie Tech, Barry Farrell taught the beginning classes, and he first introduced me to Stanislavsky's work.

I studied with Lee Strasberg in his private class for a year and a half, and then, after I directed Edward Albee's *The Zoo Story* Off-Broadway, I was invited to join The Actors Studio. I watched Elia Kazan teach and then I became his assistant, a relationship that lasted till he died. I was also Josh Logan's assistant on *Blue Denim*. I worked twice for Joe Anthony as his assistant and also observed his classes as a teacher. Around that time, I also sat in on Tamara Daykarhanova's classes, Stella Adler's classes, and Uta Hagen's. Herbert Berghof and I became good friends.

I remember my first scene as an actor for Strasberg. The scene ended, and he had me close my eyes and asked, "This woman you're acting with—what's the color of her dress? Did she have a ring on her finger? Was she wearing earrings?" I froze. I hadn't observed any of these details. The reality was that during the scene I was thinking of something else, instead of observing and responding to what was really in front of me. That first lesson is something I see so often in actors even now—the eternal problem.

A breakthrough occurred in his class when I did a different scene. Lee wasn't there; Paula Strasberg came to lead the class. In the scene, I played an emotional paraplegic on a picnic, and the girl asks me to go swimming. During the scene I tasted the sandwich I had with me, was aware of the radio that didn't work, and I became totally absorbed. I looked out onto the class, saw the faces of my class-mates, but imagined a beautiful lake, and threw rocks into the lake, and realized by the end of the scene that it was the most important moment in my acting life. That was a real experience. I was comfortable, really there, really seeing and experiencing. It's the basis of my teaching.

RR: Have you changed the way in which you teach acting?

MK: Absolutely. At first my class was all exercises. Now we emphasize scene work heavily, and the exercises are quite a bit different. One of the exercises is a powerful picture exercise, somewhat different from what Lee had picked up from Bolaslavsky. In my version, the actor takes a photo or a painting and duplicates it—to the *n*th degree. They *become* that photo, and then they demonstrate that possession by saying one line that might be the cornerstone, psychologically, of that person. The actor, in becoming the person in the picture, gains more confidence— I have him walk around, relate to other people. These exercises teach actors to investigate the details, the clothing and shoes the character wears, the behavior. That is an important key to really nailing moment-to-moment behavior and creating a character.

RR: Why should an actor study the craft of acting?

MK: Because most don't realize it is a craft. You wouldn't try to become a professional violinist without studying.

With a strong commitment to lifelong growth and development, you can go off and leave a class to work, but then come back and cultivate something new. And someone like Doris Roberts: She called me after one class—this is after a decades-long successful career—and told me, "I feel happy to be alive, I'm learning so much!" It's that desire to be better, like a quest. John Glover, a fabulous actor, has been working with me for four years and has experienced tremendous growth.

RR: How should an actor begin to work on a role?

MK: Stanislavsky said there were two areas: Work on the role and work on oneself. When the actor begins to work, he has to understand that in the end there should be a seamless connection between you and the character. A good first question to ask is, "How am I like the character and how am I different from the character?" The actor should have some sense of the answer to this. Little by little he can then merge himself into this other person.

Analyze and understand the script; develop a clarity about what's going on and your character's part in the story. Do your research. If the role is a doctor, prize fighter, architect, whatever, know the effect of this profession on the behavior, the clothes, the hair, etc.

The actor has to make choices that fire his or her imagination. The audience doesn't *need* to know—they just need to respond to the actor's hot choices.

RR: Do you place an emphasis on the actor understanding the playwright and the world of the play?

MK: Absolutely. I was fortunate enough to know Tennessee Williams very well. I had worked on Broadway on *Camino Real* and *The Rose Tattoo*. There's nothing like that kind of collaboration. Now I look for the author when I read her scripts and I try to hear her voice, the timbre, the inflection, the sense of humor, and I try to see her point of view clearly in her writing. It is very important to understand a writer. You may not know her personally, but you read all her work and read about her life to get an idea. I think actors don't do enough of this kind of research.

But that being said, actors have got to give themselves the permission in rehearsal to go where the author has not gone, to ask other questions, to provoke and challenge the writer. The actor must have freedom to develop the role.

Chekhov said something amazing about this collaboration: "Never be afraid of an author. An actor is a free artist. You ought to create an image different from the author. When the two images—the author's and the actor's—fuse into one, then a true artistic work is created."

The writer is not to be held in awe. He or she is to be studied, to be understood, excavated, and explored. And at the same time, the actor has the right to interpret, to make choices, and to emblazon a role with his or her point of view.

RR: How important is imagination in the actor's work?

MK: It's huge. I have a 1904 *Webster's Dictionary,* and I pulled the definition from there: "The will working on the materials of memory, not satisfied with following the order prescribed by nature, or suggested by accident, it selects the parts of different conceptions, or objects of memory, to form a whole, more pleasing, more terrible, or more awful than has ever been presented in the ordinary course of nature." That's the cornerstone of what we talk about with the use of imagination. That's what's necessary to elevate one's work.

Make a choice—it may lead you to some imaginative way to uncover things you never thought were possible. Try to imagine some alternatives to what the author has given you. What if Juliet didn't take the potion, and did something different instead? What would happen if Othello didn't kill Desdemona? The actor has to investigate and imagine these alternatives, so he's really moving moment to moment—not just obeying a script. Imagination has a lot to do with that.

RR: How valuable is your unique presence to the work that is actually occurring in the classroom?

MK: Actors these days flit about from teacher to teacher, spending a few months here, a few months there; this is not productive. I believe in a one-teacher concept and working out your problems with one teacher, together, over time.

I have very special teachers here at the Beverly Hills Playhouse—some have been with me for over twenty-five years. I believe that to make a difference over the long haul, we need to train teachers. I really care about the craft of acting. It's absolutely necessary to take the time and the patience to really develop an actor.

It's the artists who will change a culture. I remember Stella Adler saying to me in one of our private talks, "I'm not just teaching acting, I'm teaching actors to be people." When I heard that, I realized that's what a master teacher is doing. And that's what I'm after.

DORIS ROBERTS

Doris Roberts has distinguished herself with her versatility on Broadway, film, and television for the past forty-five years. She has won five Emmys and has received twelve Emmy nominations. She has also received the Outer Critics Circle Award for her performance in Terrence McNally's *Bad Habits*, the 1999 American Comedy Award, three Viewers for Quality Television Awards, and a TV Guide Award. On February 10, 2003, Ms. Roberts received a star on the Hollywood Walk of Fame.

RR: What drew you to study with Milton Katselas and how long did you study with him?

DR: Milton is the absolute best. He gets right to the point. I'm going to be in his classes with a walker.

He taught me something a year ago that totally changed me. He asked me to do the Empress in *Anastasia*. So I found a picture of her, and I copied what she looked like—the little dress, the pearls, I learned some sentences in Russian. I was very authentic about the accent. It went very well when we did the scene in class. When it was over, Milton said, "That was wonderful, but now I want you to be mythical."

I thought to myself, "What does that mean?" but I didn't say it out loud.

He said, "I don't like what you're wearing."

"But this is what she looked like," I explained. "It's what the Empress wore." And I showed him the picture.

"Where's Doris?" he asked me. So I changed myself, I pulled my hair straight back, made my clothes different, and when I came back out, everyone in the class was shocked. What I had done was make myself look totally different—I was "mythical." He gave me the power to permit myself to go further, even further than I had ever done before.

I am successful as an actress but I still have more to learn, and he's the man to teach it to me. He wants everyone who comes onstage to surprise people, to make brilliant choices. He just makes the whole process much more alive. He's also a brilliant painter and writer—an incredible human being. I wouldn't miss my Saturday-morning class for anything in the world. It fills me with the same passion as when I was an eighteen-year-old actress.

RR: What were you hoping to discover about yourself and the craft?

DR: To be the greatest actress! That was what I wanted to be when I started my life as an actress. As a young girl, I was taken to the Museum of Modern Art, and I saw these old films there: one was Madame Sarah Bernhardt, another was Eleanora Duse, and the third was Minnie Fiske. Duse stole my heart. I thought, "That's what I want to be!" She was so magnificent that Stanislavsky wrote about her.

RR: How would you describe what you learned?

DR: He's a great director.

It's helped me to realize I can't do the work "right on the nose" and stick to what the words are, but I should go with the subtext. Those are the choices that make it very interesting.

Whether I'm working on television or in film, whether it's a close-up or a long shot, I never approach what I do on a comedic level; I approach it from a reality level. Everything I did on the set of *Everybody Loves Raymond* I did from love, and the end is so hysterical. I wanted to live on the set: I wanted my sons to be the happiest in the world, and that's why people laughed. It's love, and that's exactly what I loved about doing the show.

ED KOVENS

Mr. Kovens was one of the founding staff members of the Lee Strasberg Theatre Institute in 1969, until he left in 1974 to form his own private class: The Professional Workshop. A lifetime member of The Actors Studio (since 1968), he has taught and used Method techniques as an actor, director, and teacher for over forty years. He is the author of the book *The Method Manual.*

RR: Who has been the biggest influence in how you teach?

EK: I studied with Lee Strasberg, first in his private classes on and off for twelve years, then at The Actors Studio after becoming a member in 1968. He changed me by making me look at myself as an actor. I had been more interested in my image. I learned from Lee who and what the character is in every part, and that "no one wrote a play about me." Lee constantly stressed Vakhtangov's principle: "What adjustments do I need to make to myself to do what the character does?" Too many actors today say, "All I have to do is play myself," which is a misconception of Stanislavsky's, "What would I do in the same situation?" This is only the beginning of the actor's work. Not going beyond that point is a major detriment to the actor's craft.

RR: Have you changed the way in which you teach acting?

EK: I was taught in a certain way, and I've developed my own usage as a teacher, director, and actor. In some ways, it's changed or it's been enhanced, modified. But I teach what I was taught.

RR: Do you stress the importance of voice/speech and body work on the actor's instrument?

EK: Someone like Tony Bennett keeps going to his teacher. An actor, like any other performing artist, has to continue to develop himself. My wife, Jill Anne Edwards, is a voice teacher, and she instructs her students on how to properly use their voice even after they have learned to sing.

I advise my students to take classes in jazz, tai chi, pilates. If they have to work on their voice and speech, I then suggest people who can help them.

RR: How should an actor begin to work on a role?

EK: The way I was taught was that you put yourself in the situation, where you and the character respond in the same way, and you leave yourself alone. You find out where you and the character differ, then you need an adjustment to do what the character does.

You have to know what you want out of the character. When I worked on the role of Harry Brock in *Born Yesterday*, the first thing I wanted people to believe was that I loved Billie, and that I wasn't an idiot. Harry Brock may be uneducated, but he's not ignorant and he can certainly be charming.

RR: Do you place an emphasis on the actor understanding the playwright and the world of the play?

EK: It's important for the actor to do his homework about the time period, the social situation. When I worked on *Richard III* in Lee's class, he asked me, "Do you have any idea what's happening in the country? People are celebrating, the war's over—so now what are you going to do?" It made me aware of the history. In the same sense, anything "classic" has to be made relevant to today, to understand the machinations of the time and how they relate to today's situation, for it to be a living thing and not a museum piece.

In Europe, there is a desire to educate the audience. I find it terribly missing here. I also want to see more work by our Native American writers, and our Hispanic, Asian, and African-American playwrights, on our stages.

RR: How important is imagination in the actor's work?

EK: Imagination must be based on reality. If you're an artist painting on a canvas, you see life and you say, "How can I put it on a canvas the way I see it?" Reality is a great springboard for imagination. Of course, without technique it can only go so far. Picasso could only distort as well as he did because he could also draw and paint realistically. Dali was an excellent draftsman. The acting process is more than "streams of the subconscious"—it is imagination with a technique. When you see Dustin Hoffman's performance in the film *Tootsie*, you don't see a man in drag. You see a woman, if Dustin were really a woman.

RR: How valuable is your unique presence to the work that is actually occurring in the classroom?

EK: Most of the time, I've tried to keep my relationship with my students as a peer who happens to know more about a particular subject. The student is coming for that knowledge. I keep it a loose workshop; I don't like the "guru" reverence thing. It's not for me. I never put Lee Strasberg in an elevated position as some students did. I gave him the respect he was due; he had incredible knowledge of the craft. I only hope I'm half the teacher he was.

In the end, that's really what an artist needs.

BETHANY BUTLER

Bethany Butler has appeared in leading roles on both television and stage. She received an NAACP Image Award nomination for her role in the *Law & Order: Special Victims Unit* episode "Lowdown."

RR: What drew you to study with Ed Kovens and how long did you study with him?

BB: I had studied at the Lee Strasberg Institute through New York University for five years. I just felt I needed a push, that my work was on one level, and I needed more layers—and I wondered how I could get there. Ed Kovens was the name I kept hearing, and that he might help. I continue studying with him. It's been three years now.

RR: How would you describe what you learned as an actor?

BB: To trust the work and play "moment to moment." I feel the technique has made me a more well-rounded person. I'm able to dive into areas that I may be unfamiliar with, and the more I trust myself, the more I can add them to my personal life. It's motivated me to do things I couldn't have imagined.

When I start working on a role, I look for similarities and differences between myself and the character. I also study with a vocal teacher outside class and we do the "song and dance" exercise from acting class to free my instrument.

Ed just knows my potential and how far I can go, even if I don't see it in myself. With Ed, I can't play "safe." He keeps taking me further.

RR: How have you been able to apply what you learned in your work?

BB: When I did an episode for *Law & Order: SVU*, I found the use of a substitution was a key tool. Recently, I went in for an audition for *Law & Order: Criminal Intent.* I called Ed beforehand and told him why I wouldn't be in class and expressed some apprehension. He gave me the best piece of advice. He said, "You don't have to go into that room proving you know how to act. Be easy, knowing that you already know how to act. Don't judge your character, love her. You just have to let go, and get out of your own way." That was a breakthrough for me.

BARBARA MACKENZIE-WOOD

Barbara Mackenzie-Wood is currently the head of acting/music theater at Carnegie Mellon University School of Drama, where she has been a member of the faculty since 1986 and is a recipient of the Hornbostel Award, given for teaching excellence in the College of Fine Arts. Ms. Mackenzie-Wood began her acting career playing opposite Raul Julia in the title role of *The Hide-and-Seek Odyssey of Madeline Gimpel*, directed by Lloyd Richards at the Eugene O'Neill Center in Waterford, Connecticut. She was a member of the acting company at the Long Wharf Theatre for five seasons and has acted in regional theater, stock, and film, and Off-Broadway. In 1983, she co-founded the Irondale Ensemble Project, where she continues to act, direct, and teach.

RR: Who has been most influential in how you teach?

BM-W: Lloyd Richards, who taught me in my senior year at Boston University and gave me the basics: talking and listening, playing actions, relaxing, being present. He showed me how to really use myself in the role. He said, "You know more than you know." That was about trusting your impulses. Lloyd gave me my first professional acting job at the Eugene O'Neill Center, playing opposite Raul Julia. I did experimental work in Boston with Caravan Theatre and the Theater Experiment Lab. I worked at the Long Wharf for five years, and I was a founder of the Irondale Ensemble Project, a New York City company rooted in improvisation. There, I became fascinated with the challenge of keeping alive the spontaneity of improvisation with a written text. That led me to work with Paul Sills.

I also studied in New York with Michael Howard and Patsy Rodenburg. Elisabeth Orion, who headed up the acting program at Carnegie Mellon when I first came here, taught me how to put a class together, how to teach actors about the arc and structure of a role. And I read so many books on acting—from Harold Clurman to, presently, Harriet Walters. In the past few years I've become very interested in the work of Michael Chekhov—the psycho-physical, the full-body connection. He's been very influential. I traveled to Poland and worked with Grotowski, and I studied with Lecoq in Paris.

RR: Why should an actor study the craft of acting?

BM-W: At the beginning of the first year of training at CMU, I say to the students, "You're very talented. You could be hired right now for just the right part in a play or film, but if you want a sustained career, and want to take on the really big roles, you have to know how to do the work." Training will expand your resources, enable you to know what you're doing and why. Training will prepare you to work in all the different fields—but it is especially necessary for work in the theater. Training helps you to understand what kind of play you are in. It increases flexibility and range and enables you to adjust to all kinds of situations.

RR: How did you decide on the exercises you use, the way in which you teach?

BM-W: The training at CMU is sequence based. Each year's work builds on what has been taught before. In the first year, I begin with impulse, then move on to actions and objectives. What do you want and what are you doing in this instant to get it? The typical class starts with a warm-up—then right into the main activity of the day—an exercise or working on a scene. We end with a game involving the whole class. In the second year, we introduce the more sophisticated techniques needed for language-driven plays. At first, we work on contemporary texts that are reasonably close to the actors' own sensibilities. Then we introduce them to Shakespeare. They learn to play "through the line," to pay attention to punctuation, to sustain longer thoughts, to really investigate a text. This is different from intellectualizing about it. Acting is experiential. Along the way, I give exercises that help them to translate their research from their heads into their work on their feet.

Every year, I see over a thousand students for twenty-eight slots in the acting/musical program at Carnegie Mellon. What I look for is a certain aliveness and a connection to their material.

RR: How should an actor begin to work on a role?

BM-W: The basics are always the same: who, what, and where—finding a connection to the material. But then you have to adjust your approach to the world and style of the play.

When I'm in rehearsal, I listen to the director, where she's moving the play. Early rehearsals for me are about going off impulse, admitting I don't have all the answers and trying hard not to come up with them too quickly. I fantasize a lot about the character. The amount of preparation necessary can also vary. If the material is very slight, sometimes all you need to do is show up and work off your partner. At the other extreme, Patsy Rodenberg said that if you're doing Shakespeare, you at least need a month before you begin rehearsals to get yourself in good enough shape to enter the physical, emotional, and vocal demands of his plays.

RR: Do you place an emphasis on the actor understanding the playwright and the world of the play?

BM-W: It's something I insist that my students do before they begin work on the play. Research must be visceral. I make my students answer questions about the play and present what they have learned to the class. Then they have to get the research into their bodies. Acting is sensual. Research is only useful if it can be translated into the acting process.

RR: How much of a role does imagination play in the actor's work on a role?

BM-W: It enables you to fill in the blanks and helps you put clothes on a role. It is what makes a part more than just an intelligent reading of the text. When I'm working with a student on a role and he says to me, "I would never do that," I say to him, "Well, this is not you. It's a character in a play." You use *you*—a part of you—through the character. That's imagination.

RR: How valuable is your unique presence to the work that is actually occurring in the classroom?

BM-W: You hope that you are able to communicate to students in a deeper way than just through the words you are saying. I think my students would say that I'm a tough, in-your-face teacher who demands a lot of them. I don't let them off the hook easily. I make them dig down and use their inner resources. Hopefully I do it with support and love and kindness. I believe teaching is about making creative human beings. I feel so responsible as an acting teacher. I hope that I am creating artists who will influence the shape and direction of theater and that some of them will go on to teach the next generation of actors.

MEGAN HILTY

Ms. Hilty made her Broadway debut as Glinda in _Wicked_ on Broadway. A recent graduate of the Carnegie Mellon School of Drama, she also appeared in _Café Puttanesca_ (City Theatre), _Suds_ (OCT) and _The Wild Party_ (Carnegie Mellon University).

RR: **What drew you to study with Barbara Mackenzie-Wood and how long did you study with her?**

MH: I had been working in Southern California, and several well-known actors said, "Get out of here and go audition!" So I auditioned for Carnegie Mellon and I got in. I entered as a musical theater major, but Barbara didn't stereotype musical students. I was treated the same as the straight acting students. I was with her for four years. She was a very intense teacher and instilled a lot of discipline in her students. She gave 500 percent of herself in all her classes and would really engage us, coming in after school hours and working with us.

RR: **What were you hoping to discover about yourself and the craft?**

MH: I was ready for something really intense to happen. Barbara's class really fulfilled what I was hoping for. She expected a lot from us; I was really open to whatever she would have us try.

RR: **How would you describe what you learned as an actor?**

MH: I felt I was prepared to take on anything that could happen, to walk into any audition, and I had all these things in my tool kit that I could use for anything they'd throw at me. I knew how to dissect a scene because they had made us do it rigorously in class.

And the fact I got through _Wicked_ eight times a week for a year is a total testament to their training. At Carnegie, they had us singing "twenty-five hours a day," and there's no way I could have gotten through the show if they hadn't presented the work to us the way they did.

RR: **How have you been able to apply what you learned in your work?**

MH: I would never have been to play Glinda in _Wicked_ unless she forced us to open our minds and work on things we thought were beyond our limits. I had instilled in me the "hunger" of always doing my best. I'd come offstage and think: Did I do my best? I grew as a person inside.

Barbara really forced us to stretch ourselves. I respect her because she believes in her students. We were all chosen to be there, and she had very high expectations of us. It was up to us to meet the bar she raised for us and to go further. It was all about committing to it.

JOANNA MERLIN

Joanna Merlin is an actor, a teacher, a former casting director, and a student of Michael Chekhov. She teaches in the Graduate Acting Program at NYU/Tisch School of the Arts and in the Michael Chekhov Association's workshops in the U.S. and in Europe. As a casting director, she is the recipient of the Casting Society of America's Artios Award for *The Last Emperor* and *Into the Woods*. As Harold Prince's casting director, she cast the original Broadway productions of Stephen Sondheim's *Company, Follies, A Little Night Music,*

Pacific Overtures, Sweeney Todd, and *Merrily We Roll Along,* as well as *Evita* and *On the Twentieth Century.* Other film casting includes three Merchant Ivory films. As an actor, she has appeared on Broadway, Off-Broadway, in regional theater, and on film and television. She is a co-founder of the Non-Traditional Casting Project and has served as a member of the Tony Awards Nominating Committee. Ms. Merlin's book, *Auditioning: An Actor-Friendly Guide,* was published by Vintage.

RR: Who has been most influential in how you teach?

JM: My first acting teacher was at the University of Chicago Laboratory Schools. She couldn't restrain herself from jumping up and down when good things happened in class or onstage. It was from her that I connected a sense of joy with acting and teaching.

Benjamin Zemach had studied at the Moscow Art Theatre and, in my mind, the M.A.T. became an almost mythological place where the actor was serious and respected and could have a creative life in the theater.

In my seventeenth year, I studied privately one summer with Morris Carnovsky. We worked on two monologues for ten sessions. From Morris, I learned about structure and how to break down a piece of text, how to use images to move through a scene.

Subsequently, it was my good fortune to work with Michael Chekhov during the last five years of his life. Chekhov combined all the elements that I had begun to incorporate earlier in a new and most inspiring and imaginative way. He created an atmosphere of permission and unlimited possibilities. We did exercises in movement and gesture that connected my mind and emotions to my body for the first time. There was great inner and outer freedom, a release of inhibition, not constrained by my own intellect or judgment. His approach led me to enlarge my image of myself as an actor, not limited by who I was, but able to use elements of self to create characters unlike myself. In a very gentle way, he created an atmosphere of playful exploration that led to creative surprises that we could not have found through analysis alone.

Chekhov was relentless in his search for the nature and art of acting. He never stopped asking questions, deepening his approach, trying to simplify the process. He searched for synthesis, a sense of the whole. As an actor and teacher, he is my inspiration and certainly my most influential mentor.

RR: Have you changed the way in which you teach acting?

JM: I had not planned to be a teacher. I had only thought of myself as an actor until Hal Prince asked me to be his casting director. I noticed that good actors didn't audition well. That provoked a need to figure out how to help actors audition better, which led me to teaching and writing a book about auditioning. I incorporated some of Michael Chekhov's ideas into the auditioning process and then started teaching the Chekhov approach independent of auditioning.

I was very nervous about teaching the Chekhov work because Chekhov was often called a genius, Stanislavsky's most brilliant student, considered by many to be one of the greatest actors of the twentieth century. How could I presume to teach the work of this genius? But as I found applications in my own work as an actor, and the courage to use myself more fully, I felt more confident about passing it on, and creating my own way of presenting it.

My work has changed over the years as I have allowed myself to become more playful and improvisational and less committed to doing it right. I think it is important for actors not to feel there is one right way, and I have tried to incorporate that idea into my teaching as well.

RR: Why should an actor study the craft of acting?

JM: Picasso said he spent his life trying to learn to paint as a child. My grandchildren become characters in a moment, with absolute belief, physicality, voice. Nothing prevents them from transforming themselves into Superman or Cinderella without inhibition. As we get older, we close down, lose touch with that most creative part of ourselves, our essential humanness, which Chekhov said yearns for transformation. Actors need to learn how to see the world in new ways, and how to incorporate what they see in the creation of theater. We learn to understand the world of the play, the point of view of the playwright, how to score our role with objectives, actions, voice, movement, speech, etc.

I feel that the work in class needs to be collaborative, so the acting choices are not imposed by the teacher, but discovered by the actor through the teacher's suggestions, which incite the imagination of the actor.

RR: Do you stress the importance of voice/speech and body work of the actor's instrument?

JM: All of these elements need to be developed in order to be useful to the actor. They are not supplemental; they are vital parts of the actor's training. Voice and speech change with each role, the body changes; otherwise, we are always playing ourselves. (Chekhov called these actors "pajama actors," because they never put on a different set of clothes—they are always wearing their own pajamas.)

At the NYU/Tisch Graduate Acting Program, where I teach, the actors spend a great deal of class time in all those disciplines, including the Alexander work, where they learn how to release physical tension. All of these abilities enhance their acting immeasurably.

RR: How valuable is your unique presence to the work that is actually occurring in the classroom?

JM: I believe that my work in the Michael Chekhov approach with actors, teachers, and directors, connecting the actor's body, mind, imagination, and emotions, enriches the training process and the development of the actor's creative individuality. It has taken fifty years for the Michael Chekhov work to be incorporated in acting training programs because he was so far ahead of his time.

Through my help in founding the Michael Chekhov Association, organizing workshops, and producing master classes on DVDs (with the help of the National Endowment for the Arts), I feel I have helped pass this very rich approach along to the theatrical community.

DAWN ARNOLD

As artistic director of the Moving Dock Theatre Company, Dawn Arnold teaches with the Chekhov technique in their rehearsal process. She has directed/devised *Celestial Mechanics—Or the Questionable Attraction of Entities*, directed *Savage/Love*, and co-directed/adapted *Galway Bay*, *Einstein's Dreams*, *Ocean Sea*, and *The Quiltmaker's Gift*. As an actress, she has performed with the Moving Dock in *Galway Bay*, *Ocean Sea*, and *Undercurrents*, with Alchymia Theatre in *Flood*, and with other companies in *The Cherry Orchard* as Ranyevskaya, *Heartbreak House*, *Mud*, and *Richard III*. Ms. Arnold also teaches at colleges and other theater companies.

RR: What drew you to study with Joanna Merlin and how long did you study with her?

DA: I got connected with Joanna Merlin through her incredible work with the Michael Chekhov Association.

RR: What were you hoping to discover about yourself and the craft?

DA: I had only briefly gotten to know the Chekhov technique through a movement teacher, Denise Gabriel. She told me, "I think you'll like this." It was planted in my mind at that time. Since then, I have explored Viewpoints, Laban, and a lot of body work. The summer before, I went to the MICHA conference and studied Laban in England with Jean Newlove. I kept trying to find out how movement work relates to acting.

Coming to the Chekhov work, I wondered, "What will I think about this?" At that point, I had a lot of questions; I was a teacher as well as an actor. The first workshop blew me away.

RR: How would you describe what you learned as an actor?

DA: I finally had a workshop with Joanna at the conference and we worked with the psychological gesture. It's when the essence of the Chekhov work came to me. It was the way of finding the character through gesture. Up until that point, the preliminary training exercises seemed to me very much like the movement work I had been doing, ways to awaken the actor's body. But then, with Joanna's teaching of the psychological gesture, we really got into the development of the character. Joanna is practical in that she really gets to what the actor has to do.

RR: How have you been able to apply what you learned in your work?

DA: It's become my artistic life. I've become a Chekhov teacher. My theater company has become a Chekhov theater company. I bring the Michael Chekhov work right into the process in our rehearsals. With each show, I start every rehearsal process teaching the basic concepts, forming a vocabulary with the cast with ideas from the Chekhov work.

When we adapted a novel, *Einstein's Dreams*, we used Chekhov's idea of the character's imaginary body in our process.

Michael Chekhov's psychological gesture intrigues me—I continue to delve into it more and more, seeing what this "door" will open for me as an actor and for my students.

ROBERT X. MODICA

Robert X. Modica has been teaching in his Carnegie Hall studio in New York City since 1966. After serving in the Marine Corps in the Korean War, Mr. Modica attended Adelphi University. While going to school and playing football and lacrosse, he discovered his passion for theater. As an actor, he studied privately with Sanford Meisner and then co-taught with him at the Neighborhood Playhouse. He is one of the few teachers teaching today who was chosen by Sandy Meisner to carry on his work. Mr. Modica has worked as an actor in film, television, and theater; however, he feels that teaching is his calling. In his over forty years of teaching, Mr. Modica has inspired many actors, including John Turturro, Louise Lasser, Tyne Daly, Scott Cohen, and David Duchovny.

RR: Who has been most influential in how you teach?

RM: Unquestionably, Sandy Meisner. The work Sandy did, his humanity, his incisive insight into the actor's work, certainly applies to how and what I teach. He inspired me to discover, realize, and apply all that was in me to use and draw upon as a teacher.

The U.S. Marine Corps, the men I served with in Korea, as well as the coaches and players that I admired and respected while playing football and lacrosse in college—these have all played a significant role in my approach to teaching, for in all these endeavors, it was always hard work, perseverance, courage, and love that produced results.

RR: Why should an actor study the craft of acting?

RM: This work is about truth, which is then enhanced by the imagination and individuality of the actor. It is necessary for the actor to learn how to trust themselves and give themselves completely over to the work.

RR: Have you changed the way in which you teach acting?

RM: You start out with a principle technique you believe in, in this case, Stanislavsky's principles, and they have to be processed through your own humanity, your own awareness and skills. I have a different background, a frame of reference about life, and it becomes part of the approach. The actor has to find their approach to truth, it's a matter of finding themselves through technique.

Over the years, my teaching has been deepened, broadened, and enhanced by my interaction with the students. I have learned a great deal from them, and it is incorporated into my work.

This work has always come out of a mutual commitment of trust and respect with my students. This leads me to constantly evolve and learn as a teacher.

RR: How valuable is your unique presence to the work that is actually occurring in the classroom?

RM: My presence in the work and passion for the work will only continue to be important and valuable if I stay available, involved, insightful, sensitive, and aware of the sensibilities, talents, and unique individuality of the students I work with.

I try to convey to my students that to be part of a process that leads to realizations and revelations of the human condition is very significant—that in transforming themselves as characters in a play or film, they are serving a higher purpose, touching and awakening people to their own lives, hearts, and minds.

JOHN TURTURRO

John Turturro created the title role in John Patrick Shanley's *Danny and the Deep Blue Sea* at the O'Neill National Playwrights Conference and reprised the role the following year Off-Broadway, receiving an OBIE Award. He has also enjoyed a collaboration with the Coen brothers, appearing in their films *The Big Lebowski*, *Miller's Crossing*, *Barton Fink*, and *O Brother, Where Art Thou?* His film and TV work includes *Quiz Show*, *To Live and Die in L.A.*,

The Color of Money, Five Corners, Do the Right Thing, Men of Respect, Anger Management, and *Monk.* Mr. Turturro was the producer, director, and star of *Illuminata,* opposite his wife, Katherine Borowitz.

RR: What drew you to study with Robert X. Modica and how long did you study with him?

JT: I first met Bob at New Paltz when I was studying there. A friend, Todd Thaler, who was best friends with Louise Lasser, had come up with Bob [Robert X. Modica] to see a play I was in. I was struck by his voice, how he talked, where he came from. And in the course of the conversation I learned he had played football against my uncle on Long Island. He told me he had been in the Vietnam War; my father had been in the war.

I had had good teachers at the State University of New York, New Paltz—Richard Bell and Beverly Brumm; they worked out of the "Uta Hagen tradition." Studying with them, I had learned how to break down characters and play objectives. Beverly had brought in a very exciting group of people to teach us. Julian Beck and Judith Malina came to work with us, and Christopher Martin. Harold Clurman had also come to speak at the school; he made a deep impression on me. At New Paltz in 1975, they were a great group of talented people, especially Beverly—she was a great advisor to me.

I began studying with Bob after that, for over a year. I was doing construction work while I was performing Off-Broadway. In his class, I was at first shocked at the primitiveness of the exercises; I had already been doing plays by then. In class there were a lot of good actors, like Rachel Ward. I really liked Bob a lot; he had a special kind of presence.

RR: What were you hoping to discover about yourself and the craft?

JT: I really wanted to know how to go "moment to moment" in the work—and when I did a show, where I should put my attention. I didn't know how to hustle, how to get an audition; I was very shy at that time. But I was a very hard worker. Sometimes he'd yell at me after I worked: "What are you doing?" I wasn't used to it—his brutal honesty. It took a lot to master an exercise in class unless I worked on it a lot. After a while I got better. I'd work a lot on doing independent exercises in class. I didn't know how to stay alive in the exercise, how to "keep the juices flowing." I was so used to using myself, but it's much harder to do exercises truthfully and to honestly live moment to moment.

RR: How would you describe what you learned?

JT: I had never felt like I had mastered those exercises. It takes a lot to stay alive moment to moment. Bob and I struck up a friendship. If I had to work on something for a particular role, he and I would talk about it.

I also brought my brother, and my cousin, and Aida, my sister, to Bob. And my wife, Katherine, she also learned a lot. I even got Beverly to come and watch Bob work, and she was very interested in the work he was doing.

RR: How have you been able to apply what you learned in your work?

JT: I've always been the kind of actor who wants to stay "at the table" and keep reading the play over and over and keep talking about it.

Actors have the tendency to start performing when they get up in class. But I want to go through everything first, make as many discoveries as I can.

In the movies, it's incredibly important. Sometimes as the character, I might have nothing to say—I'm just responding to what's happening. I might find an activity. For me, it's about being totally believable, totally alive every moment.

I worked with James Gandolfini, and when you watch the way he works—the way he puts his entire attention on the other person all the time—it seemed so simple, but he's very hard on himself; he's totally in the moment.

When Robert De Niro directed me in a film there were times I wanted to take in what had just happened in the moment, and he'd say to me, "Don't do that."

"But I don't know where I am," I'd answer.

"If that's the moment, it's okay. The next moment will come and it will lead to something."

ERIC MORRIS

Eric Morris began his involvement in theater at Northwestern University. His acting career includes over one hundred plays, twenty films, fifty network television episodes, and running roles on two syndicated TV series. His books, *No Acting Please; Being & Doing; Irreverent Acting; Acting from the Ultimate Consciousness; Acting, Imaging and the Unconscious;* and *The Diary of a Professional Experiencer* (*An Autobiographical Journey into the Evolution of an Acting System*) are used in colleges, universities, and private schools all over the world. Mr. Morris founded the American New Theater, a company of bicoastal actors who have a common approach to acting and a common goal of carrying that approach into theater and film.

RR: Who has been the most influential in how you teach?

EM: I'm a Method-based teacher. I got a degree in speech and theater from Northwestern University. Then I read all of Stanislavsky's books, but I was very frustrated because I couldn't figure out the "how" of his principles. He left a lot of questions unanswered. Starting in 1959, I studied three years with Martin Landau, who was a protégé of Lee Strasberg, and I attended The Actors Studio for seven years, where I watched Lee teach. Lee was a modern-day genius, very specific, very focused. I respect him a lot.

So I went from A to D in a process that I got from Marty and Lee, and in the next forty-plus years, I went from D to S on my own—and I expect to go to Z before I die! My teaching goes way beyond the Method, because I saw so many actors struggle unsuccessfully to apply Stanislavsky's very general ideas. My system of acting came out of the work I was forced to create.

RR: Have you changed the way in which you teach?

EM: Oh yes. My system evolved over forty-six years of teaching. I'd see an acting student become very frustrated, unable to break through, and I would invent an exercise right there on the spot, to address the obstacle and free the actor to function naturally. At one point I'd created seven hundred instrumental exercises, which I pared down to about three hundred in a "tool kit" of goodies that an actor can choose from. Most of these are included in the five books I've written.

RR: Why should an actor study the craft of acting?

EM: Human emotions are to actors as muscles are to dancers—they must be exercised every day, strengthened and loosened up so they're easily available. It takes years of training.

My goal is to teach every actor to be a "professional experiencer," meaning that he or she must use his or her own life experiences to fulfill the obligations in a script. The actor must first determine the playwright's intentions for how the character is feeling in a particular scene, then go on a "Choice Hunt" through his own personal life to find parallel experiences that might produce those same feelings. At the same time, the actor is selecting from thirty-one "Choice Approaches" to find the one or more approaches that bring the choice alive.

RR: Do you stress the importance of voice/speech and body work of the actor's instrument?

EM: Speech and body work are very important. Many actors can't speak the language properly, can't enunciate, can't project. I will tell an actor that he or she has to learn how to articulate and project and, when needed, to fulfill the vocal demands of classical material.

But what concerns me is that when actors start studying voice, they could short-circuit the natural connection between their voice and their emotions. Most actors become vocally dependent, using their voice to communicate without real emotional content. This causes a split between the voice and the emotion.

RR: How should an actor begin to work on a role?

EM: It's all laid out in my book *Irreverent Acting*. First, the actor should Relax, Sensitize, and do Personal Inventory. Then, without any preconceived ideas, read the material several times. Then begin to determine the various obligations of the play in seven areas: Time and Place, Character, Relationship, Emotional, Historic, Thematic, and Subtextual. Then ask yourself: What do I have to address first? If it's the Character obligation, select choices to create that character. And remember, all the choices the actor makes to fulfill the obligations of the play must come from his or her own real life.

Imagination has the extraordinary capacity to create fantasies. In using one of my choice approaches, called Believability, the actor combines a few true facts with imagined realities to create the emotional impetus that fulfills an obligation. Also, imagination is a fundamental aspect of the many techniques for developing what I call the Conscious-Unconscious Connection. My fourth and fifth books deal exclusively with this connection, because it's a gold mine of powerful truth in an actor's performance. It creates inspired, electrifying acting.

RR: How valuable is your unique presence to the work that is actually occurring in the classroom?

EM: My personality is kind of charismatic and I have a good sense of humor, but the work is not dependent on me. I've trained others who are using it all over the United States and in eleven other countries. My books are translated into several languages. Through many years of teaching, I've seen countless actors break out from socially conditioned barriers to full, natural, and compelling expression. I find that very satisfying. I do what I do because I believe in it.

JOAN HOTCHKIS

Joan Hotchkis debuted on Broadway in *Advise and Consent*, followed by other Broadway and Off-Broadway plays. Regionally, she performed lead roles at the Oregon Shakespeare Festival, Milwaukee Repertory, Cincinnati Playhouse, Tennessee Repertory Company, L.A. Theatre Works, and Odyssey Theatre Ensemble. She co-starred on *My World and Welcome to It* and guest-starred on numerous TV shows, including *The Odd Couple* as Oscar's girl-friend. Ms. Hotchkis toured in her two solo performance plays: *Tearsheets:*

Rude Tales from the Ranch (Fringe First Award at the '92 Edinburgh International Theater Festival), and *Elements of Flesh or Screwing Saved My Ass*. Her feature films include *Ode to Billie Joe, Breezy, Old Boyfriends* and an independent feature she authored entitled *Legacy*, which won prizes at festivals abroad and was distributed in 18 countries.

RR: What drew you to study with Eric Morris and how long did you study with him?

JH: I met Eric in 1969 in a scene study session at The Actors Studio West in Hollywood. I performed a scene from a solo play I was writing, and in the members' comments afterward, Eric spoke. I saw this slim, fair-haired man in the back row. He had an aura of calm about him and a "lightness of being," as if he were seated on a cloud of possibilities.

He said, "Your talent is like a line of silver Rolls-Royces trapped in a tunnel, because the opening is blocked by a rusty old Ford." He spoke about my tension and lack of trust in myself. "Your motor is running fine," he said, "but then you keep turning the ignition." Later I discovered that cars are one of Eric's hobbies, and in his teaching he often makes analogies to them. Lee Strasberg (I studied with him for three years) loved to cook, so drew his parallels from the kitchen. Lee used to say, "Darling, you keep lighting the match and then blowing it out," describing the same problem in my acting that Eric observed.

The next day, Eric and I met in a coffee shop. I wanted to take his classes and he wanted to direct my play. He told me about the "instrumental" exercises he invents in class and the necessity for actors to do them, besides working on scenes. We also talked about sense memory as a "foundation skill," demanding daily practice, because most dramatic material requires an actor to create realities that aren't really there.

I began my first class that same week. For five years, I took a five-hour class once a week, plus a series of one-hour private lessons and occasionally a twenty-four-hour marathon.

RR: What were you hoping to discover about yourself and the craft?

JH: Eric seemed to know how to break down the magic and mystery of acting into concrete, do-able steps. I hoped to learn how to broaden my range of characterization beyond the conventional housewives that made up the bulk of my professional roles. I hoped to acquire more confidence in myself as an actor, more courage to take risks and try original interpretations.

Years ago, in my admission interview with Sanford Meisner (I took his class for two years), I remember feeling almost desperate explaining why I wanted to act. Sandy's wise blue eyes studied me. He said, "You want to fly, don't you?" I was astonished by his insight.

I hoped with all my heart that Eric would teach me how to fly.

RR: When you left the class, how would you describe what you learned as an actor?

JH: During the time that I was studying with Eric, he and I were coauthoring his first book, *No Acting Please*, and he was directing me in my first play, *Legacy*. My work as a student was enriched by both of these projects. I began to sense the difference between choices that engaged my guts and choices that stayed cool in my head. I became more vulnerable and spontaneous, allowing the lines to come out of whatever I felt at the moment.

No Acting Please was published in 1973. In 1974, Eric and I produced *Legacy* at The Actors Studio West. Karen Arthur, an independent filmmaker, saw the play and made it into a prize-winning feature film. This would never have happened had my acting not gone through a transformational change.

GEORGE MORRISON

George Morrison has worked extensively as a director on Broadway and Off-Broadway, in regional theater, and on network television. In 1988, with Mike Nichols and Paul Sills (two classmates from the University of Chicago), he founded the New Actors Workshop, a two-year conservatory program in New York City, where he continues to serve as president and principal instructor of acting. He studied at the Yale School of Drama and extensively with Lee Strasberg at The Actors Studio, maintained a private studio for twenty years, is professor emeritus at the State University of New York at Purchase, and has taught at Juilliard. He has trained Edie Falco, Scott Glenn, Gene Hackman, Barbara Harris, Dustin Hoffman, Ron Leibman, Ving Rhames, and Stanley Tucci.

RR: Who has been most influential in the way you teach?

GM: It's been a long and winding road, beginning as a child in Evanston, Illinois, where I learned to act under the tutelage of Winifred Ward, a pioneering professor of children's theater at Northwestern University. I graduated from high school into three years of summer stock under the charismatic guidance of Alvina Krause. By seventeen, I was playing Orlando in *As You Like It*, by eighteen, Shylock in *The Merchant of Venice*. I spent two years at the University of Chicago, and that was where I met my two partners in the New Actors Workshop, Mike Nichols and Paul Sills. I studied for two years in Lee Strasberg's private class and then for an extended period at The Actors Studio. Both Mike Nichols and I were influenced by Lee's brilliant ability to analyze the acting problems in a scene. His work still informs the technical base of my teaching.

In 1965, I studied the improvisational theater games developed by Viola Spolin and then taught them to many hundreds of students over the next ten years. This unique approach to performing is still a featured component of my school. I inherited a powerful curiosity from my father, and I have, over the years, continued to study, gradually integrating into my teaching bits and pieces of neuro-linguistic programming, psychological theory, Mihaly Csikszentmihalyi's concept of flow, and a number of physical and vocal disciplines. Towering over my patchwork of influences stands the heroic figure of Stanislavsky and his placement of "experiencing" at the center of acting training.

RR: Have you changed the way in which you teach acting?

GM: The only constant in my teaching is change. I have never been fully satisfied with what I do. I am constantly reassessing my procedures and seeking out and studying what is new in fields related to creative functioning. My ongoing project of reflecting on my own personal experience in the classroom is a crucial part of my evolution as a teacher, even at 78.

RR: Why should an actor study the craft of acting?

GM: Stanislavsky called his system "notes for the moment of difficulty." If all goes well in rehearsal—if the actor's intuition stimulates the imagination, and the imagination leads to experiencing, and the experiencing expresses itself outwardly so that it can be seen and heard by the audience, and the whole process is repeatable—then there is no need for craft. But if the imagination falters, if it fails to lead to experiencing and expression, or it is not repeatable, then there is a need for a conscious process. Craft is developed through the practice of repeatable technical procedures accompanied by the working through of resistances to the flow of imagination, experiencing, and expressiveness (Grotowski's *via negativa*). In training, this project must be contained by a context in which the student feels safe to explore, and has access to accurate, non-judgmental feedback. This is the essential process of mastering any art. The great educator A.N. Whitehead wrote: "The canons of art are merely the expression, in specialized forms, for 'depth of experience.'"

I am open to whatever works. Samuel Beckett wrote, "Ever tried. Ever failed. No matter. Try again. Fail again. Fail better."

RR: Do you stress the importance of voice/speech and body work of the actor's instrument?

GM: In my school, we require extensive work on voice and speech and three modes of body training: Feldenkrais, Alexander, and Improvisational Group Movement (unique to us). In addition we teach, again uniquely, a class in differentiating voice from body from face, a technique based on the work of Wesley Balk, an opera coach, as adapted by me to acting.

RR: How should an actor begin to work on a role?

GM: Not by analyzing, not by excessive interpretation, not by discussing the script with the partner. The rehearsal process should strive to keep the door open for intuition and spontaneity as long as possible. Premature closure is the death of creativity, and the student must learn to tolerate the anxiety of "not knowing" for as long as possible. While in school, the best place to begin is to sit down with the partner, lift the words off the page, and talk and listen without deciding in advance what anything "means." More easily said than done, but this is a technique that can be learned.

RR: Do you place an emphasis on the actor understanding the playwright and the world of the play?

GM: Such an understanding is essential for an effective performance, but it's not the beginning place for a dynamic rehearsal process. In professional work, interpretation is largely left to the director, and most actors are content with that division of labor. Rehearsing scenes for a class, the student must play the role of both actor and director and learn to alternate between them.

RR: How important is imagination in the actor's work?

GM: Imagination is the soul of the process. The enormous challenge is to allow the body to bring forth one's imagination. At its highest reaches, it's only, as Laurence Olivier said, the most difficult job in the world.

RR: How valuable is your unique presence to the work that is actually occurring in the classroom?

GM: Perhaps the most vital contribution my presence makes to the students is that they witness me struggling with the difficulties of teaching acting, difficulties I do not hide from them. They see me evolving in front of them, and consequently I serve as a role model for their own artistic development. Actually, over the two years I strive to reduce the importance of my presence by teaching them to give feedback to their classmates. It takes time and effort for them to learn to distinguish evaluation (good/bad, truthful/indicated, and so on) from feedback, which requires the audience member to articulate the subjective rather than the judgmental experience of witnessing a performance, including the thoughts, feelings, fantasies, identifications, and sensations of the witness.

I teach because it's in my bones. Witnessing each individual student's awakening, as they shake off their culturally induced numbness and begin to appreciate their own complexity, is a daily reward for me.

GENE HACKMAN ·

Mr. Hackman made his debut Off-Broadway in *Children at Their Games,* **earning a Clarence Derwent Award.** *Poor Richard* **followed, and** *Any Wednesday.* **Mr. Hackman's films include** *Bonnie and Clyde* **(Oscar nomination),** *Marooned, I Never Sang for My Father* **(Oscar nomination),** *The French Connection,* **(Oscar, best actor),** *The Poseidon Adventure, Scarecrow, The Conversation, Superman, Reds, Under Fire, Hoosiers, No Way Out, Mississippi Burning* **(Oscar nomination),** *Class Action, Postcards from the Edge, The Firm, Unforgiven* **(Oscar, best supporting actor),** *Crimson Tide, Get Shorty, The Birdcage, Absolute Power, Enemy of the State, Antz,* **and** *The Royal Tenenbaums* **(for which he received his third Golden Globe Award).**

RR: What drew you to study with George Morrison and how long did you study with him?

GH: As an apprentice in summer stock in Bellport, Long Island, I was given a small part in Arthur Miller's *A View from the Bridge,* directed by Ulu Grosbard, starring Bob Duvall. Getting to know Ulu and his wife, Rose Gregorio, was a godsend. In the fall, Ulu sent me to his friend George Morrison (Ulu's wife, Rose, was also a Morrison student.) Ulu and George attended Yale Drama together.

RR: What were you hoping to discover about yourself and the craft?

GH: I was with George off and on for seven or eight years. My previous training, such as it was, had been at the Pasadena Playhouse in California, where one's scene performance, makeup, costume, and movement were all graded on a scale of 1 to 5. I don't think I ever achieved higher than a 3 for any category, so my expectations for something better were extremely high, and I certainly wasn't disappointed.

RR: When you left the class, how would you describe what you learned as an actor?

GH: Because of George's work at Yale and with Lee Strasberg, our work almost always dealt with the explorations of our senses and how that applied to the work of the actor. The application of sense memory and how it affects the actor, to me, is probably the most important aspect of the craft of acting—the various explorations of sense memory and effective memory, along with a particular song exercise and, maybe most importantly, the relaxation exercise.

RR: How have you been able to apply what you learned in your work?

GH: I felt at the time, and still do, that maybe the actor is most effective when not completely objective about his work, that *results* are best left to others, and that the important thing being the *work*.

LARRY MOSS

Mr. Moss studied his craft with Stella Adler, Sanford Meisner, and Warren Robertson. He began his career at the famed New York cabaret Upstairs at the Downstairs and went on to appear on Broadway in numerous productions. After teaching in New York at Juilliard and Circle in the Square, he founded The Larry Moss Studio in Los Angeles. It was there that he directed and developed Pamela Gien's *The Syringa Tree* (world premiere, ACT Theatre, New York City; OBIE Award for best play; Drama Desk, Outer Critics Circle

Awards for outstanding solo performance). Mr. Moss also developed and directed Bo Eason's *Runt of the Litter* (Manhattan Class Company). Off-Broadway he directed *Who Is Floyd Stearn?*, *Beast on the Moon*, and *RFK* by Jack Holmes (The Culture Project). Mr. Moss directed the award-winning short film *Dos Corazones* and is directing *Clint Holmes Live and On Time* for Broadway and April Daisy White's *Sugar* Off-Broadway. His coaching students include Helen Hunt (*As Good As It Gets*); Hilary Swank (*Boys Don't Cry*, *Million Dollar Baby*, *Black Dahlia*); Jim Carrey (*The Majestic*); Tobey Maguire (*Seabiscuit*); Leonardo DiCaprio (*The Aviator*, *The Departed*, *Blood Diamond*). Mr. Moss is a founding director of the Edgemar Center for the Arts in Santa Monica. His book on acting, *The Intent to Live*, was released by Bantam Dell.

RR: Who has been most influential in how you teach?

LM: Stella Adler, Sanford Meisner, and Warren Robertson.

What I got from Stella was her understanding of the social/political ideas in a play, to look at the social changes of a society, the upbringing of the character, and his education. What role money plays in the character's life.

I wrote about it in my book, *The Intent to Live*. When Stella talked about Maggie in *Cat on a Hot Tin Roof*, she made it clear that an actress playing the role of Maggie the Cat has to understand what Maggie means when Tennessee [Williams] has her say, "You can be young without money, but you can't be old without it. . . ." The way Stella discussed the play was a breakthrough for me, and it was also how she "broke down" George Bernard Shaw's *Pygmalion* in her script analysis class. At the time of the play, 1916, a woman of Eliza's class had two choices: to have a menial job or to be a whore. When Eliza is forced to take a bath in Professor Higgins's home, she is terrified that she'll be submerged in ice-cold water because the lower classes had no hot-water pipes.

All these things meant so much to me. Once I grabbed this from Stella, it made me ask all the right questions as an actor and as a director.

Sandy [Meisner] was my first teacher, when I was nineteen. I think the Meisner technique is the best way to start teaching acting to a young student.

I studied with Warren [Robertson] in the seventies, and what he did was considered controversial at that time. He took people to their most emotionally vulnerable areas. Warren's exercises were very physical, almost like Gestalt therapy.

All three of these teachers, combined, were really a complete education for me. Later, I worked with Patsy Rodenburg—a superb teacher of vocal production technique and Shakespeare.

Harold [Clurman], director, writer, and teacher, had the most extraordinary vitality. When you see him in interviews or you read his books, you are inspired. That's what I attempt to do—inspire. I teach with tenacious vitality.

RR: Why should an actor study the craft of acting?

LM: Because the actor has to grasp and explore the full range of his possibilities. Young actors need to get into a good class and work on their voice, their body, and their imagination. It takes discipline, dedication, and consistency of effort. They must do it because they have a passion to participate in the powerful and important world of good plays. They have to learn how to be still and simple, as well as how to create movement that reveals aspects of the character that are not expressed in the text. Actors must read plays, good fiction, history, philosophy, and psychology, as well as haunt every museum they can. The more actors learn about the world and their own inner selves, the better actors they become.

John Malkovich wisely said, "If I can find the character's point of view of the world, I can play him."

How we view the world is very specific and deeply emotional and based on our life experiences. How do we walk through the world? I was sitting in a café in Paris, watching people walk by. I suddenly saw a woman whose walk captured and disturbed me in one instant. She seemed to have just been through a deeply tragic event; her gigantic eyes stared straight ahead. She trudged forward as if she were in a terror trance and her head weighed a hundred pounds; her two children followed behind her, lost and trembling. Looking at her face and body, and then looking at the two children, my heart began to beat very fast and I became short of breath. There was no language, just despair; it was all in the body.

It is a lot like Michael Chekhov's way of thinking, when he talked about the physical center of a characterization. Chekhov also said that the best actors have a muscularly released body with a volcano inside.

RR: Do you stress the importance of voice/speech and body work of the actor's instrument?

LM: A great deal. There should be a complete commitment to finding the full range of the voice. The actor has to approach speaking like singing. Actors have to build their vocal range from their lowest note to their highest and exercise their vocal instrument every day. Actors have to be able to use their voice in as many different ways as possible. Laurence Olivier famously dropped his voice a complete octave to play Othello. Joaquin Phoenix did much the same thing for *Walk the Line*. The fascinating thing is, the more you explore your voice, the more you learn about yourself.

Every actor should take different kinds of dance classes, some jazz, ballet, and tap. In the fifties, most of the important film talent came from the stage. Many of the stage actors took Afro-Cuban dance classes with the great Katherine Dunham—the actors worked barefoot and danced to live drumming. This connected the actors to the ground.

Pamela Gien, who starred in *The Syringa Tree*, which I directed, plays twenty-four different characters. Pamela did two vocal warmups a day for a year. Judi Dench has talked about the work she has done on her voice and body to be able to do what she does. When I worked with Leo [DiCaprio] on *The Aviator*, he worked diligently on his voice in order to play Howard Hughes. Hilary Swank in *Boys Don't Cry* continually worked on her voice through the filming, and of course it made all the difference.

RR: How should an actor begin to work on a role?

LM: First he has to read the script, three times at the minimum, and get an overview. The first time the actor reads it as an audience, purely for entertainment; the second time it should be read silently on the lips to involve your body and your breath; and, the last time out loud to hear the play and all the different characters' points of view. The actor has to get to the story to find out why the character is in the script. What would be missing if that character weren't there? Go scene by scene and find out as much information as you can from the writer: all the obstacles in the way of getting what your character wants, and what is going on in all the relationships emotionally, and how they change. This is the "meat and potatoes" understanding of a play. Obviously, how high the stakes are for your character is vital to understand, as well as when and where a play takes place, the economics of the play and the nationality of their characters, and lastly, how a character tries to get what he wants. Playing active intentions reveals to the audience who the character is.

RR: How important is imagination in the actor's work?

LM: It's tremendous. I always say, start with the imagery that the writer gave you and imagine that first, but if images from your own life fill you with emotion, of course you should listen to that.

If you've done your imagery work during the rehearsal period, you will be amazed at how the images join you in performance. Just like you don't need to bring up images in your life—they are just there. But this is not the same thing as an emotional trigger (which you may use to create a specific emotion at a certain time); it's the imagery that the character is sharing with himself or another character.

RR: How valuable is your unique presence to the work that is actually occurring in the classroom?

LM: Having begun as an actor and worked all over the country on Broadway, in films and television, and teaching in front of classes for many years, I have to admit that what you might call my unique presence is simply that I'm a "ham." I love to express myself. I love language. I love the courage of acting. A teacher needs to feel the drama in himself.

PAMELA GIEN

Pamela Gien, playwright and performer of *The Syringa Tree*, won the OBIE Award for best play in 2001, the Drama Desk Award for best solo performance, the Outer Circle Critics Award, and numerous others. With extensive international theater and television credits, she recently completed the novel *The Syringa Tree*, published by Random House.

RR: What drew you to study with Larry Moss and how long did you study with him?

PG: I was cast in a play with Ron Orbach. He asked me one day, "Have you ever studied?" I had studied briefly with Jacques Lecoq in Paris and admitted that I had never gone to any kind of a class. He told me that Larry Moss, with whom he'd been studying, had been to one of our performances, and he could speak with Larry on my behalf. The next day Ron told me that Larry said I should come right away, so I did.

RR: What were you hoping to discover about yourself and the craft?

PG: When I came into the class, there were well-established, breath-taking actors, like Jason Alexander, working on scenes. I sat in the back row for months. I saw instantly that Larry was a special human being, and a brilliant, gifted teacher. I knew there was something more I needed to know and learn.

Suddenly, I was in a place where I could safely discover how to work at my best. When I was performing at the American Repertory Theatre and I did a good performance, I'd try the next night to recapture what I had discovered. I didn't know why I often couldn't.

One of the great things about Larry is that he doesn't teach just one way of working. He has studied in depth with legendary teachers, he has a lifetime of theater experience, and he's done so much psychological work on himself. Deeply, and with uncommon skill, he understands the actor's psychology. It's an incredibly personal, deep journey with Larry toward authenticity. And that means authenticity within yourself *and* within the character you're portraying. Larry will say often in class, "Take whatever works for you from the great acting methods. Take what resonates uniquely for you, for your instrument. We're all so different."

RR: How would you describe what you learned?

PG: The great and deeply lucky thing of my life is that I got to study with Larry and be directed by him in *The Syringa Tree*. Everything I learned in class I've been able to apply in every performance. I understand intention in a way I never did before, how to marry instinct with technique, how to protect my heart and be courageous at the same time, how to access gold, and, how not to pay dearly physically and emotionally when I work.

Larry is the greatest mentor of my life, and I wouldn't have had the experience of *The Syringa Tree* without his vision, his profound understanding of what I had to say as an artist before I realized it in myself. I would never have given myself permission to write without Larry.

When I brought in the first piece of *The Syringa Tree*, he said, "You have to write this as a play. We need to know these stories, to understand the world and one another better." Eight weeks later, I handed him the text, and we started to stage it. He often says it's up to us to take responsibility for being creative, to not wait for the bus to stop *for* you, but to be the driver of your own life.

The Syringa Tree actually grew out of an exercise in class. I had been studying with him for over three years, and one evening when he came into class, he said, "We're not doing the usual relaxation tonight. Turn to the person next to you and tell her a story. It can be anything—start speaking." I turned, and roaring into my mind came the picture of my grandfather's farm in South Africa. I hadn't thought of it in close to thirty years. I immediately tried to think of something else to tell. But Larry then said to the class, "Don't censor whatever comes into your minds; tell *that* story, *it will choose you*."

I will never forget those words. I slowly started to speak, out of deep, foggy childhood memory. Larry said to us all, "Take the story you just told and bring it back next week in a staged form—physicalize it." I went away thinking, "I'll never go near that!" But as the little gate of memory opened, I remembered songs we'd sing around the tree at the back of our house, little glimpses in my mind.

I was dealing with something so buried, so painful. When I finished, Larry said, "Can you see how emotional your colleagues are? This is extraordinary material."

I said, "It's just my life," still thinking I had nothing in the world of value to say.

He said to the class, "The more personal it is, the more universal it is, and the more it affects us."

RR: How have you been able to apply what you learned in your work?

PG: To stand on the stage, you'll always be frightened, but technique is one's safe harbor, the path to freedom in your instrument, and ultimately, in your soul. Larry always reminds me, as long as you're a bit more excited than you are afraid, you'll be okay. Most important, Larry taught me what it means to "be of service." When I might be really frightened, I remember that it's not about me. I *get to be* the vessel that serves the story, that tells this story of people who gave their lives in South Africa, for freedom. I remember I don't have to be anything other than who I am. When I remember that it's not about succeeding, but about serving, I'm able to deeply immerse myself in my job as an actor. Larry gave me that, and so very much more.

ELIZABETH PARRISH

Ms. Parrish trained with, and was inspired by, Stella Adler, Harold Clurman, and Martha Graham. She has taught at the Stella Adler Studio of Acting, Yale School of Drama (associate professor adjunct), Yale University (summer term: "Introduction to Acting as a Performing Art"), the Metropolitan Opera Studio (to help young opera singers to act), Circle in the Square, High School of Performing Arts, American Academy of Dramatic Arts, North Carolina School of the Arts, and the Eugene O'Neill National Theater Institute, and was the artistic director of Theatre in Education's training program. As a performer, Ms. Parrish has had featured roles on Broadway, Off-Broadway, and in regional theaters, summer stock, films, and television. She has written and given solo cabaret performances.

RR: Who has been most influential in how you teach?

EP: Stella Adler and Harold Clurman. And, in a way, Martha Graham. I was very lucky to have taken classes with her. She told us in class that she wanted to make us "acrobats of God." She would teach us that the contractions we did in class were spasms of faith. She would talk about Greek myths, and what it meant to be a creative being, and a "searcher."

It filled me with a deep, respectful awe at the miracle of being alive, of the importance of searching for truth.

Harold's wild passion and his adoration of theater as a way of life was truly exciting. He also had a great kindness. I took his midnight classes and he was wonderful for me. He would tell these wonderful stories and they gave me enormous faith in the theater.

Bobby Lewis—he had a great passion for the theater.

It was their enormous talent that made such an impact on the theater and on me.

RR: Have you changed the way in which you teach acting?

EP: I teach acting according to Stella, which is according to Stanislavsky. I probably have changed, but fundamentally what I teach comes from her. I try to keep her legacy alive and, of course, the students have changed because of the times. They don't know a great deal of their tradition. We're at the end of a different age. There was a time when you didn't speak to Ethel Barrymore unless she spoke to you.

I only began to teach because Stella wanted to go to Europe and she said to me, "Darling, you can do it. Here are all my books." Well, I organized them and taught and discovered I could do it.

RR: Do you stress the importance of voice/speech and body work of the actor's instrument?

EP: They're extremely important. A balance has to exist between the wild freedom that you need to have and the enormous discipline that's required. So your body responds to your ideas, so that you're not stuck in your own time. The voice is essential. One of the things we lack is the appreciation of the power of language, not just the intellect. Language is power. An actor better know how to use his voice if he wishes to do Tennessee Williams or Shakespeare. You need variety, pitch, resonance.

John Gielgud once said, "I didn't have a wonderful voice, but I did everything I could to develop my voice."

RR: Do you place an emphasis on the actor understanding the playwright and the world of the play?

EP: Yes, it's vital. There is such a desire by young actors to pull the material down to themselves, but you have to find out what is going on in the playwright. With a writer such as Tennessee Williams, you immediately become aware of the demise of the aristocratic point of view. Stella Adler woke us to what Williams meant through her script interpretation class. Anyone who decides to act in his plays had better know first what Tennessee was after. When Blanche covers the light bulb with a Chinese lantern in *Streetcar*, she's raising herself with some beauty. Stella fought for us to understand. Ideas like these flowed out of Harold Clurman too.

RR: How important is imagination in the actor's work?

EP: Tremendous. It was one of Stella's convictions, that as artists we are here to say something, and what you have to say comes to life through our imagination, our insights from living. So you better have an enormous imagination if you're going to say something important. Through this art form we're able to say something about who we are, with meaning because of the power of our imagination.

RR: How valuable is your unique presence to the work that is actually occurring in the classroom?

EP: I try, consciously, to continue what Stella and Harold worked so hard for. Most of us who teach know hard it is. I sometimes feel like I'm one of the "last of the Mohicans" because of the deep dedication I have. As I come to understand what I do, I keep having more and more fun. I love teaching. There's an enormous amount of strength I gain from teaching.

ROBBIE SUBLETT

Robbie Sublett is a graduate of NYU/Tisch School of the Arts, where he received the 2006 J.S. Seidman Award for most outstanding graduating theater artist. In 2005, he won the National Society of Arts and Letters Acting for Comedy Competition in Honolulu, and in 2002 he won the National Poetry Slam Championship. His one-man show, *Calacas*, was optioned for an Off-Broadway run after its first workshop run at the Stella Adler Studio and in the Harold Clurman Festival of the Arts.

RR: What drew you to study with Betsy Parrish and how long did you study with her?

RS: I studied character with Betsy through the Stella Adler Studio of Acting in the undergraduate program at New York University. Since then, our relationship has grown, and I worked with her on her cabaret show. I've also been working on my own one-person show.

RR: What were you hoping to discover about yourself and the craft?

RS: I had the privilege of studying with Betsy once a week at the Stella Adler Studio. I also studied with Ron Burrus three times weekly, along with classes in voice and movement.

The first time she came in, she immediately told all of us to sit up on the edge of our seats and said, "Ready, set . . . live this way." For her it's all about the energy of who you are, and in your acting. She hooked me from that moment.

I had become familiar with the Adler technique when I auditioned for New York University. The Adler technique is focused around the principle that growth as a human being is inseparable from and conducive to one's growth as an actor. That as an artist you must nourish your soul through an understanding of all the arts, and those rich experiences foster personal growth and inspiration, and all of that feeds your acting.

I wanted to learn that process of deepening and cultivate it in myself. I understood I had an affinity for acting, but I knew there was much more to learn, especially if I wanted to have a career in acting.

RR: How would you describe what you learned?

RS: My class with Betsy was about how to close the gap between this person who is not me and discovering an entry point (vocally, physically, or with costume) into what about them is like me or does exist in me. When I played Vershinin in *Three Sisters*—and I'm not someone who comes from a military background—I had to transform my external world into something I could literally see when I looked in the mirror. Betsy put us right into that world from the beginning, with military boots and a uniform, and had us marching around the room in single-file lines, standing at attention. Prior to class, I studied the photos of the period, read history books, to have a sense of how to stand, to move, to talk with the same sense of power and discipline that is inherent in Vershinin's office. And what came over me was totally different, out a different time period than my own. Altering the external totally transformed and refocused my internal life.

RR: How have you been able to apply what you learned in your work?

RS: As I've sharpened my imagination, I've been able to put myself more fully into the life of a play onstage as these characters.

In order to create my own one-man show, *Calacas,* I drew from my own life, my own encounters with different cultures, and my imagination. The whole piece is a construction that parallels an artist's process of creation and how imagination is a living, breathing tool. I experimented with physical circumstances and then expanded out through a resourceful exploration of what's possible for the characters at any moment. Working with Betsy gave me enormous freedom.

ROBERT PATTERSON

Robert Patterson has been teaching acting at the Robert Patterson Studio in New York City for the past thirty-three years. He had a successful career, primarily on Broadway, Off-Broadway, and at major regional theaters throughout the country. During the late 1960s, Mr. Patterson spent eighteen months in the U.S.S.R. studying its theatrical traditions.

RR: Who has been most influential in how you teach?

RP: Many people. Of course, Sanford Meisner, who discovered a doable approach based on what is universally human.

A great speech teacher, Robert Neff Williams, because he employed discipline in his classroom and his work, and the sense of protocol came through the process of what he taught.

Harold Clurman, our great theatrical giant, who in many ways surpassed George Bernard Shaw.

Martha Graham, who in tandem with Meisner at the Neighborhood Playhouse, taught American actors how to move in a truly theatrical way.

Stella Adler, who is uncompromising in her vision of theatrical truth versus emotional truth.

RR: Have you changed the way in which you teach acting?

RP: After thirty-three years, I would hope so. In the beginning, I basically taught what Sanford Meisner had taught at the Neighborhood Playhouse. Because of the selective nature of my classes, which never exceed seven people, I began to realize after three or four years that a more complete process of approaching the role was beginning to evolve from the fundamentals of what Meisner had taught. From the outset I resented the idea that American actors cannot do classical work and dedicated myself to developing a process that dispels that idea. Having enormously gifted students has made that possible.

RR: Why should an actor study the craft of acting?

RP: What is essential to a theatrical experience are the playwright, the actor, and the audience. Only in the theater can actors truly practice their craft, and from the outset of that journey they must understand their moral obligation to the playwright and to the audience.

RR: Do you stress the importance of voice/speech and body work of the actor's instrument?

RP: It is an absolute necessity for the real actor to be schooled completely in the externals of his craft. It is a never-ending process. Everyone who studies at my studio must study dance at the Martha Graham School of Contemporary Dance, Limón Dance Company, the Alexander Technique with Tom Vasiliades, and singing with Rob La Rocca. Today's young actors must understand the importance of the physical aspect of their craft.

RR: How should an actor begin to work on a role?

RP: The actor's job is to re-create the specific independent life of the role through the selectivity of what he is doing. Therefore, he must have a complete, concrete emotional understanding of the particular society that is depicted through what the playwright wrote. After reading the play, the first thing the actor must do is subject himself to the physical, emotional, and moral atmosphere of that particular society so that he has a complete, active understanding of that one human experience, endemic to that particular society, in which to begin interpretation. It is only the first step; do not confuse this with research. Research belongs in a scientific laboratory.

An actor's task is to live through the participatory life of the role within a concrete set of governing emotional conditions. No matter what the playwright is writing about, the actor must make use of all his inner and outer resources with a sense of taste to bring it alive. Vladimir Horowitz, perhaps the greatest pianist who ever lived, said, "Beyond technique, an understanding of life experience must be brought to the music."

RR: How important is imagination in the actor's work?

RP: The realization of the role must be the by-product of the dramatic imagination emanating from the actor's sense of truth.

RR: How valuable is your unique presence to the work that is actually occurring in the classroom?

RP: A teacher's obligation is to set his students free with a complete understanding of the work they were taught. In that sense, I would say what I do is relevant.

My wish is that everyone who completes my class is secure in their abilities and can work to their fullest capacity in whatever situation they are placed in, no longer dependent upon a teacher or anyone else to approve of them.

JO BETH WILLIAMS

JoBeth Williams was a member of the Trinity Repertory Company and made her Broadway debut in *A Coupla White Chicks Sitting Around Talking*. She has starred in several television shows, including *24* and *Guiding Light*. Ms. Williams's film work includes *Kramer vs. Kramer, Stir Crazy, Endangered Species, The Day After, The Big Chill, Teachers, Switch, Dutch, Wyatt Earp, Jungle 2 Jungle, It Came from the Sky, Fever Pitch, Poltergeist*, and *Poltergeist II: The Other Side*. Ms. Williams also directed *On Hope* (Oscar nomination for best live-action short film).

RR: What drew you to study with Robert Patterson and how long did you study with him?

JW: I was doing an Off-Broadway play, *Moonchildren*, in New York City, and several of the actors in the show kept talking about their acting teacher—Robert Patterson. They talked about how demanding he was, but they also described his method of teaching as the most concrete that any of them had ever studied. I was very intrigued. I had done theater at Brown University and then gone into Trinity Repertory Company. I had been working both in regional theater and in New York for a couple of years, but I had never really studied with an acting teacher. So I decided to sit in on his class. I was amazed at the exercises and the scene work the class was doing. I knew this was what I was looking for.

Bob demanded a two-year commitment and would not allow you to miss class, even for work. I had gotten a part on a soap opera, which allowed me to take his class at night and work during the day. There were a couple of times during the two years that I had to miss class because of a job. Bob actually kicked me out of class for it, but I persuaded him to let me back in. It was very important to me that I finish. I think the Meisner technique (which is what Bob teaches) is a brilliant method. I love the specificity of the exercises, from the repetition exercise to scene study and character work.

RR: What were you hoping to discover about yourself and the craft?

JW: I was hoping that Bob's class would give me a technique, a craft. I felt, as I am sure many young actors do, that some nights I was really "tuned in," connected emotionally to the role, and some nights I wasn't. I wanted to find a concrete way to reconnect with a role night after night.

RR: How would you describe what you learned?

JW: I think I went into the class with a natural talent, but I didn't really have the skills I needed. When I left Bob's class, I had a whole different way of working. I knew how to really work moment to moment off other actors, how to do an emotional preparation, how to break down a script and a character. Before his class, I was already a professional actor and working, but I needed training. I didn't know how to make things happen consistently. Bob gave me a craft, a technique, to do the work.

RR: How have you been able to apply what you learned in your work?

JW: I was able to apply what I was learning in Bob's class right away because I was working on the daytime show *Somerset* while I was studying with him. I even had the luck of working with Ted Danson on *Somerset,* who had also studied with Bob. So we had a lot of fun on that show because we had a very specific way of working together, speaking the same "language," you could say. And to this day, I use what I learned in Bob's class. It's a technique you can apply to stage, film, or television.

CAROL FOX PRESCOTT

After a fulfilling and varied acting and directing career, Ms. Prescott began teaching as a member of the faculty at the American Academy of Dramatic Arts and, later, the T. Schreiber Studio. In 1990, she created her own studio: Carol Fox Prescott Acting Classes. She has taught at the Naropa Institute in Boulder, Colorado; Elat Chayyim, a Jewish center for healing and renewal (Accord, New York); Shantigar, an arts and healing center (Rowe, Massachusetts); the National Association of Gender Diversity Training;

Deconstructionist Rabbinical College (Philadelphia); Artistic New Directions Annual Summer Improv Retreats; and the State University of New York at New Paltz. In her own private creativity workshop, Inspiration into Expression, in Woodstock, New York, she works with clergy, attorneys, medical doctors, PTA presidents, therapists, and others.

RR: Who has been most influential in how you teach?

CFP: So many people.

Peter Brook, although I never met him. I saw his *A Midsummer Night's Dream* production on Broadway in 1968; it literally blew my mind. Everything I thought I understood about theater was thrown up in the air, along with the actors on the trampolines and trapezes. In the seventies, when I was traveling in London, I saw his company perform *Pere Ubu* in French. Although I don't speak French I understood it all and saw that human communication was deeper than language. I began to search for what that might be.

Morris Carnovsky. When I was in college, I spent a summer at the American Shakespeare Festival in Stratford, Connecticut, and I saw his Prospero, his Feste, and his Lepedius over and over and over; it was the experience of greatness. The following year I wrote a college paper on the Method and Shakespeare. I interviewed him, and as I sat in his living room, while he shifted from one character to the next, he described what he did when he played these different characters; it was like pyrotechnics. I told him that he kept changing and he became angry at the thought, saying, "I am only me. There's only me here!" That planted an important seed, which I never forgot.

Robert Smith taught me to be easy and lighthearted around Shakespeare.

Michael Moriarty was the first person I heard say, "It's all about the breath." He changed my life. He introduced me to this way of seeing the creative process. It's what I've spent my life working on—understanding the work through the breath as an instinctive knowing, an immediate definition of truth.

Joshua Shelley, my first acting teacher, taught me about concentration. Charles Nelson Reilly, my second acting teacher, made it all seem simple, clear, and attainable in a musical theater class at HB Studio. He taught us: "If it's not fun, it's not worth it."

Gary Austin. Eleven years ago I met Gary and taught with him. We recognized that we had a lot in common. I had had no improvisational background. He had no understanding of the power of the breath. We started teaching together so we could learn from one another; it's been incredible. I learned about saying "yes" to everything, which is a clean, clear way of teaching how to stay in the moment. I discovered that improv and acting with text are the same art form.

Edward Strauss, the colleague with whom I teach musical theater workshops. He teaches me to trust the underdeveloped musician in myself, listening to the music in the spoken word.

And two performers: Kim Stanley—I saw her performance in *Bus Stop* on Broadway when I was sixteen years old. She cast a spell over me filled with energy and love—like sparkles of light coming out of her eyes and causing everyone in the audience to catch the glow.

Barbara Cook, from whom I learned that there's no difference between singing and acting and the joy in the doing trumps everything else.

RR: Have you changed the way in which you teach acting?

CFP: I had been working for two years at the American Academy of Dramatic Arts teaching what I had learned: straight Method work—sense memory, personalization, etc. I came to believe that there was a missing element.

RR: Why should an actor study the craft of acting?

CFP: It's the job of the actor to know how to mine the human experience. It's the actor's obligation to know himself, to explore himself as the acting instruments he is, inside all the possibilities of experience. A well-trained actor should be able to do two hundred performances or twenty takes in a row and keep them all fresh. He should have the flexibility to enter into the emotional and physical lives of all kinds of people. Knowing the instrument gives the actor the confidence to know how to approach a role.

Once the craft is well developed, it's invaluable to keep coming back to class to have an outside "eye" one can trust when working on a role.

RR: Do you stress the importance of voice/speech and body work of the actor's instrument?

CFP: One of the valuable things about breath work is that it makes demands on the actor's voice and body as well as the emotions. I'm not an expert in movement, but I have some background in dance, yoga, Pilates, and other physical modalities. I'm not a voice teacher, but I am a trained singer and have some working knowledge of the muscles and mechanisms of the voice. It's all included in my work. Without an expressive body and voice, feelings don't get communicated. I always suggest more specific training in both.

RR: How should an actor begin to work on a role?

CFP: With freedom and openness to all possibilities. I ask an actor to explore the play, to enter into the world of the play, not only looking for literal meanings, but listening to the music—sounds and rhythms that cause responses in the body. We're looking to work with the whole piece. A part in a play must be read over and over, every day, with the goal of knowing the world of the play as well as one knows one's own world. Research into the things that are not easily accessible to the actor is essential here. After each rehearsal I suggest keeping a journal, writing down every feeling, every experience, making no distinction between what one perceived as the character's feelings and as one's own feelings. The assumption will be that everything felt belonged to the character. On another page, write: "What did those feelings and experiences teach me about the character I'm bringing to life?" So that each lived-out moment can be explored, learning about the three-dimensional life of the character. Then, sign off with one's own name, marking the place where rehearsal is over as one goes back to one's own life and circumstances. It's an experiential way of learning about the character.

RR: How valuable is your unique presence to the work that is actually occurring in the classroom?

CFP: One of the challenges in being a teacher on my own is that I have to constantly work to keep myself present, centered, alive to each moment in class. At the same time, I don't want it to be about me. My only mirror is the response of my students.

There's a special "love affair" between me and every person in class. I make a conscious effort to work with positive energy and to include everyone in the room. To set up an environment where risks are the general rule and take the preciousness out of the work. Having spent a good part of my life as an actress, I see the students as courageous, special people. I demand a lot of truth.

I make no real distinctions between my spiritual and artistic lives, where the highest goal is to sensitize myself to the energy, breath, and experience of each human soul I encounter.

LIBBY SKALA

Libby Skala wrote and has performed her one-woman play, *LiLiA!*, across North America and in Europe, including productions in New York with the Mirror Repertory Company, in Vancouver as the season opener for Pacific Theatre, at the Edinburgh Fringe Festival Fringe and at the Georgian International Festival of Art (GIFT) in Tbilisi, Georgia. Her new solo piece, *A Time to Dance*, was developed with a fellowship from the Field Organization and premiered at the Fringe of Toronto Theatre Festival. Her other credits include playing Viola in *Twelfth Night* at the St. Lawrence Shakespeare Festival in Canada and appearing in Jonathan Glazer's film *Birth*, with Nicole Kidman.

RR: What drew you to study with Carol Fox Prescott and how long did you study with her?

LS: I signed up for a week-long improvisation retreat in 1996 sponsored by Artistic New Directions, and Carol was one of the teachers. She was teaching an acting technique based on breathing, awareness, and joy. I had a breakthrough in one of her classes. She instructed us to find a partner, to stay aware of our breath, and to make ourselves physically comfortable while looking into our partner's eyes. I sat there looking into my partner's eyes, faking acting comfortable with all my might, inwardly chanting, "He's my father. He's my brother," because I refused to visit the place calling out to me—that he was my lover. I'd spent my life barricading myself against exposing my heart for fear of appearing foolish. Carol spotted this immediately, came over, gently shook my tense hand, and said, "Doesn't he have beautiful brown eyes?" My cover blown, tears flowed. Amazingly, the world didn't implode. By the end, I felt I'd experienced firsthand a deeply committed long-term relationship without any embarrassment or confusion about the feelings being exclusive to the exercise. It was powerfully cathartic. I continue to study with Carol now.

RR: What were you hoping to discover about yourself and the craft?

LS: I expected to continue to expand and free myself as an actor; to expose and overcome fears, limitations, and preconceived notions about myself and others; to learn how to effectively apply the breath technique to the work of great playwrights; to discover everything beautiful, rich, and deep about humanity. My expectations are constantly fulfilled.

RR: How would you describe what you learned?

LS: Carol talks about the breath as inspiration and expression—both literally and figuratively. I've learned that working with the breath in rehearsal means becoming a free channel for the inspiration and expression to flow through. That my job isn't to analyze or judge, but to discover. When I listen and breathe with a text, I'm informed of how to dance, something like a jazz improvisation. By following the breath, there are an infinite number of ways to play the sequence of notes written by the playwright.

I've learned that any feelings that come up during rehearsals and performance belong to the character. Carol calls these feelings "intimate but not personal." Understanding this distinction permits me to embrace thoughts and feelings that come up in rehearsal without identifying them as belonging to me. I keep a rehearsal journal for writing down feelings that come up and what they teach me about the character.

RR: How have you been able to apply what you learn in your work?

LS: When I played Viola in *Twelfth Night*, I came into rehearsal with a lot of judgments. None of the productions I'd seen before had worked for me. Once we started rehearsal, I so fully occupied myself with finding and following my breath within the rhythm of the verse that I didn't have time to worry about making sense of the story. In the process, I discovered layers of truth beyond words pervading my being. It was extraordinary. I've learned that live performance is about moment-to-moment truth, not about making intellectual sense for the audience. If it were the latter, we could all stay home and read the play.

When I first performed *LiLiA!*, I would have an inspired performance followed by an uninspired performance. Carol pointed out that every audience is different. That's what makes live theater thrilling. Holding on to what worked for me yesterday cuts me off from the inspiration of this moment. Mary Baker Eddy writes: "God expresses in man the infinite idea forever developing itself, broadening and rising higher and higher from a boundless basis." For me, the breath work is a wondrous metaphor and tool. When I follow the inspiration, my energy is released, the playwright is served, the audience follows, and we all breathe as one. Then theater is illuminating and powerful.

JOANNA ROTTÉ

Joanna Rotté is a writer, teacher, director, and actor. Her books include *Scene Change—A Theatre Diary: Prague, Moscow, Leningrad* and *Acting with Adler*. As professor of theater in the graduate program of Villanova University, she specializes in teaching script analysis and scene study. She regularly directs and performs on Villanova's main stage repertory theater and has directed featured productions for the Philadelphia Fringe Festival, including two of her own plays: *Art Talk* and *Prajna*, which is based on a script by the Tibetan meditation master Chogyam Trungpa Rinpoche. She is a yoga instructor and meditation practitioner. Her comments on acting are published regularly in *The Soul of the American Actor* newspaper.

RR: Who has been most influential in how you teach?

JR: Stella Adler and Harold Clurman. Most important was Stella's sense of theater as a life path—that acting is potentially more than a career or a profession. I inferred this to mean that acting can be a way, or a Tao—though she would not have used that terminology—a path of spiritual discipline. I believe she recognized a spiritual dimension to the art of acting, insofar as acting can transcend the corporeal and materialistic. She would say that as artists grow older, they change, their heads change. She meant that the artist deepens and improves as a human being. She would recall how Stanislavsky intimated that he started out to become a better actor and became a better person.

I was affected by Stella's insistence that the performance be grounded in the given circumstances. In my teaching, the avenue to the given circumstances is script analysis: examining the text in detail, line by line, discovering the playwright's intentions for deciphering the role, because it contains all you need to activate the body and imagination.

Harold Clurman influenced me differently. He introduced me to the New York theater. I had the good fortune of being his student. The doctoral program at the City University of New York had invited Harold as a guest professor, and in his class, "American Theater between the Wars," he would tell stories of the American theater from the 1920s and 1930s.

At the break during the very first class, he asked me if I'd like to go to the theater with him. (He was the theater critic for *The Nation*.) I said "yes," and over several years, from time to time, I'd accompany him to opening nights.

In his company I learned the possibility of the moment of truth, that in any instant of live theater, something startlingly genuine may happen. In relation to the theater, Harold had what Zen calls "beginner's mind." He looked at art with fresh eyes and managed to refrain from cynicism. I assimilated a kind of faith from his erudition and his appreciation of playwrights—his respect for Ibsen and his love for Chekhov.

RR: Have you changed the way in which you teach acting?

JR: In the beginning I heard Stella Adler's voice inside my head. By now I've broken away and made the teaching my own. Also, my teaching developed in clarity through my experiences as a director, and more recently through returning to the stage as an actor. My studies in Asian culture and Zen Buddhism, as well as my yoga and meditation practices, have deepened my capacity for understanding acting and the nature of being human.

The radical change has been to articulate a perspective on the place of ego for the actor. I've come to profess that there is no place for ego—that shedding the ego is crucial in honestly attempting to embrace the role, to being a creative contributor to the production, and to being an artist.

RR: Why should an actor study the craft of acting?

JR: Because it's the handed-down set of instructions for using the tools—it's the legacy. There's a craft, and one becomes a journeyman. Today, on-the-job training doesn't really exist as it once did, where a young actor could apprentice to a theater company. Today, an actor attends a conservatory to learn to use the tools of the trade. The tools are the actor's material with which to practice the craft—the imagination, the energetic aspect, the body, the movement, the voice, the speech, the mind—bringing their beauty to bear.

RR: Do you stress the importance of voice/speech and body work of the actor's instrument?

JR: It's what's essential to manifest the inner work and allows the professional to change and endure. If you're a painter, you don't want to leave your watercolors in the rain. The voice and the body need to be cared for and persistently cultivated. They need to achieve their best expression. The actor's entire being needs to be made strong and flexible.

Stella told an impressive story of Olga Knipper-Chekhova, whom she met during her encounter with Stanislavsky in Paris. After their initial conversation, he turned to Olga and scolded her: "Madame Chekhova, you're late for your speech lessons." And she was eighty!

RR: How should an actor begin to work on a role?

JR: When Georgia O'Keefe began painting her flowers, she sensed that the critics looked at her flowers and saw their own flowers. They didn't write about the flowers she had painted because they hadn't seen them. For the actor, there is always the danger of saying, "I know what this is, I know this situation, I know this character"—without really seeing what's in front of you. Allow the script to speak its nature; take in the facts and gather first impressions. Begin by opening your heart and mind. In *Creating a Role*, Stanislavsky wrote: "...invite one's soul to buoyancy."

RR: Do you place an emphasis on the actor understanding the playwright and the world of the play?

JR: Yes! Envisioning the world of the play is one of the greatest joys of theater because we're actively creating, like gods or children. We're creating a world that is not our everyday one. All together, the actors, director, and designers are making an alternative reality so the characters have a world in which to live.

RR: How valuable is your unique presence to the work that is actually occurring in the classroom?

JR: My presence is indivisible from the work because my job is to assist the actor's job.

I try to model the practice of creative craft. My intention is inspiration. What's most important is that the students find an avenue for realizing their highest human nature. My function is to guide them through an evolution of consciousness.

SAXON TRAINOR

Saxon Trainor is a professional actor living in Los Angeles.

RR: What drew you to study with Joanna Rotté and how long did you study with her?

ST: I met Joanna at Villanova University when I was cast in a production of Frank Wedekind's *Spring Awakening*. I had never studied acting; I worked on pure instinct. Needless to say, I was terrified, and hoping for divine intervention. It came in the form of Joanna Rotté. Her calmness and compassion, and the power of her presence, drew me to her. I was an undergrad studying philosophy but I was allowed to take her voice and movement class for two semesters.

The fundamental theory behind her class was what some might refer to as "being present in the moment." She also included yoga and meditation in the work. She really introduced me to what acting was all about. She advised me to go study with Stella Adler in New York City. I had the honor of being in Stella's scene study class for a year. Joanna introduced me to the concept of theater as an art form. I had no idea what "the craft" was; I was a complete beginner. It was a profound awakening that acting was my path in life.

RR: How have you been able to apply what you learned in your work?

ST: For me, it's always been about the story and the truth of the person's story—that's what sustained me and kept my desire alive. Joanna talked about The Group Theatre and the power of what they did, politically and socially.

I believe theater and the art of acting should be respected—the humanity, intelligence, artistry, and compassion involved in it keeps me in love with my chosen path.

I teach now and try to instill in my students that it's a noble profession, that it's not about getting fame or fortune but about getting to the story in all its glorious dimensions. That it's first and foremost about artistry. I was very fortunate to have had Joanna instill in me a passion about the theater. She gave me an understanding of who the great playwrights are and what they mean to us.

TERRY SCHREIBER

Mr. Schreiber founded the T. Schreiber Studio in 1969. Mr. Schreiber has directed *The Trip Back Down*, *Devour the Snow*, and the Tony-nominated *K2* on Broadway. He has directed Off-Broadway, in regional theater, and for international productions in Tokyo, Japan. His most recent book is *Acting: Advanced Techniques for the Actor, Director, and Teacher*.

RR: Who has been most influential in how you teach acting?

TS: Michael Howard—I spent four years with him. He helped me experience the joy of acting and the work. I came to New York City with seventy-five plays under my belt, with terrific energy, incredible enthusiasm. Michael gave me an insight into the work—ways of finding my way inside a written character. Up until Michael, my approach had been from the outside in; he helped me reverse that process. His exercises were inventive and opened up my imagination. Michael was my introduction to breaking down defenses and opening up to all the possibility within myself.

RR: Have you changed the way in which you teach?

TS: I think over these last few years I have become more text-conscious, attempting to help the actor hear the music of different writers—rhythm, punctuation, and, most of all, recurring theme. You cannot play David Mamet, Sam Shepard, John Shanley, and many writers after 1960 the way you would play Miller, Inge, Williams. We are here to serve the text, and an actor's own natural rhythm has to be adjusted to accommodate the rhythm of the playwright's language.

I keep encouraging actors to take risks and chances and not to play it safe. We establish a safe, nonjudgmental, supportive atmosphere at the studio; a safety net for the actor to take those chances and risks. I continue to pursue more and more of this in my classes.

RR: Why should an actor study the craft of acting?

TS: It's an art form that you must seek growth in during your entire career. Stanislavsky, near his deathbed, had just begun to explore yoga.

Actors can get very lazy about expanding their craft. To be a good creative actor, you need constantly to challenge yourself. As Stanislavsky said, "Love the art in yourself, not yourself in the art."

Recently Eli Wallach and Anne Jackson spoke at the T. Schreiber Studio, and Eli stressed how he works to keep the "acting muscle" strong. I think it was the great Edwin Booth who said, "Acting is like sculpting in snow." It is vital to keep fine-tuning the instrument, to have a class where you can work on problem areas and challenging material.

Over thirty-eight years, the curriculum has evolved at the studio. I believe the actor's instrument must be open and full to express colors, rhythms, feeling, and emotion—to take on the body language of individual characters.

Initially I incorporated yoga into the acting classes, then added vocal production and movement work. Body Dynamics replaced the yoga classes. Taught by Carol Reynolds, the class uses bioenergetics and other forms to identify and loosen body tension produced by the body's muscular defense system. Our vocal production class, taught by Lynn Singer, also uses a bioenergetic base to help actors put their voices on their breath. Peter Miner teaches the on-camera class, and we have added an on-camera commercial class taught by Angela Maltabano, a voice-over class, a monologue class, and improv, and Sam Christensen teaches a four-day intensive, The Actor's Image.

RR: Do you place an emphasis on the actor understanding the playwright and the world of the play?

TS: Yes. It's absolutely vital that actors become better read. Every writer has his theme, and actors can see that in interpreting the playwright. I want them to read biographies of writers, and to see the influence Chekhov had on Williams, Ibsen on Miller, and Beckett on Pinter and Albee. The actor's job is to transcend the page and make a playwright's words come alive. The more you know about the playwright's theme, writing style, and music/rhythm, the easier the task of bringing the words alive.

RR: How important is imagination in the actor's work?

TS: The imagination is equated for me with the subconscious. The work is about tricking the subconscious to behave spontaneously. When that step happens, the imagination takes over. When actors give themselves to completely pursuing their objective, there is a giving up of control and the objective becomes the be-all and end-all. Obviously, giving over to an objective frees the imagination to create with aliveness and spontaneity. Helping the actor learn tools to free the imagination is a vital and key ingredient in the work of my studio.

RR: How valuable is your unique presence to the work that is actually occurring in the classroom?

TS: My presence is to help actors expand and grow. I want to create a nonjudgmental environment where actors can trust, take chances. I assign exercises and scenes that will help the actors open up their talent to the fullest. I love the work and exploring the art of good acting. I hope my enthusiasm inspires them, promotes confidence, and encourages them to go after their dreams with all their heart and soul.

EDWARD NORTON

Mr. Norton began his acting career performing Off-Broadway in the world premiere of Edward Albee's *Fragments*. His film work includes *Primal Fear* (Golden Globe Award, Academy Award nomination), *The Painted Veil*, Woody Allen's *Everyone Says I Love You*, *The People vs. Larry Flynt*, *American History X* (Academy Award nomination), *Rounders*, and *Fight Club*. He played himself in a cameo role in the experimental comedy show *Stella* and was the leper king in *Kingdom of Heaven*. In 2000, he made his debut as a film director with *Keeping the Faith*. He directed an adaptation of the novel *Motherless Brooklyn*.

RR: What drew you to study with Terry Schreiber and how long did you to study with him?

EN: An acting teacher I met in college taught at the T. Schreiber Studio, and I sought her out when I moved to New York. Terry's studio was on East 4th Street back then, next door to New York Theatre Workshop and across the street from La

Mama, E.T.C. He basically had an old brownstone that had been converted. There was the lobby down from the sidewalk level and then a creaky old seventy-five-seat black box theater upstairs. Classes were held up there. I started out taking a class with this other teacher, but she pretty quickly suggested to Terry that I should join his class. We talked and I liked him right away, and it turned out he was going to direct a production of a Tennessee Williams play in Tokyo and needed some basic Japanese. I spoke it well enough to coach him and so that was how we started—trading acting classes for Japanese lessons. I studied with Terry off and on for two or three years.

RR: What were you hoping to discover about yourself and the craft?

EN: I hoped the environment would be serious and practical, which it was. I remember that I wanted to find ideas to bounce my own instincts off of and get a feeling for where I was technically weak.

RR: How would you describe what you learned?

EN: In the broadest sense, I think Terry expanded my toolbox. He had a very pluralistic approach to the challenges an actor faces. He recognized that actors in the modern world of theater and film and television are going to be confronted with wildly divergent types of material and that no single, narrow technique was going to give you the key to all of it. He was very well versed in many of the well-known schools of actor training—Adler, Strasberg, Meisner—and he had many of his own ideas, too. He brought elements of all of that into class, along with just good basic text analysis. He would introduce you to a lot of these different ideas through exercise work, and then that would evolve up into working on actual scenes from plays. I liked this because it seemed highly practical to me—not that he in any way denied the magic of the process or that of intuition and instinct, although you really can't teach that stuff. I walked away with a much clearer understanding that you might have to pick the lock of a character a different way each time and feeling like I had some idea how I might go through that process on my own. He was there to arm you with craft and get you out there, and if you weren't looking for work, he didn't want you in the class.

RR: How have you been able to apply what you learned in your work?

EN: It's hard to say. Time goes by and your process changes, to be honest, because your relationship to doing the work changes. But I certainly still remind myself now and then to be sure I'm actually listening to the actor across that space from me, taking in what he or she is offering, and responding to it, as opposed to playing out some idea I had of the scene on the way to work that morning or assuming that it's going to be the same play that it was the night before. Terry was always stressing that listening was half of the job, and I agree. And I think, too, that I still use a lot of what Terry was teaching in his "private moment" exercises. He helped me have confidence that behavior without words can be as revealing and riveting as the best speech. And I always look for those moments in a piece—the moments when a character, alone, reveals himself.

SANDE SHURIN

Ms. Shurin authored the book *Transformational Acting: A Step Beyond* (Limelight Editions). She currently teaches in New York City and in Woodstock, New York. She was seen on *The Oprah Winfrey Show*, *Faking It*, and *America's Next Top Model*. Ms. Shurin was the acting coach for Robert Margolis' film *The Definition of Insanity*, featuring Peter Bogdanovich and Bruce Levy. She has directed *The Price of Genius* on Broadway, several Off- and Off-Off-Broadway plays, the cabaret show *You, Me and Sammy D*, and the cable series *Working Actors*. Ms. Shurin has coached and directed many actors, including Anthony Rapp, Matthew Modine, Daphne Rubin-Vega, Sylvia Miles, Adam Pascal, Ty Treadway, Tripp Hanson, and the Manhattan Rhythm Kings. Ms. Shurin developed the Break-Thru Workshop, a powerful transformational event that supports organizational leaders as well as actors and business people of all kinds in personal and career breakthroughs. She is directing her first feature film, *Feminine Protection*, by Emily Duff.

RR: Who has been most influential in how you teach?

SS: Actually, I was more influenced by the period of time, the culture, and our need to change and was impacted by other art forms around me more than by a particular teacher. I was impassioned by breakaway, innovative new art forms, and riveted by the "new" cutting-edge work of Joe Chaiken, Claus Oldenburg, John Cassavetes, Federico Fellini, Robert Rauschenberg, Andy Warhol, Allen Ginsburg, and Bob Dylan. I had taught a very strong Stanislavsky-based acting technique over thirty years ago for Irene Daly to some of the day's celebrities, like David Soul and Kathleen Quinlan, and I used this technique myself. I found something missing. I loved rock concerts like the Rolling Stones and David Bowie—such electricity between the performer and the audience. How could I get that electricity between a serious performer and the audience? Thus, my technique, Transformational Acting, was born.

It's not a traditional technique. There's no sense memory—only what is going on in the moment. It's not an objective-driven technique. It's based on the actor's presence, his uniqueness, and using his current feelings.

Although my technique doesn't sit on the shoulders of any Stanislavsky-based technique, without this brilliant teacher's contribution to acting, I could not have veered from it to create my own acting technique.

RR: Have you changed in the way in which you teach acting?

SS: Yes! My technique started to focus on creating individually signatured artists working with the truth of the actor, rather than just the truth of the character. I became acutely aware that all emotions are made of the same energy, with different-colored filters over that energy to create an emotion. Any real true current emotion will give the actor the fuel, the electricity. It's learning how to use these filters.

I also discovered psyche work: altering the actor's blueprint from his own to become that of the character's. This new blueprint actually becomes a filter. It doesn't dictate the emotion; it changes the psyche (attitude, point of view, and perceptions) of the character and how the character utilizes energy through new thought patterns.

There is another very strong component of my work: Don't act! For actors not to preconceive what they think their character is feeling, but to use what is current and true for them. To let their emotions flow naturally. To use these psyche filters and allow for surprises and quick shifts of emotions, which I feel is much more life-like than predetermining the character's emotions.

RR: Why should an actor study the craft of acting?

SS: I consider acting an art and I develop artists. I believe acting is a muscle. An actor must be alive and in the moment, in peak condition, at the top of his form, and be willing to take risks. When the director calls "action," or you get your countdown for TV, or "places" for theater, you have to jump through the hoop—no building time, just be in perfect condition, in the moment and at the height of emotion, listening and responding and following your impulses.

Acting and teaching are creations. I create new exercises all the time to keep my actors excited and fresh and more deeply connected to themselves and to transforming into character. But more importantly, I watch to see what they need and create the appropriate exercises and new distinctions to allow them to grow where they need to grow. I also recently developed a set of exercises for the auditioning experience, to help my actors with their auditions.

RR: Do you stress the importance of voice/speech and body work of the actor's instrument?

SS: Every actor needs to be able to be heard; I don't believe in artificial speech. If you need to do a dialect for a certain role, then a dialect coach is a must. Also, the actor must learn the relationship between breath and voice. But it is my experience that when an actor truly transforms into character, becomes that character, he will usually be appropriately heard.

The body is the physical support system for the actor's instrument. Keeping it toned and trained gives the actor the support he needs to naturally transform into character. First comes the psyche transformation, which then dictates the physical transformation. A well-trained body can accommodate that transformation more easily. Also, our jobs are rigorous, with long hours, and we need stamina and endurance. We need our body to support us through arduous hours.

RR: How should an actor begin to work on a role?

SS: The short of it is "impressions." What does the script evoke in you? The art of the work is in being aware of and using what the script evokes in you and how the script helps trigger your transformation into character, as well as helping the actor create the life under the words—not playing the scene. The script is your partner—you should feel the changes, the tones, and the various rhythms.

Read the material and use a four-color pen to underline or notate:

All given circumstances, including information regarding your character—the circumstances are the springboard for your creativity.

What is going on in the scenes, including actions?

Theme, and how your character fits into the whole picture—including intentions, relationship, needs, and your ongoing through line. For film, you need a well-constructed arc notating all time lines so that you are freed up to be creative, move to move.

What is relevant to you in your own life evoked by the script. Note all personal connections, including associations with dreams, music, images, and current life explorations.

Allow all of this information to "work on you" and then let it go and begin your transformation into character.

RR: Do you place an emphasis on the actor understanding the playwright and the world of the play?

SS: The emphasis is on the actor "experiencing" the writer and the world of the script, not intellectually understanding the writer, reasons, and world of the script. The difference is between an artist and a technician is to learn about what the writer is saying and what the script is all about. What the writer has written is the world the character lives in and the "reality" the actor expresses. However, this learning experience should not land on the actor as an intellectual pursuit, but as experiences to be used to create from.

RR: How important is imagination in the actor's work?

SS: You soar when your imagination is connected to your impulses. You can get stuck in repeating when imagination is linked to planning.

I'm always in favor of creative pursuits—your imagination linked to creative impulses gives the actor the license to say whatever the character says or does. When does your character get up in the morning? Does he water his plants, put on music, or put on the news? The actor has to trust whatever information and images comes to him. Go with your first impulse. You can always change it later. You will eventually discover a gut way of knowing what works.

RR: How valuable is your unique presence to the work that is actually occurring in the classroom?

SS: I am honored to be able to make such a difference in the lives, work, and careers of so many talented actors and am grateful for my unique presence, which allows me to do it.

My work, whether as a teacher, director, or writer, is always looking to break new ground while exploring the truth of one's self. I am looking to my students to do the same and to inspire audiences to do the same. It is the reason I do what I do—to inspire. I hope this will be my legacy.

JICKY SCHNEE

Jicky Schnee appeared as Franciska in the New York premiere of *Arabian Night* by Roland Schimmelpfennig at Classic Stage Company. Her film and television roles include *The Afterlight*, directed by Alexei Kaleina and Craig MacNeill; *Dedication*, directed by Justin Theroux; *Flavors*; *The Shake*; *Hope & Faith*; *Law & Order: Criminal Intent*; and *The Jury*.

RR: What drew you to study with Sande Shurin and how long did you study with her?

JS: A friend, an artist, brought me to one of Sande's classes initially. I had taken classes previously with Marcia Haufrecht and Susan Batson, they both taught the Method or their own version of the Method. Both Susan and Marcia gave me a great foundation for working: Marcia taught with a more classical Stanislavsky approach; Susan expanded my emotional range by pushing always to find the "need" of the character.

I can still hear her screaming at me to get to the "bottom" of the character. I felt prepared to work, but a sense of ease was missing, and this is why I ended up looking for another teacher and how I met and started working with Sande. I've been working with her for about two years.

RR: What were you hoping to discover about yourself and the craft?

JS: I was hoping to open myself up to a greater sense of ease when working, being as truthful as possible in my work without it being painful, which can be one of the pitfalls of sense memory work. Sande teaches her own technique, Transformational Acting. She believes every character is inside you. If you can access more parts of yourself and "fire them up," then you can play any character.

RR: How would you describe what you learned?

JS: It's expanded my repertory. For example, I'm a very shy person and I had always had trouble doing flirtatious or sexually motivated characters.

In class I worked on the character of Curley's wife from *Of Mice and Men*. She's very different from me, how I was raised, the mores that were ground into me as a child, and I originally found great difficulty being open to that energy. But Sande somehow helped me open up that part of my own psyche and to compassionately give it to the character. It really expanded me as an actor to figure out not only how to be okay in that energy, but to thrive in it.

In another class, we were given an exercise to share three different aspects of our own psyches. Sande had us stand in front of the class in each of the three aspects and asked us questions about ourselves. What we like to do, wear, buy, eat, etc. It became clear to me that each different psyche aspect had different behaviors.

RR: How have you been able to apply what you learned in your work?

JS: Sande keeps telling me to expand past what I think I am. I never thought of myself as a particularly funny person, but I auditioned and got a small but very funny role on *Hope & Faith*.

MELISSA SMITH

Melissa Smith appeared as Rebecca McKeene in *Continental Divide* at Berkeley Repertory Theatre and throughout BRT's Birmingham/London tour. Other Bay Area performances include Susan in *Holiday* at Napa Valley Repertory Theatre. Ms. Smith has also worked extensively Off-Off-Broadway and in regional theaters across America. Since 1995, Ms. Smith has served as American Conservatory Theater's conservatory director and as the master acting teacher in its MFA program. She was the director of the Program in Theater & Dance at Princeton University and taught acting at the Caymichael Patton Studio in New York City and in various high schools, colleges, and universities in New York, New Jersey, Honolulu, and Florence, Italy.

RR: Who has been most influential in how you teach?

MS: I was trained by Earle Gister at Yale, and his approach to identifying actions/objectives in a text is a layer of my foundation. Lloyd Richards directed me at Yale, and rehearsal with him was a master acting class for me.

Caymichael Patten became my mentor. With Cay, I learned how to bring myself more fully to my acting, to access and use my instincts and intuition in creating a role and, subsequently, how to teach others to do this as well. I studied with her at the perfect moment in my life—she spoke directly to what I needed to learn then. In retrospect it may have been important that she is a woman.

I've also been influenced by the students of Peter Kass, especially Dennis Krausnick, head of training at Shakespeare & Company, and Ron Van Lieu, head of training at Yale Drama. From them I have learned the importance of getting a young actor to experience and acknowledge both his fear and his desire to act in order to develop a passion for doing undefended, transformational work.

Earle Gister—I appreciated the value of my work with him much later.

RR: Have you changed the way in which you teach acting?

MS: I pay more attention to what is actually happening in the room than to the plan I made before I got there. Increasingly, I think it matters less what technique I am employing—be it the Meisner "repetition" exercise or the "five questions"—and more what kind of person and presence I have in the room. Recently I came across the term, "undefended presence," and I recognized that as something I try to cultivate in my actors.

If I come into a class tense, unapproachable, or unavailable, I can't expect them to be open and undefended with me. The enterprise of teaching acting—and making theater—is a collaborative game between people. How they interact with one another, in ways small and large, matters more than their expertise in terms of the life of the final product. I have come to subscribe more and more to the thinking: The way you rehearse it is how you will perform it.

When I first started out, I was teaching scene study the way I had been trained: by breaking a scene down into actions and objectives. I happened to visit a class that Joan MacIntosh taught where the work was messier than that in my class and much, much more alive. I realized in that moment that I was interested in acting that made me listen—listen to the actors and to the words they said. I believe that we go to the theater to listen to a play as much as to see it. (After all, the word "rehearse" contains the word "re-hear"). The way I teach has everything to do with getting actors to listen deeply to one another, to develop an interactive life between themselves and the text. When that life happens, we—the audience—are drawn into the life of the play.

RR: Do you stress the importance of voice/speech and body work of the actor's instrument?

MS: It's very important. Acting is an athletic endeavor, involving a body/thinking process. Physical and vocal training, done properly, will release an actor's talent, deepening and broadening his range, helping to develop in him the stamina necessary for the rigors of sustained live performance—just like practice drills heighten the athlete's performance in the real game. I frequently co-teach with a voice or movement teacher to help actors understand that voice and body work can open up an actor's mind and emotional life.

RR: Do you place an emphasis on the actor understanding the playwright and the world of the play?

MS: Yes, but as John Gielgud said, "Style is knowing what kind of play you are in." That knowledge can be gleaned through reading history, seeing films, looking at paintings, reading other plays by the same writer, and listening to the director and dramaturge of a production you are in. I encourage actors to experiment with a variety of research tools and to learn what kind of research is most helpful to them.

RR: How valuable is your unique presence to the work that is actually occurring in the classroom?

MS: I believe I can promote certain values with my gifts and my presence. Helping another human being lead a creative life, guided by humanistic values—that feels like a huge contribution, one I'm proud to make.

DANIEL BEATY

Daniel Beaty was seen on *Russell Simmons Presents Def Poetry, Showtime at the Apollo,* and *106 & Park.* His solo show, *Emergence-SEE!,* had its Off-Broadway premiere at The Public Theater in New York City. Mr. Beaty has performed at the White House and at the Kennedy Center in a tribute to Ruby Dee and Ossie Davis. He was the 2004 Nuyorican Grand Slam Champion at the Nuyorican Poets Cafe and the Fox Networks National Redemption Slam champion and has also performed with Jill Scott, Sonia Sanchez, MC Lyte, Mos Def, Tracy Chapman, Deepak Chopra, and Phylicia Rashad.

RR: What drew you to study with Melissa Smith and how long did you study with her?

DB: I did my undergraduate study at Yale, graduated in 1998, and looked at graduate programs. I spoke with Melissa about her program, and during the audition process, I was pushed to an emotional place of "letting go." I felt vulnerable, in a way, out of control, by what I was asked to do. She encouraged me to go further.

I received a full scholarship to study at American Conservatory Theater and was very happy to be there for three years in the Master's program. Melissa was my primary acting teacher the first year, and then I worked with her during my third year. She'd evaluate my work in class; she was a constant presence, always available for consultations.

RR: What were you hoping to discover about yourself and the craft?

DB: I began to discover, during my senior year at Yale, a feeling of truth emanating from my soul. I could feel the ability of being totally engaged, of being focused on an objective, that I was *making* it happen. I was hoping to find a safe place to explore at A.C.T. And I did.

I was aware that I didn't have a technique or the vocal training I needed to have. I could feel I was carrying a lot of tension in my body; I was beginning a relationship with my body. I had been an opera singer and had a concept of training, but it wasn't entirely what it needed to be for acting. At A.C.T. I learned the Linklater technique.

RR: When you left the class, how would you describe what you learned as an actor?

DB: I had a very strong relationship with Melissa; my life was changed in terms of doing the process. One of the techniques I learned was the Meisner technique; she really had developed her own version of it.

For me, the Meisner technique has a lot to do with not censuring yourself. It has to do with the ability to "give over" completely to the moment and affecting another person.

I had moved through my life censoring my responses as a human being. As a black man, in my life I had devised a way of censoring myself, making sure my words communicated my thoughts "correctly." I had the experience of being in certain situations, of being in front of people, where I had to mute my impulses.

In the process of using the Meisner technique, the "giving over" wasn't easy. I had censured myself for so long, controlled my actions, and now I was in a situation of being pushed beyond that place; it was scary. I had felt safe being disconnected.

Melissa was unrelenting in her insistence. We worked on opening me up—that was really the core for me. That's what acting is really about—the alive, vibrant energy between people.

As the training progressed, we'd work on character, beginning with the "self." Allowing my own emotional palette to be as broad as possible, to really explore certain areas—authentic anger, authentic joy—to be "emotionally naked."

She saw my ability to fake it, and I knew I had enough ability, of actions, of beats, that I could "self-create" whatever emotions were required. But she pushed me to be organic. I was terrified, frustrated. It took a while to be able to do it. I felt it contrasted to my experience in my own life, and I shared these thoughts with Melissa. It was my deep inability to get the Meisner work as quickly as the others that challenged me.

I found a place in A.C.T. where I could create. I found also my particular strength in transforming into a character. A space was also created for exploration of my own work. I'm a playwright, and it allowed my ability to come through—uncensored and authentic in my expression, and it's how I began work on my own solo show: *Emergence-SEE!*

RR: How have you been able to apply what you learned in your work?

DB: What I discovered was that it's about being present, being open, and trusting the intelligence that comes from my body, my feelings, myself. Melissa's influence impacted everything I did. The basic way I can describe it is that synthesized acting is energy between people.

If I'm too focused on myself, I'm not fully present. I'm not really melting into the other person or the audience, and the exchange of energy definitely won't happen. At A.C.T., I began to understand a clear sense of my purpose as an artist.

ROBIN LYNN SMITH

Ms. Smith is a founding partner and artistic director for Freehold Theatre Lab Studio in Seattle. She has worked for the past twenty-five years acting, directing, and teaching in Chicago, Boston, Seattle, and New York. She has directed Off-Broadway (*Curse of the Starving Class* at the Promenade Theatre) and at regional theaters and is presently directing Freehold's Engaged Theatre program, which tours Shakespeare productions to prisons, projects, and tent cities. She served as an artist-in-residence with Dan

Sullivan at the Seattle Repertory Theatre, where she directed several productions, including *Marvin's Room, Frankie and Johnnie in the Claire de Lune, City of Gold,* and the developmental workshop of Elizabeth Chiffon's *New Patagonia.* She has also directed in Seattle at the Empty Space Theatre, New City Theatre, On the Boards, ACT Theatre, and Seattle Children's Theatre, and she is presently an affiliate artist with Bartlett Sher at Intiman Theatre. At Freehold, she directed the award-winning laboratory investigations of *The Seagull, An Altered Life* by Elizabeth Heron, *Three Sisters, The Winter's Tale,* and *The Tempest.* She is the director of Freehold's annual residency in the development of new work with the inmates of Washington State Women's Penitentiary. Robin has been a guest director and instructor at New York University/Tisch's Graduate Acting Program and the University of Washington's Professional Actor Training Program and is presently on the faculty of Cornish College of the Arts.

RR: Who has been most influential in how you teach?

RLS: A few different teachers: Ron Van Lieu, Joseph Chaikin, and Sanford Meisner (indirectly). Interestingly enough, my karate master, Tadashi Nakamura.

With Ron it was his ability to see what was going on in each individual student. What I learned, what I am still learning, is that you have to see what is going on in the actor. The most important thing for an acting teacher is to somehow develop an eye for what is authentic, organic, and connected in the actor and be able to sense the places of disconnect and ask questions to help the actor find his way back in. Ron is a master at that—that sense of really watching and asking questions. It empowers the actor.

Joe Chaikin was a very important influence. As a performer, I learned to use a physical path to intuition, instinct, and internal inspiration. The whole thing for a performer is to have tools, techniques to access something deep inside, a deep river. It is a powerful thing. Joe's way through physical impulse was an alternative to the ways I had learned in more traditional Stanislavsky-based training. Really, both ways are going for the same deep source. The physical work helped me tap into astonishing images and dream spaces. I have found that for some actors and students, it is the most useful way to get hooked up.

The Meisner work brings that deep, mystical imagination into the present moment and a truthful response to the life around you. I have learned so much about availability, transcending blocks and defenses, and getting past hiding through Mr. Meisner's work.

What I learned from my karate master was that art is a practice. In theater, as in the martial arts, there is a sense of ongoing, lifelong practice, and there is always further to go toward mastery with techniques. It is exciting as a teacher to work this way. I am not some font of knowledge, but a practitioner, facilitating others in this practice.

RR: Have you changed the way in which you teach acting?

RLS: It is continually changing, always with the intent of finding more effective ways to help actors access and develop their individual inspiration. One thing that was confirmed for me from working with a Stanislavsky-based Russian teacher in the late 1990s was that there is a force, a creative force, in us—natural inspiration. In teaching, we help people access that, their talent. Once you start to respect something larger than yourself, you open up to more depth and range. Actors become a vessel for that larger force to move through them. The more I work with it, the more I'm astonished and in awe at how profound the imagination is. So much of my work is to make our imagination visceral. That is something I trust— that it is there, available to us.

The other change is in continuing to experiment with form as a way to free the intuitive, inner life. The form of verse, or a strict physical score, can be a spring-board to release spontaneous inspiration into living in imaginary circumstances. I used to think of them as corsets; now I understand that they can be mini tram-polines to meaning.

RR: Do you stress the importance of voice/speech and body work of the actor's instrument?

RLS: It is enormously important. You need organic, truthful roots to live in imagi-nary circumstances and vocal and physical technique for extraordinary expres-sion. If you are not manifesting the mystery specifically and clearly, the audience cannot receive it. That communion is the point.

RR: How should an actor begin to work on a role?

RLS: By reading the play several times. At the beginning, the actor needs to find a way to place himself/herself in the circumstances. Look into the context of the world the playwright has created.

The point is immersing yourself psychologically, politically, socially, economi-cally, spiritually in that world. Whether it is Ibsen's realism or an absurdist play, the world has a set of specific rules. You have to look at the events, the actions, and their meaning. What does the character do, and how does he/she do it?

What language is being used? How is it being used? Is it used to reveal or cover the truth of the moment in the character? The structure and intent of the language tells you how the person is functioning in interaction with his own inner life and with the larger community around him.

Then, most essentially, you have to find a way to genuinely engage your heart in the circumstances, to identify with the character's crisis and to bring your soul to fight for him. You need to find what is at stake for him, what he needs in essen-tial human terms, and then find where you personally connect with that. And then look at the relationships—what everything and everyone means to you in that context.

RR: How much of a role does imagination play in the actor's work on a role?

RLS: A thousand percent. How can you go to the place you need to go to inhabit, embody this life, and live spontaneously in imaginary circumstances without it? The imagination is enormously important. The visceral imagination inspires the subconscious. Even when starting from a physical place, you need to engage the imagination.

RR: How important and valuable is your unique presence to the work that is actually occurring in the classroom?

RLS: It's not about me. There is something that one does by creating a space, by creating the "crucible," so that people can risk and have extraordinary experiences. I try to create a space where actors are challenged to risk and grow. A space to facilitate those experiences. A place to go further. I feel that is what is important.

I know that I am incredibly tenacious about seeking out a certain sense of truth and going after the organic core, encouraging the actor to come from a place of inspiration and deep imagination. As teachers, we must have faith that we can make the work better and change the world just a little bit.

KATE WISNIEWSKI

An actor, instructor, and a private coach, Ms. Wisniewski has appeared on several Seattle stages and at the American Repertory Theatre in Cambridge, Massachusetts, where she was in *How I Learned to Drive* with Debra Winger, and in the world premiere of Mac Wellman's *Hypatia*. Ms. Wisniewski is a graduate of the American Repertory Theatre Institute for Advanced Theatre Training at Harvard University. She is a certified associate teacher of Fitzmaurice Voicework and also teaches at Seattle University.

RR: What drew you to study with Robin Lynn Smith and how long did you study with her?

KW: I first became acquainted with Robin when I was living on San Juan Island in the Pacific Northwest. I became involved in producing workshops for local actors and I wanted to produce some workshops for acting training. When I was in Seattle I came across Robin's name.

RR: How have you been able to apply what you learned in your work?

KW: What I try to do in my theater classes is give the students a sense of what I've learned, to understand the kind of risk it takes, the personal bravery for an actor to be truthful onstage.

They're so used to having a "cool" attitude, to not wanting to be expressive. I try and give them an appreciation of the art form—to experience an "authentic moment." I feel it's vital to get them to understand that this is a live art form and what that can mean for them as audience members.

Robin inspired me and has inspired a lot of people in Seattle. She's a committed teacher, stubbornly committed to being human in a world that wants to shy away from it. She's willing to be very brave, and I admire that—to never shy away from the human experience.

ALICE SPIVAK

Having trained at the HB Studio with Herbert Berghof and Uta Hagen, Ms. Spivak was made a teacher there in 1962 and taught on their faculty for fifteen years. She has been a popular freelance acting teacher and acting coach, coaching on numerous feature films, Broadway shows, regional shows, TV mini-series, and pilots. She also taught film directing workshops on the faculty of NYU/Tisch Film & Television Program's Graduate Division and was given the Indie Award by the Association of Independent Video and

Filmmakers in 1977. She is the co-writer and director of a short film comedy, *Working for Peanuts*, and completed a screenplay, *No Right Turn*. Ms. Spivak's book, *How to Rehearse When There Is No Rehearsal: Acting and the Media*, is published by Limelight Editions.

RR: Who has been most influential in how you teach?

AS: Herbert Berghof was the one who inspired me. To hear him speak had a deep impact upon me; his profound sense of ethics and aesthetics in the art of acting has influenced me as an actress and as a teacher. Herbert and his wife, Uta Hagen, gave me a worldview, which proved useful to me as an actress and an acting coach.

Uta Hagen gave me a very practical way of working. She had a deep sense of excitement and a joy about acting. She had a marvelously logical approach to solving the problems of performance that might come up, a way of analyzing the script in terms of the character, in terms of the emotional results required. She laid the foundation on which I could build my own interpretation of the best acting approach and, very importantly, how to treat students respectfully and as colleagues. She gave me an unending joy in the search for the performance.

Bill Hickey gave me a sense of humor, a relaxed way of dealing with students, letting them discover the objective. Uta was very strict about choosing it, but Bill was the opposite. He'd say, "I'm interested in the process of acting, the process of discovery, in letting it happen."

RR: Have you changed the way in which you teach acting?

AS: My thinking is always changing. I remain an actress, I go on auditions, I coach on sets or backstage. The technology of today, with its lack of rehearsal time, required me to have to expand on the ways I teach preparation for a role. I stick to Stanislavsky's basic rules, but my approach has become more practical, attempting always to avoid "instant" characterization and yet being ready with very little time.

RR: Why should an actor study the craft of acting?

AS: In the United States, we see actors from Canada, from Ireland, from England, and Australia, so the American actor had better have a solid background in acting technique.

With Bill Hickey and Stephen Strimpell, we forged a technique program for the HB Studio, using a basic object exercise and improvisations touching on all the specifics of how to make a fictitious situation real to you, and therefore to the audience. Over the years, I've stuck with it, improved on it—it's the basic toolkit the actor has to have for the work.

RR: Do you stress the importance of voice/speech and body work of the actor's instrument?

AS: I wish to give to the actor, at the beginning of his study, some sense of who he is, and how eventually to inhabit a character. Only then do I make him aware of his voice, his speech, his body, so he can improve on them. I make the actor understand that only with confidence in his physical and vocal skills can he truly become somebody else, a character—but I do this only after he has a foundation in the acting experience. I have found that if, at the beginning of his training, the actor obsesses on voice, speech, and physical behavior, it makes the actor so self-aware that it will stall his progress. I have often observed actors lose regionalisms in their speech and change their physicality as they succeed in their work on scenes and characters. Learning to build a character from the inside out, à la the Stanislavsky System, will often provide the actor with a good sense of his body and his voice and what he will want to do to refine them.

RR: How should an actor begin to work on a role?

AS: One of the things I do in my scene study classes is to give the students a way to rehearse. I give each of them a handout of a step-by-step rehearsal process—this is what you do when you first get together, the second rehearsal, and so on. In effect, I'm overseeing their rehearsals for class.

RR: Do you place an emphasis on the actor understanding the playwright and the world of the play?

AS: In the beginning, yes. Because that's the way to understand the play. I encourage them to know American theater history and our dramatic literature, as well as the classics, and, of course, Stanislavsky. They should know about The Group Theatre, where Stanislavsky's theories first arrived from the Moscow Art Theatre, so they, too, can feel some tradition. To understand why a playwright writes the way he does. Writers such as O'Neill, Odets, Williams, and Miller put America on the map. The actor has to learn to be sensitive to the music in the language of writers, their origins, their politics, and their passions. Only then, by having something to refer back to, can they tackle all the peculiar and complex problems.

RR: How important is imagination in the actor's work?

AS: It plays a huge role. Because imagining yourself in the situation is a primary way of getting into the character. The actual work begins by breaking down all the elements that make up the scene in a step-by-step process. I believe, as Uta did, that we are making substitutions all during rehearsal, often unconsciously, as we grow more familiar with the material. The choices you will make should come not just from the script, but from your imagination, your experience, and your instincts. Ask yourself: What if I were in this situation? In Herbert's first lecture, he asked, "Where else but on the stage can you have a relationship, get married, rob a bank, even kill someone, and when the curtain comes down, there are no strings attached?" It all begins with imagining yourself there.

RR: How valuable is your unique presence to the work that is actually occurring in the classroom?

AS: I think it's very important. Because the actor needs a guide, a third eye. It's my role to free the student. There are no shortcuts when you are working out a scene for my class, no formulas, just hard work.

JAMES DALE

Mr. Dale's Off-Broadway appearances include *Getting into Heaven* and *Burleigh Grimes*. He has been seen in the films *The Departed* and *Lord of the Flies*, among others. He has extensive television credits.

RR: What drew you to study with Alice Spivak and how long did you study with her?

JD: I still study with her. I've been with Alice off and on for six years. She's very flexible, and it's a great place to work. My family is in the theater, and my father was good friends with the actress Carol Lawrence. Carol Lawrence said Alice was the best. When I came to New York, Alice took me under her wing and she brought me into her class.

RR: What were you hoping to discover about yourself and the craft?

JD: I've learned it has a lot to do with what your goals are as an actor. I had done plays in school and worked a little, but I didn't know how to act. I thought I did, but I didn't have an approach. I was in the theater program at Manhattanville College when I hooked up with Alice. I had been reading a lot of books on the theater—Bolaslavsky, Stanislavsky, Uta Hagen's *Respect for Acting*.

RR: How have you been able to apply what you learned in your work?

JD: She's been pounding into me that I have to be brave and gravitate toward parts that will allow me to do that. What I try to avoid is doing something predetermined. It's a matter of making it personal for myself, knowing who a person is, a place or a thing, feeling the objectives, and finding the beats. Once I do, it grounds me and gives me confidence and security in the script. Alice always says, "Do your work, stay with the process."

JOHN STRASBERG

For forty years, John Strasberg has had an international career in the theater. He has worked as an actor in theater, film, and television, including roles in *Mound Builders*, *The Rose Tattoo*, and *Butterflies Are Free*. He has worked as a director, designer, and master teacher in New York at the Mirror Repertory Company with Geraldine Page, at John Strasberg's The Real Stage, and currently at John Strasberg Studios, the Accidental Repertory Theater, as well as in Paris at John Strasberg Studios, Atelier. He has also worked in Montreal, Spain, Italy, Norway, Germany, Argentina, and Peru. He is the author of *Accidentally on Purpose: Reflections on Life, Acting and the Nine Natural Laws of Creativity*, and *The Shooting Party*. He has also been a producer, designer, and critic. An award-winning documentary of his teaching was produced, called *Organic Creative Process: Accidentally on Purpose*. Mr.

Strasberg has directed award-winning productions by Shakespeare, Aristophanes, Ibsen, O'Neill, Lope de Vega, Clifford Odets, Kaufman and Hart, Arniches, Guimera, Pirandello, and Beckett, including *Richard III, Ghosts, Beast and Virtue, La Senorita de Trevelez, Happy Days, Long Day's Journey into Night, Paradise Lost, Alice in Wonderland,* and *Don Juan Tenorio.*

RR: Who has been most influential in how you teach?

JS: My father (Lee Strasberg) and myself. My teaching evolved from my own perceptions and the conflicts I had because of how I was taught to think about acting by my father. I had to battle to understand what I was doing, as opposed to how I was taught to think about acting. My father was a brilliant teacher whose work was methodical and specific. I learned to work that way, and parts of the Method are wonderful, like learning how specific and real imaginary reality can become with sense memory exercises. But when I actually acted, and was inspired, acting was what I dreamed it to be. And it wasn't what I had been taught. My life, my imagination, seemed to merge with the character's. Spontaneously, I was living in another world. I couldn't explain what happened then.

As I matured, I wanted to know what I had done—and how to do it consciously. It led me to discover a deeper foundation to the creative process. I doubt that I would have been able to do that without my father's work coming before me. Or without the personal conflicts I had in my work due to the fact not only of the way I worked, but that my teacher was also my real father. This interaction has led me to understand what the Organic Creative Process is. It is an advance from the Method and other systems of training.

I also think that growing up in the theater has been a major influence on my teaching. There are times I know things without knowing how I know them.

Dr. Elsworth Baker was fundamental to my development. He was a medical agronomist, the man Wilhelm Reich chose to carry on his work. Dr. Baker knew more about life and human behavior than anyone I've ever known. He helped me affirm my own intuitions and sense of truth.

My mother, Paula Strasberg, and Peggy Feury were also important in my development as an actor.

Franchot Tone, who was my godfather, because he was a wonderful actor, a renaissance man, and he loved me.

RR: Have you changed the way in which you teach acting?

JS: More than once—and I probably will again. As I live, I learn, and my work evolves. I began experimenting, moving from classical Method work to improvisation and the theater games of Viola Spolin. I began to teach without using sense memory exercises, working directly from the play, because I realized that everything is already in the play.

Life is an improvisation. And I'm developing the actor's natural capacities, spontaneity, intelligence, real thought, involvement, sense of truth, knowledge of himself, while he is working on a scene. I call my work Organic Script Analysis.

But I continued to evolve. I've even begun to teach sense memory again, after twenty-five years of not teaching it. Because it helps actors learn how to prepare, concentrate, and understand how specific they have to be. It also enables them to take the necessary time to discover that they can actually make an imaginary reality real and build a habit that will accelerate their involvement in the imaginary world of the play. I don't consider sense memory, or any technique separate from the play, to be the fundamental way to act. Acting isn't a recipe where you think about ingredients—sense memories, substitutions, actions, objectives—to cook up life. It's being able to use your imagination, focusing on the play and the character, to really live another life. I want actors to be spontaneous. Too many actors think acting is directing themselves.

When I was young, many people in New York seemed to think that it was necessary and normal to scream at actors. I never liked doing that; I thought there was something wrong with me until I realized that teachers like my father often got mad because they took an actor's difficulty as resistance to them and reacted personally. One day I realized that the actor wasn't trying to be difficult or trying to resist—he just didn't understand. I relaxed and felt more confident to teach in my own way. Also, working in many countries with actors who have very different traditions, ideas, and philosophies of acting led me to discover that talking about life overcame any differences. This led me to insist that actors think like human beings.

RR: Why should an actor study the craft of acting?

JS: Acting is a natural process. We are born with the capacity. The only reason to study is if you really want to be able to create life, and become able to do it on cue, consciously—to transform oneself, put yourself in someone else's shoes, and go beyond yourself. Actors need an environment in which to explore and develop their creative process.

Should we ask why a painter should study painting? Or a musician study music? A dancer study dance? Why do we ask it in acting? Probably because most of what we call "acting" is entertainment, a question of personality. One can enjoy it, but it has nothing to do with the art of acting. Studying acting begins from that perception.

I work directly from the text. My classes feel closer to rehearsing than most acting classes. The difference is that the objective is to develop the actor's creative process rather than preparing a play for opening.

I teach that the fundamental reality of an acting technique is about the actor knowing himself and learning how to become deeply involved in an imaginary world that develops through the actor's interaction with the play. What's the technique for learning to dream on your feet while you're awake? I think that technique is about believing that what you imagine is real. One can learn that by working directly with the play; it's more natural and direct.

RR: Do you stress the importance of voice/speech and body work of the actor's instrument?

JS: If your body and your voice aren't capable of being spontaneous, and being able to be inspired and express what you feel, it's impossible to get to the end of the process. Voice and speech are essential. One wants to train the actor's voice to be able to express what he or she feels. To know this is true, work on Shakespeare. Whatever feeling you get, it must be expressed in the voice.

RR: How should an actor begin to work on a role?

JS: By reading the play, and then dreaming. One dreams, focusing on some particular reality. In any creative process, in any human endeavor, creativity begins with a dream.

RR: How valuable is your unique presence to the work that is actually occurring in the classroom?

JS: I think that who I am, and how I behave, is 50 percent of what I'm teaching. I think it was the same with my father, or Stella Adler, or Sandy Meisner. But I think that it's about being the most human you can be. I, like my father and Stella, have a love and a passion for what I do.

I teach what I know. I teach what I do. I teach what I am. It's probably the most important part. If an actor has that, then technique, learning, means something. My knowledge, my awareness of problems comes from my own talent and my own experience. How else will I recognize the problems that an actor is having and be able to help? I create an environment in the classroom that enables actors to go beyond themselves, to learn what they need to learn.

STEVE BUSCEMI

Mr. Buscemi is an associate member of the experimental theater company The Wooster Group. His film work includes *Reservoir Dogs*, *Armageddon*, *The Big Lebowski*, *Fargo*, *Slaves of New York*, *King of New York*, *Miller's Crossing*, *Barton Fink*, *The Hudsucker Proxy*, *Pulp Fiction*, *Con Air*, *28 Days*, *The Grey Zone*, *The Laramie Project*, *Coffee and Cigarettes*, *Charlotte's Web*, and *The Island*. In 2004 he joined the cast of *The Sopranos*; he has also directed different episodes of the show. Mr. Buscemi directed the films *Trees Lounge*, *Animal Factory*, *Lonesome Jim*, and *Interview*, and the television drama *Oz*.

RR: What drew you to study with John Strasberg and how long did you study with him?

SB: I first took John's class when I was enrolled at the Lee Strasberg Theatre Institute. I think I sat in his class for about four months before I found the nerve to actually work on a scene. It was from Neil Simon's play *Come Blow Your Horn*.

The first thing I remember John saying to me was that he could see that I clearly enjoyed acting and being onstage. I don't know why, but I found that encouraging. I mean, he didn't exactly say that *he* enjoyed watching me.

I also joined John and his then-wife, Sabra Jones, when they broke away from the Institute and started teaching their own private classes. I studied with John on and off for about two years.

I liked John's basic philosophy that an actor should do what works for him. He didn't adhere to a strict method or a certain way of doing things. He cared about finding the truth of the scene; it didn't matter so much the method used to find it. He also liked to do improvisation exercises, which I loved.

RR: What were you hoping to discover about yourself and the craft?

SB: I was very young, about eighteen. I didn't have any expectations of being a serious actor. I was always interested in comedy and hoped to someday be a stand-up comic, with the thought of getting cast in a sitcom. I never thought I would be interested in Shakespeare, O'Neill, or Miller. I had never heard of Chekhov. I learned a lot about the history of theater, what was important. I discovered I liked drama as much as comedy, and that it was okay for me to think of myself as an actor.

RR: How would you describe what you learned?

SB: I think I learned to trust myself more. To look for clues in the play to help me with the character I was playing. To ask myself questions, and to have fun exploring and taking risks.

RR: How have you been able to apply what you learned in your work?

SB: The improv work I did in John's class was especially useful when I began working with Mark Boone Junior in the early 1980s. We would write and perform our own short plays, which grew out of improvisation. Later, when I got more film work, I always depended on the script to look for answers to any questions I had. With good writing, you don't really question, you just do. You feel it. I don't like to analyze it too much. When it works, it works, and I don't question it.

PENNY TEMPLETON

Ms. Templeton's artistry is the culmination of four generations of theater actresses. She studied under such masters as Paul Sorvino, Jack Garfein, and Wynn Handman. Her acting career includes starring in Joyce Carol Oates's *I Stand Before You Naked* at the American Place Theatre and as Paul Sorvino's wife in *All the King's Men*. In 1990, she began coaching actors privately, and in 1994 opened the Penny Templeton Studio. Ms. Templeton has offered her expertise in national magazines and served as a finalist judge for the Cable

Ace Awards, the Daytime Emmy Awards, and the New York Film Festival. Ms. Templeton was chosen by Kristin Linklater, head of the Columbia University MFA Drama Program to teach the third-year acting candidates. Among her directorial credits are the one-man shows *The F Train* and *The Idiot's Guide to Life* and staged readings in Los Angeles and New York of the play *The Rise of Dorothy Hale*. She has recently added online coaching to enable actors to work with her outside of her studio. Currently she is writing her acting book, *Acting under Fire: Creating Acting Lions*.

RR: Who has been the most influential in how you teach?

PT: I have had great role models who taught me valuable lessons as a teacher. My grandmother and mother were both professional actors. They *loved* theater and had a passion for acting, so it must be in my genes because I seemed to have inherited that passion.

Paul Sorvino taught me the Meisner technique at the American Stage Company. He was also an accomplished actor who brought an actor's perspective to the teaching of the craft. He taught me not to have a timetable, but to move at the pace of the actor's development; not to teach "classes," but to teach people.

When I studied the Method with Jack Garfein, his ingenious exercises inspired me to think outside the box when creating my own exercises.

Patricia Grantham, also a Method teacher, instilled the gift of discovering how unique each of us is and the power of understanding how we are perceived when we are onstage or walk into an audition. Her sensory exercises were amazing in that they gave us the keys to unlock the heart of our emotions.

Wynn Handman taught me to understand the style of a piece, the importance of researching the historical context in which the play is set, and the use of imagination to set it free. Wynn also handed down the joy of working with each and every one of his actors.

But the most important influences are my students because through them, I am constantly evolving as a teacher.

RR: Why should an actor study the craft of acting?

PT: Fear stifles creativity.

First and foremost, great actors are consistent and know how to create and how to *re-create* their work by keeping it alive and fresh. My goal is to cultivate working artists, so they know how to use their craft to work in today's world, where the pressure is to "act fast."

My technique has two interlocking and inseparable parts. I teach actors to do in-depth script analysis before they begin to apply their craft to create the character and serve the writer's intent.

I provide ongoing master classes for the working professional, along with a specialized on-camera class. I also have an intermediate and a beginning class. The curriculum inside the four-hour ongoing technique/scene classes is broken into an "acting barre," a series of exploration exercises to develop, stretch, and strengthen the actor. The second part is on camera (including the actor using his own video camera) and may include monologues, cold scenes, sensory exercises, etc., which are shown back on a film screen to enhance the actor's awareness by "seeing" his work enlarged. The third part is in-depth work on theater scenes. I choose scenes for each actor based on his strengths and weaknesses, to challenge and spark the unique fire in each actor.

RR: How important is imagination in the actor's work?

PT: The imagination allows the actor to see all those possibilities of how a scene can be brought to life; the very first thing an actor must do is *start with himself.* This is the cornerstone of what I teach.

The actor learns to use his personal substitutions to connect the emotional needs of the character to his own experiences, and improvisation to set it free. When an actor uses his imagination to fully commit to his choices, the audience is taken on a journey that brings the truth of the human experience home to them.

RR: How valuable is your unique presence to the work that is actually occurring in the classroom?

PT: An artist must be willing to put himself on the line and build himself through exploration. I do my best to be an encouraging teacher, and guide the actor to see and enhance his uniqueness while at the same time gently challenging and addressing weaknesses or limitations.

Truth. That is what art is about. We each have our own individual life experiences. At the same time, there is a universality to those experiences that is shared by all humankind. I hope I have succeeded in inspiring my actors to dig deep to find the truth within themselves. All I can do is help the actors find the truth. *They* send it out into the world!

SARAH WYNTER

Sarah Wynter grew up in Australia. She is most widely known for her television role as Kate Warner on *24* (for which she was nominated for a Screen Actors Guild Award) and starred as Beth on the NBC series *Windfall.* She also had a role on the *Sex and the City* pilot. Ms. Wynter appeared in *The Sixth Day* and *Lost Souls* and had a recurring role in *The Dead Zone.* Her Australian feature film debut was in *Three Dollars.*

RR: What drew you to study with Penny Templeton and how long did you study with her?

SW: I wanted to become a better actor. I really loved her class. In addition to working on our technique and theater skills, we also did a lot of on-camera work to prepare us for working in television and film. Penny focused a great amount of attention on having me audition for TV and film—it was a new world to me. We'd "audition" in front of a camera in class, which was extremely helpful. I've been studying with her now for twelve years.

RR: What were you hoping to discover about yourself and the craft?

SW: I was just starting out; I didn't know how to get the kind of work I wanted. I had only done theater work before, so I had to learn how be subtle in front of a camera, to learn that certain things were enough, and trust that the camera will pick them up. Still, it's absolutely important to learn acting from a theatrical base.

RR: How would you describe what you learned?

SW: The most valuable thing was to know how to do my best in an audition. It's a necessity to work in this business. Penny taught me how to feel confident and powerful in an audition and not to "fear" a casting director.

When I've landed jobs, I'll go back to Penny to work with her. We work together on the sides of the script and break the scene down. Her method is very specific. It starts with the basic questions: What is the character's "core"? It generally comes down to one of three things: love, power, or control. The core strongly affects the character's driving question in the scene. Then it's what motivates the scene.

I always break the scene down into beats with separate actions and tactics. What am I doing with this line, and how am I doing it?

We worked on an audition scene recently where I played a waitress. In walks a biker gang, which I have to serve while keeping the other patrons calm. So my driving question became: How can I save this situation? I'd "personalize" it and ask myself: What does this mean to me, Sarah?

It gives me more than what appears on the page; it gives me an inner life.

When Penny and I work together, we mark the script in pencil using symbols that are simple but that have very specific meaning. For example, we use a bull's-eye for a "take in," meaning specifically: to take a pause and react to what has happened. Other symbols include a bomb—for when someone drops a "bomb." This kind of work with Penny has given me the confidence to do my best work at an audition or on a set.

RR: How have you been able to apply what you learned in your work?

SW: I was on the TV series *24,* and the lingo is expositional. So you really have to be sure you've done your homework, know what the purpose of the scene is and what you need to bring to it. To know what the driving question is in each scene. They might be rewriting the script while you're shooting it, and they'll hand you the script a minute before you film the scene! So you need to be able to work quickly with your choices.

Recently I finished shooting thirteen episodes for an NBC show, *Windfall*, about a group of friends who win the lottery. It explores all the good things and bad things that come out of something like that. You never know what will happen. I'm pleased with the work, the cast, and the writers. All those things contribute to a very rich working experience. I've been blessed to have so many creatively fulfilling moments in my career.

What I love about Penny is that she never lets you forget what's special about you. But she still makes you work very hard. She made me feel that it was okay that I had an Australian accent but also found me a speech teacher who taught me an American dialect. This was imperative for me to become an employed actor in this country. But instead of focusing on a weakness, Penny found a solution. And Penny is *all* about finding the solution, making things work.

It makes a world of difference to have a teacher who believes in you and makes you feel that, with hard work and determination, you're just as good as anyone else. That's why I keep coming back to Penny and that's why I keep working and loving what I do.

RON VAN LIEU

Mr. Lieu was trained at New York University/Tisch School of the Arts. His acting credits include several major regional theaters and leading roles Off-Broadway, at the New York Shakespeare Festival, Public Theater, and Playwrights Horizons, and he was a company member of the Milwaukee Repertory Theater. His directing credits include Playwrights Horizons, Public Theater, Syracuse Stage, Greer Garson Theater in Santa Fe, and fifty productions at the NYU/Tisch Graduate Acting Program. For twenty-nine years he was a master teacher of acting at the NYU/Tisch Graduate Acting Program, where he also served as chair of the program. In 1993 he was awarded the New York University Distinguished Teaching Medal, the university's highest award for classroom teaching. He was a founding faculty member of the Shakespeare Lab at the New York Shakespeare Festival and for ten years was the acting teacher there. He is a founding faculty member, member of the board, and currently a master teacher of acting at The Actors Center, New York City. Since 2004, Mr. Van Lieu has served as the Lloyd Richards Professor of Acting and chair of the acting program at the Yale School of Drama.

RR: Who has been most influential in how you teach?

RVL: I began my acting training at Bowling Green State University in Ohio—my first real teacher of the craft was F. Lee Meisle. I was lucky to start out with someone who loved the theater and imparted to me his sense of passion, his sense of discipline, and a work ethic. The most influential teachers to me as an acting student at NYU/Tisch's Graduate Acting Program included Omar Shapli (who taught theater games), Olympia Dukakis, Lloyd Richards, Peter Kass, and Joe Chaikin. Also Joseph Anthony—my first professional teacher. He taught me the Michael Chekhov technique. From Omar I learned how important spontaneity was, how to find freedom within the form. I believe theater games are useful for the actor in regard to impulse, the release of spontaneity, for the imagination. With Olympia, the great thing I got from her was how necessary it is to bring yourself into the work. It is imperative that you release yourself from clichéd ideas and not be hampered by judgment or fear. Lloyd taught me the nature of character, how to "mine" a text, how to begin the process of transformation. Peter Kass was a master teacher of objectives and actions. What he did affected me the most. He taught objectives as a very visceral pursuit from the body rather than from the intellect.

And Joe Chaiken just worked from a very deep center. I learned the necessity of concentration, depth of focus, simplicity, truthfulness.

RR: Have you changed the way in which you teach acting?

RVL: Yes. Time takes care of a lot of things. I've become more involved in the study of the text of the scene as a way of teaching acting. Before, I was more involved with the person in front of me. I put the person first, and the obligation to the text second. Now I give them equal focus. When the actor is young, he wants to theorize about everything. What I've learned is that only the actual experience teaches you, not the theory. The best teachers lead you to an experience, to a visceral event. It's what I try to do with my students, and lead them to an experience.

RR: Why should an actor study the craft of acting?

RVL: So he can equip himself to have a life in the theater for fifty to sixty years. Training doesn't finish an actor; it starts him in the right direction. If he's lucky enough to be employed on a steady basis, he will learn and grow as an actor. Actors need to learn a craft that supports them in rehearsal. The hallmark of successful people is that while they were training, they learned how to get out of their own way.

RR: Do you stress the importance of voice/speech and body work of the actor's instrument?

RVL: A great deal, especially as connected to the breath. Without breathing you can't access an emotional life. Actors battle their entire lives not to be overcome with fear. The best way to do that is to breathe through the fear. I put a great emphasis on the vocal work, on the physical work.

One of the greatest things revealed to me by Kristin Linklater was that I was a "chest-breather." She redirected my instrument toward a more natural way of breathing through my diaphragm. The discovery of breath was an earth-shattering event for me. It opened up my emotional and physical life.

RR: Do you place an emphasis on the actor understanding the playwright and the world of the play?

RVL: I want the actor to read the entire body of work of the playwright. Then they'll be able to uncover the themes that haunt the writer, the questions that the writer revisits from play to play, and the obsessions the writer is concerned with. Enter into the playwright's unique vision of the world in order understand who the character is and how he experiences the world.

RR: How valuable is your unique presence to the work that is actually occurring in the classroom?

RVL: If an actor is able to illuminate the human condition while I'm sitting in the theater and lead me to understand something in a visceral way, in a way that touches my feelings and my thoughts and awakens my understanding, then there is nothing more important to me. When people gather to watch a play, they collectively want that to happen. Actors should disturb the air, not put people to sleep.

I teach from an authentic sense of self because I want the students to tell the truth. As I've grown, I've allowed more of myself to be revealed as I teach. That's the only way if I expect my students to reveal themselves.

BILLY CRUDUP

Billy Crudup starred on Broadway in *The Pillowman* opposite Jeff Goldblum and in Lincoln Center's production of Tom Stoppard's *The Coast of Utopia*. He also appeared on the New York stage in *Arcadia* (Lincoln Center Theater), *Three Sisters, Oedipus,* and *Measure for Measure* (New York Shakespeare

Festival). He has acted in such films as *1996, Princess Mononoke, Sleepers, Inventing the Abbotts, Grind, Snitch, Without Limits, The Hi-Lo Country, Jesus' Son, Almost Famous, World Traveler, Charlotte Gray, Birdseye, Big Fish, Stage Beauty, Trust the Man, Mission: Impossible III, Dedication,* and *The Good Shepherd.*

RR: What drew you to study with Ron Van Lieu and how long did you study with him?

BC: I auditioned for graduate schools, and New York University had the best reputation. I was fortunate to be audited by Ron and then studied with him for three years.

RR: What were you hoping to discover and how would you describe what you learned?

BC: My expectation was to be built from the bottom up as a working actor. Little did I know that Ron's process is about forcing you to create yourself. He made me figure out which of the many skills he had a command of teaching were suitable for me to be using to be a better actor.

I learned from him to think critically about my instrument. I learned rudimentary questions to ask when I get stuck and what sorts of things I do to get in my own way in the journey to giving a free and insightful performance.

I learned almost everything from him about who I am in order to become a more complete actor.

WENDY WARD

Director of the Ward Acting Studio, which she founded in 1996, Ms. Ward received her B.A. in drama in 1981 from Duke University, where she has served on the advisory board for the university's drama department. Ms. Ward continued her training at the National Theater Institute with Rudi Shelly, Morris Carnovsky, Joanne Pattavina, and Peter Lobdell, and in New York with Anna Deavere Smith, James Price, Larry Arrick, and Vivian Matalon. She has taught the Meisner approach since 1989, first at The Acting Studio, where she served as associate director with Mr. Price. She has directed over fifty plays, half of which are original works built in her studio's Advanced Performance Workshop. Recently, Ms. Ward has served on the faculty of University of the Arts in Philadelphia, teaching the Meisner technique to sophomores.

RR: Who has been the most influential in how you teach acting?

WW: After I completed my own Meisner training with James Price, James asked me to teach for his studio. Traditionally, Meisner teachers are hand-selected and then asked to work with a master teacher for many months before being given their own classes. This is how I learned to teach the Meisner approach under James's tutelage. So while I did not study with Sandy directly, obviously his approach has had the greatest impact on my own teaching methods.

RR: Have you changed the way in which you teach acting?

WW: Sandy Meisner said it takes twenty years to make an actor—the same may be true for a good teacher. After eighteen years, I can say that I'm mastering the art of teaching Meisner—I know when to push an actor, when to ignore a problem and just let the actor experience the work, when to be strict and when to let up, and when to help an actor retain a sense of humor about himself. I've learned that when an actor feels the most dismayed, it is frequently a sign that he is about to have a breakthrough. I've become better able to inspire young actors, who seem to suffer from a significant lack of imagination and curiosity, and to help experienced actors suffering from a results-oriented approach get back to the organic, fully connected experience of the imaginary circumstances. Acting is hard work requiring training and tenacity.

RR: Do you stress the importance of voice/speech and body work on the actor's instrument?

WW: Voice and speech are extremely important in developing actors into skilled professionals. Actors who have been blessed with beautiful, strong voices and the ability to handle language have a huge advantage. The moment someone with good speech and a resonant voice comes onstage, we are drawn to them.

Many young actors are interested in becoming film actors and don't believe that their voice is going to matter because they will be miked. What they fail to realize is that our voices have much to do with the presence that we command. Additionally, voice and breath have much to do with being centered in our bodies—relaxed and concentrated—and these are qualities that all actors need, whether they're acting onstage or in front of a camera.

RR: How should an actor begin to work on a role?

WW: The actor's first responsibility is to be able to put himself in the circumstances of the play. Actors must find their own humanity in the role if they are going to bring the role to life. It is important that they understand the circumstances, the specific relationships with other characters, and are able to live in the appropriate emotional reality. Our courses train actors to analyze the script in a way that keeps them out of their head and grounded in their intuition, in their heart. While the text provides details about the circumstances that the actor can particularize—and of course the actors must begin working on any physical or vocal adjustments necessary for the role—it is important that the *core* of their performance comes from the simplicity of being able to experience the imaginary circumstances.

RR: Do you place an emphasis on the actor understanding the playwright and the world of the play?

WW: As an actress and director, I have always valued learning about the playwright and the background of the play's origins. I find it can bring greater clarity to the role. However, all actors are different. I think you have to permit each individual actor to work in his or her own way. An actor's performance will not be compelling if the heart and soul are left out. And I have seen many a smart actor who could not bring a role to life because he was so cerebral in his approach. All the intellectual analysis and conversation about the play, the playwright's intentions, etc., will not help at all unless it is then translated into a deep emotional connection with the circumstances that the actor can then bring to life.

RR: How important is imagination in the actor's work?

WW: Imagination is critical. The actor has to know how to use it *well*. I really drill my students in how they can get more compelling results by making more specific choices, which will ignite their imaginations and bring their feelings alive. There is no sense memory or emotional recall work in the Meisner training; rather, our emotional preparation training is based on effective use of the imagination.

RR: How valuable is your unique presence to the work that is actually occurring in the classroom?

WW: What I do best as a teacher and as a director is help actors abandon their external personas and bring their deeper, truer selves to their roles without using their own history as the resource. I help actors understand that their imaginations are infinitely more resourceful than their past experiences. I carry this work over into my directing in our Advanced Performance Workshop by including actors in the building of our original works. Our studio is intimate, passionate, and compelling. That is the tradition I intend to build upon in our next ten years as a training institution.

CLAYTON DEAN

Clayton Dean Smith appeared opposite Jodie Foster in Neil Jordan's *The Brave One*, on *Law & Order: SVU*, *The Sopranos*, *One Life to Live*, and numerous commercials. New York theater includes *Outward Bound* (Keen

Company, Drama Desk nomination for best revival), Charles Ludlam's *Conquest of the Universe* (Salt Theater), *1984* (Synapse Productions), and the bluegrass musical *The Blue Flower* (NYMF). Training: Uprights Citizen Brigade, Anne Bogart and SITI Company, LAByrinth, Kristin Linklater, and Ward Acting Studio.

RR: What drew you to study with Wendy Ward and how long did you study with her?

CDS: I studied with Wendy for a year and half in the fall of 1999, two to three nights a week. A friend encouraged me to meet with her. As Wendy guided me into the advanced program, we were putting up productions and I felt I had found what I was looking for. Since then, her presence in my life continues to remind me of her principles, her values. When I had an audition for *Thom Pain* in New York City, she worked with me on my preparation.

RR: What were you hoping to discover about yourself and the craft?

CDS: When I first met her she made it clear she wanted actors at the Ward Acting Studio who wanted to do the work. For her it's all about commitment and genuineness about the work. A clarity of the intention in what we're doing in this business. That appealed to me. I didn't come to New York for fame or money or any illusions of the business; I came to learn the craft and to work with like-minded people, to create work that I wanted to be a part of. When I met Wendy, I knew I was in the right place. She excited me. She knows what she wants her classroom to be, and will do whatever it takes to foster that environment.

RR: How would you describe what you learned?

CDS: By the time I was performing, what I was doing didn't feel like acting. The preparation is the hard work; the acting is the reality of existing in the circumstances. Wendy got me to understand the importance of keeping it real. It got to the point where I didn't think about what the director wanted or what the audience wanted, but what my responsibility was to the character. In her classes, a hundred times over, she would force us to respond to what it was that we really stood for.

What really matters to me is to really light a fire so that my commitment to the integrity of the work is paramount, as well as my commitment to life. I gained an honesty from Wendy about what I bring to my work. She said, "You're a complete person; you don't have to come up with anything better than yourself. By the time I'm done with you, you'll embrace who you are and it will be wonderful and exciting." She's totally uncompromising as a teacher.

RR: How have you been able to apply what you learned in your work?

CDS: What I learned is always with me. Last year I did a production with the Keen Company of *Outward Bound*. I played a minister on board a ship. At one point I go out on deck (offstage), and when I come back onstage I was supposed to have seen that there is no water, that we are on a ghost ship and we're heading nowhere. Well, I struggled with what to do offstage. What was I supposed to imagine? Finally, I realized I was too self-absorbed. It was just like one of Wendy's repetition exercises. When you're struggling, it's because you're focused on yourself. Throw the focus on your partner; that's the way to unlock the true alchemy of the scene.

In that particular scene, the interesting part of my character's journey was coming back on the ship and seeing everyone looking to me for guidance. I put all the attention on them. When I did, and I took in all these wonderful actors' fears, their anxiety, their hope and doubt, it allowed the story to be told as it was written. It was all in their eyes. And that's when I stepped up as the character and I could be responsible for that moment. I learned that from Wendy Ward.

LOYD WILLIAMSON

Loyd Williamson is the creator and author of the Williamson technique, a two-year system of training for the body and the communication process. In 1975 he founded the Actors Movement Studio in partnership with Philip Burton. Mr. Williamson served as artistic director until his retirement in 2002. In 1979, at the invitation of William Esper and Dean Jack Bettenbender, he joined the faculty of the newly formed Mason Gross School of the Arts at Rutgers University, remaining its principal professor of the actors' physical training for twenty-two years. In 1995, he created the Tamarack Lodge Retreat Center, which has hosted over fifty retreats in its first ten years, including Kristin Linklater's teacher certification program; Lenard Petit's Michael Chekhov workshop; and Mitchell Karp's retreats for corporate trainers. He spent eleven years on the faculty of the HB Studio in New York, beginning his work there as an assistant to Anna Sokolow, his mentor. He was a guest teacher at the Tisch School of the Arts of New York University and has taught at Northern Illinois University, The Juilliard School of Drama, Ensemble Studio Theatre, Pearl Theatre Company, and Princeton Shakespeare Company.

RR: Who has been most influential in how you teach students and direct actors?

LW: Sandy Meisner. His connection between actors, his work in realizing that the actor's behavior comes from the impulse of the other actor. It comes from the understanding of who you are, why you're there, and then giving it away—living moment to moment.

Harold Clurman. He was a great talent. He gave you the idea you could do anything according to the dictates of your talent. That you need not necessarily follow rules.

Anna Sokolow. Her understanding of art and the connection between music, movement, and poetry.

Michael Shurtleff, because of his understanding of scene structure.

RR: How have you changed the way in which you work with actors?

LW: I've become clearer. Our lives are fed by the contact between people, places, and the things that surround us at any given moment. As I've matured, the depths of these moments have given me experiences that are simply complete, leading me to understand that elusive experience of living in the current moment. I teach with an empathetic connection with the experience of actors when they're acting and the role the body plays—the physical instrument in processing these experiences.

RR: Why should an actor study the craft of acting?

LW: Because it is an art. And an actor has no room for the accidental clutter of everyday life. Acting must be clear, direct, and true.

RR: Do you stress the importance of voice/speech and body work of the actor's instrument?

LW: You cannot act except what's processed through the body—from the body's connection to the world and the behavior that flows from that experience. It means being centrally alive, experientially vulnerable, and allowing behavior to fall from that truth completely in the moment. Behavior includes every impulse of the body's response to experience. It may be a blush, which can be a pivotal moment in a motion picture, or the extended lushness of sound that flows from a Tennessee Williams line. The body must reopen, reduce all sound, emotion. The shape of the sound is the voice and diction. The openness of the voice and emotion is the provenance of movement class, and of the voice. Of the mastery of the movement. Shape is the heart of Stanislavsky's book, *Building a Character,* in which he says, "The heart of the actor's art is line and form." Experience gives rise to this. And in the master craftsman's acting, emotion and sound effortlessly merge in a completed art.

RR: How should an actor begin to work on a role?

LW: The actor makes contact with his world, then his body comes alive to his world through the experience, and that experience gives rise to the behavior.

RR: How important is imagination in the actor's work?

LW: It is everything. Actions, intentions, meanings of moments, relationships, character choices, emotional explorations or preparations will only come to life if the actor creates a vivid imaginary world that can bring his body to life.

Jodie Foster is one of the most talented people I have ever coached. She is also an extremely private person. I think it would be most helpful to share her grasp of this technique that happened over three sessions. She has a natural vulnerability when she is acting that makes her almost transparent—fearless, willing to take any risk. She would go straight from the coaching sessions to the set of the film *Nell.*

When she first arrived at my apartment, she asked, "How does this person walk?" And so our work began. I asked her, "What is most important for you in creating a role?" If I remember correctly, she said that it was struggles, the challenges that the character must face. I set out to begin to allow the physical life of character to evolve from Nell's connections to her world.

"Why does Nell place daisies on her mother's eyes?" I asked. We looked at several possibilities. Finally we settled on the simple fact that they were flowers, instead of coins. Where did they come from? "The forest. They grow wild in the forest." All of our work, then, began with Nell's connection to a specific element in her world: wildflowers.

From there we went to the script: Nell's entire existence has been spent alone in the forest at night. It is there that she comes to life. She seems to live a happy life in her forest. She also has never seen any people other than her mother and her twin sister. Later, in the courtroom scene, where the state is challenging her ability to survive on her own in her forest, she summarizes her life: "My world is very simple." She is a person of total openness to her world.

This central idea defined her experience of every moment that followed. That's why she's completely in awe when first sees a man's naked body when she is swimming one night. The core of the entire film was Nell's sensory connection to and experiences of this world.

Now we were ready explore what behavior would evolve as she traveled through her forest at night. Jody began by stepping out of the apartment door onto the metal stairs that dropped into the garden that surrounded the apartment, and because of her vivid imagination, she "stepped into the world of her forest," so her behavior became that of a child living in wonder. She moved down the steps with a light grace and freedom, and through the garden like a young deer.

She was completely open, responsive to all of her impulses, and finally able to produce behavior that was clear, direct, and true.

RR: How valuable is your unique presence to the work that is actually occurring in the classroom?

LW: It's essential because the actors can only experience what the teacher himself has experienced. The depth of an actor's experience is dependent on the depth of the teacher. Bringing to life the entire inner body in my work means bringing to life the vital organs, the skeletal systems. I define experience that way.

KRISTIN DAVIS

Kristin Davis appeared as Brooke Armstrong on the Fox television series *Melrose Place* and starred on HBO's *Sex and the City* as Charlotte York, opposite Sarah Jessica Parker, Cynthia Nixon, and Kim Cattrall. Ms. Davis and the cast received a Screen Actors Guild Award for outstanding performance by an ensemble in a comedy series in 2002. Her other television work includes the films *Atomic Train, Deadly Vision, Murder in Mind, Three Days,* and *The Ultimate Lie.* She has guest-starred on *Seinfeld, Friends, E.R., The Larry Sanders Show,* and the adaptation of *The Heidi Chronicles.*

RR: What drew you to study with Loyd Williamson and how long did you study with him?

KD: I studied with Loyd when I was enrolled in the acting program at Mason Gross School of the Arts at Rutgers University. They had a very well rounded program and we had Loyd for three years. It was an important part of our training, partly because it was so rigorous physically. Since we were so young (nineteen to twenty-one), it really helped us to understand how hard we needed to work to be trained for the stage. As we progressed, we learned Elizabethan dance and worked with period costumes in our classes. It was so much fun, but also good preparation for the discipline needed to succeed in our profession.

RR: What were you hoping to discover about yourself and the craft?

KD: I knew intuitively how important your body is when you are acting, and I hoped that Loyd would help me learn to carry myself in a more open and powerful way. He focused on unlocking physical patterns that blocked full emotional expression. And though it was difficult, and I remember crying tears of frustration, he succeeded in ridding me of my teenage slouching. He also encouraged me, and all of the women in our class, to prize strength *and* grace in movement. Which meant a lot to me as a young woman.

RR: When you left the class, how would you describe what you learned as an actor?

KD: What I learned from Loyd took a while to really sink in. He incorporated so many different techniques, I would find myself thinking, "Oh, I understand what he meant." Years later, it still happens when I'm on a set sometimes. I remember that I need to pay attention to my breath and open up physically to really be present in my performance. I think that, as all good teachers have, Loyd had a vision of me that I didn't have when I began studying with him. It actually took me many years to grow into that vision. And that is really his biggest gift to me, to have pointed me toward the future of who I wanted to become as an actor.

RR: How have you been able to apply what you learned in your work?

KD: I'm happy to say that people often ask me if I used to dance and compliment me on my posture. This is all from my training with Loyd. And in terms of day-to-day work, I use specific techniques I learned from Loyd on a daily basis. The central idea that he gave me is that you can't separate your performance from your body—they work together when you've taken care of yourself. And when you haven't, your body can work against what you want to express in a scene.

PART II
ACTORS WHO TEACH ACTING

OLYMPIA DUKAKIS

An actress, director, producer, teacher, activist, and author of her best-selling memoir, *Ask Me Again Tomorrow*, Ms. Dukakis received an Academy Award in the best supporting actress category, the New York Film Critics Award, the Los Angeles Film Critics Award, and the Golden Globe Award for her work in the Norman Jewison film *Moonstruck*. Ms. Dukakis has received two OBIE Awards, for Bertolt Brecht's *A Man's a Man*, and Christopher Durang's *The Marriage of Bette and Boo* at Joseph Papp's Public Theater. On Broadway, Ms. Dukakis starred in the solo play *Rose*. She starred as Clytemnestra in *Agamemnon* and has also performed at Actors Company Theatre in *The Mother* (world premiere) by Gorky, adapted by Constance Congdon. As a founding member and producing artistic director of the Whole Theatre in Montclair, New Jersey, for nineteen years (1971 to 1990), she directed and appeared in many productions. Ms. Dukakis received the New Jersey Governor's Walt Whitman Creative Arts Award. A founding member of the Actors Company and the Charles Playhouse (both in Boston), she has appeared in over 130 productions Off-Broadway and regionally, at venues including A.C.T., Shakespeare in the Park, Albany's Studio Arena, American Place Theatre, APA Phoenix, Circle Repertory Company, and the Williamstown Theatre Festival, where she also served as associate director. Ms. Dukakis taught acting at New York University/Tisch's Graduate Acting Program for fifteen years and currently teaches master classes at various universities and colleges throughout the country.

RR: Who has been most influential in how you teach?

OD: First, the students.

From watching Peter Kass—his clarity, his commitment, his originality. How he presented the information and the way in which he conducted a class. It could change wildly from one day to the next. I saw how engaged he was with the students. It was Peter who got me involved at New York University.

RR: Have you changed the way in which you teach acting?

OD: Yes, I have. My acting has gone through a number of changes, and all of those changes have informed me. My experiences have definitely influenced my teaching. The initial effort was to have a craft that I could depend upon, skills that I could own. A craft and skills are certainly what you care about with young beginning actors. Those who have been working for ten years are looking to deepen their work to handle complex demands.

When I first started out, I taught from having observed other teachers. I began to find my own way and understand the students have to be able walk away from you. They have to figure out how to take total responsibility for their work. The effort for me is to look at who is in front of me and adjust and shape my approach.

With the older actor it's really important that when you come to the theater, you're really coming to a part of your life. That's it's not only a job—that acting continues to be an opportunity for discovery. Why you're continuing to act becomes more and more an issue as you get older.

Many people who have been in the business for a while find their expectations have been shattered, so the question becomes: Why do you continue? It has to be found, discovered anew. Where do I want to go in my work? What do I want to make of myself? What do I need to do to confront the work?

RR: Why should an actor study the craft of acting?

OD: Some people learn as they go along. That's probably a lot easier in movies than on the stage, because in movies they're able to do things in small sections and there's no audience. Mistakes can be fixed. Many people in film and taped TV haven't studied. Bright, ambitious, self-motivated people really figure out how to do it, learning from those around them. However, if you want make a collaborative process happen every night in a play for several months, it's quite something else.

When I teach, I talk about discipline as something you do for yourself. What works against it is the cynicism and the despair that "the business can evoke."

RR: How should an actor begin to work on a role?

OD: There is no "should." Every actor will change from the way he was taught. Learning is a constant. The process evolves. Sometimes a director says, "I don't want to sit around the table and read the play. Let's get up on our feet." A choice has been made for you.

It's a collaborative experience; you're working with people who have their own concerns, insecurities, and needs. In time you become confident, less adamant that "This is how I work," and become flexible instead of standing rigid. And then, of course, comes the moment when nothing works.

I did a television series. Usually I have a feeling that whatever comes up, however difficult, I'll find my way. Satisfy my expectations. Well, this time I couldn't find a way. I was constantly running ahead of this feeling of failure, of humiliation, and no amount of telling me I was doing really well would satisfy me. There is no process, no rehearsal for the actor in doing sitcoms. Each actor has to find his own way. In a strange way my feelings of failure were liberating, not as devastating as I anticipated.

Ed Asner, who was on the show, kept telling me to come in and have a good time. I wanted to come and do a good piece of work. Learning to tolerate the humiliation actually freed me, made a good time possible, not every day but some. I still feel grateful to him.

When I was young, it was so important for me to lay it all out: I'd map out the structure of a part. I'd lay out the "bones." I'd ask. I'd get the information and become a "good spy." I became a good plumber, fitting one pipe into another one. Eventually turning on the water.

RR: Do you place an emphasis on the actor understanding the playwright and the world of the play?

OD: Yes, I do. However, I'm aware that that kind of information is not going to be helpful for all actors, some of whom will find that the larger picture is too overwhelming, and they become lost. I absolutely need to understand why someone wrote a play. I work my way to that answer through all the questions that present themselves, each answer opening up to more questions.

RR: How important is imagination in the actor's work?

OD: There are roles you feel unable to play, moments for which you have no reference, so you have to imagine what might be. What's needed is a willingness to go to that place. Peter [Kass] once remarked that he believed we have felt every strong feeling, reasonable or unreasonable, by the time we are thirteen years old: love, murder, altruism, hate, revenge—it's all there, waiting to be tapped. Some actors want to tap into this well; others prefer to imagine, to play "as if."

RR: How valuable is your unique presence to the work that is actually occurring in the classroom?

OD: First we have to define what my "unique presence" might be. I've taught, directed, produced eight shows in eight weeks, performed on TV, film, Broadway, Off-Broadway, regional theater, ran a theater for almost twenty years, have three children, been married for forty-three years.

I went toward what I needed, wanted. To be alive, fully engaged. I'm grateful to the theater that it exists, that transformation is a possibility. I started three theaters, the last of which lasted for nineteen years. I was aware how important the theater was to the community, that it mattered to people, that they wanted to come and be a part of it.

This piece by García Lorca hung next to my desk at the theater:
> The poem,
> the song,
> the picture,
> is only water drawn from the well of the people,
> and it should be given back to them
> in a cup of beauty
> so that they may drink
> and in drinking
> understand themselves.

It's been gratifying for me to see the young people whom I taught make a living and do good work as actors or as playwrights or as directors. I'm always moved by that and I've taken the opportunity to work with as many of them as I can, or to hire them as actors or directors on a project I was working on. There's a real satisfaction.

ALEXANDRA GERSTEN-VASSILAROS

Ms. Gersten-Vassilaros wrote the play *The Argument* (premiered Off-Broadway at the Vineyard Theatre), *The Airport Play* (Ensemble Studio Theatre's Marathon 2005), *Omnium Gatherum* (finalist for the 2004 Pulitzer Prize for drama, co-written with Theresa Rebeck, premiered at the Actors Theatre of Louisville, produced Off-Broadway, at regional theaters, and internationally), *My Thing of Love* (Broadway, Steppenwolf Theatre Company, Joseph Jefferson Award), *Supple In Combat* (Steppenwolf Theatre), *I Never Told Anyone: A Short Play* (McCarter Theatre and *Mother of Invention* (Steppenwolf Theatre, Williamstown Theatre Festival). As an actress, she appeared on Broadway in *Beautiful Child* (Vineyard Theatre) and at Ensemble Studio Theatre, Second Stage, and Primary Stages. She is a member of The Actors Studio, HB Playwrights Foundation, and PEN.

RR: What drew you to study with Olympia Dukakis and how long did you study with her?

AV: I wanted to go to a school where I might have a chance to be taught by working theater professionals. My mother and Olympia had acted together in *The Breaking Wall* at the St. Mark's Playhouse in New York City in the early sixties. The first time I saw Olympia onstage was unforgettable. She was in *Peer Gynt* at the New York Shakespeare Festival in Central Park. She played many parts, but the character that made an indelible impression on me was the riveting Princess Troll, a lavish, lush, three-breasted half-goddess kind of she-beast, who danced and wiggled in an anything-but-tepid fashion, and when she spoke, ribbons of red silk literally unfurled from her mouth in great airborne arcs of color. This image became emblematic of many of my experiences and memories of Olympia over many years as teacher, mentor, colleague, and friend.

I auditioned for the Graduate Acting Program at NYU and got in. During my second and third year, Olympia taught a marathon acting class, to accommodate her own acting schedule. She was appearing in *Curse of the Starving Class* at the Public Theater, so they invented this exhausting marathon acting class that went from 2:30 in the afternoon until midnight.

RR: What were you hoping to discover about yourself and the craft?

AV: As an aspiring actress, I mistakenly thought acting was more about *performing* than anything else, and I just wanted to be liked too much. My first year at NYU was confounding, mysterious, odd, sleepless, bizarre, psychedelic, demanding, discomforting, and, needless to say, crucifying. If ever I needed a guardian angel to tempt me from the edge, and securely guide me, it was now, and she appeared once again, this time as a supremely wise and knowledgeable she-beast of an acting teacher, with a veritable miner's lamp upon her head, ready to guide us all through the heights and lower depths of graduate acting school.

The first year I learned about trying to expose or reveal myself (so to speak) fearlessly, intimately. In the second year, we would be encouraged to lift out of ourselves and learn to explore character. Olympia let us know that we were not at the mercy of our own history. We learned to play actions, identify character objectives and super-objectives, and in a sort of mathematical and architectural way, develop a solid technique that was enlivening and fun and practical at the same time.

RR: How would you describe what you learned as an actor?

AV: I learned how to challenge myself to make lively choices and to at least try committing to them with gusto. Olympia asked that we search for "good verbs" or specific objectives to pursue. At one point we got a list of two hundred verbs on a single white piece of paper. Olympia asked an actor playing Trofimov in *The Cherry Orchard* what action he was playing, and he said, "I'm trying to convince Anya to leave her entitled life behind and go away with me." Olympia said that to "merely convince" Anya would not be as compelling or as fun to play as "fomenting a revolution within her." Would Trofimov simply ask her to join him and his cause, or could he "conjure her curiosity" or "seduce her with ideals," or could he win his objective by "shaming her entitled lifestyle"?

Olympia was always interested in an actor's originality. She was a tireless cheerleader, a "birther," a wisdom-giver. It was her objective to help us all discover all our colors and parts of ourselves we didn't yet know about. "Get out of the small choice,"she'd yell out, "and explore your imagination!"

She had a great exercise using four chairs, with each chair representing a strong emotion: "sad," "glad," "mad," or "bad (devilish)," and, depending upon which chair you were sitting in, you'd have to commit to be unceasingly sad, or insatiably mean, and it really pushed me to explore the extent of how far I could go in one chair before I switched to another, or how interesting it would be to use the "sad" chair when the text seemed to indicate the "glad" chair. I mean, here was a chance to explore extremes and out-of-the-ordinary choices, and it was thrilling. Olympia wasn't concerned with the audience per se. "You're not onstage to be loved," she'd say, "you're there to act and *serve the play*! You have a responsibility to something greater than yourself—the play!"

Her passion was invigorating. Her belief that acting was a way to explore *life* gave meaning to the entire enterprise—an expressive and meaningful way to experience all of life's complications.

RR: How have you been able to apply what you learned in your work?

AV: I worked a lot with Olympia right out of school in plays with her at the Whole Theatre, her theater in Montclair, then on Broadway and Off-Broadway. When I first acted with Olympia, I saw her technique in action and was awed. At one point in George Walker's play *Better Living*, Olympia's character was digging a bomb shelter in the back yard, so Olympia explored being full up to her ankles with mud. Making her first entrance, she laid out a newspaper for every step she took, trying to take care not to muddy up the "house." It was really hilarious. Well, she really is also a hilarious comic. She gave herself over completely to the experience. Some actors would only give themselves boots that had telltale signs of mud on them, and that would be that, but she worked with the idea of mud *thoroughly*. She also had a shovel and a hard hat, also appropriately muddied, so that when she came onstage, her offstage life came with her. She also wore work gloves (more mud) and spent time dealing with taking them on or off. It was like a play within a play, a rare opportunity to see just how far and brilliantly an objective of a character could be pursued. Because of my early training with her, I have a determined desire to explore the aching hearts and embittered humor of all the characters I write or portray.

ANDRÉ DE SHIELDS

André De Shields has established himself as an award-winning actor, director, and educator. He is best known for his showstopping performances in the original Broadway productions of *The Full Monty*, *Play On!*, *Ain't Misbehavin'*, and *The Wiz*. He has distinguished himself in such roles as Graham, the gorilla, in *Prymate*; Henry Drummond in *Inherit the Wind*; Louis Armstrong in *Ambassador Satch*; Vladimir in *Waiting for Godot*; Willy Loman in *Death of a Salesman*; Sheridan Whiteside in *The Man Who Came to Dinner*; Jacob Strand in *Ghosts* (starring Jane Alexander); the Stage Manager in *Our Town*; Makak in *Dream on Monkey Mountain*; and the title role of *Caligula*. Educated at both the University of Wisconsin—Madison (B.A.) and New York University's Gallatin School of Individualized Study (M.A.), he holds doctor of fine arts degrees *honoris causa* from the University of Wisconsin and the State University of New York at Buffalo. He has been honored with his portrait at Broadway's Sardi's Restaurant. Mr. De Shields has served as both distinguished visiting professor and adjunct professor at universities and colleges across America, including Southern Methodist University, Morehouse College, the University of Michigan—Ann Arbor, New York University, and the City University of New York—Hunter College.

RR: Who has been most influential on the way you teach?

AD: As a graduate student at NYU's Gallatin School of Individualized Study, I was fortunate to have been mentored by Professor John Carroll, who introduced me to the fascinating concept of innatism. It is a philosophical construct that argues that we know everything we need to know; we simply do not know that we know it. That concept continues to be the fundamental strategy in my process. It is an unsettling proposition to American students particularly, since when faced with hard questions, they are used to responding with "I don't know," or expect the teacher to provide the answer. That concept continues to be the fundamental strategy in my process.

Professor Michael Dinwiddie, a distinguished member of Gallatin's tenured faculty. His specialty is dramatizing history, and his influence on me was the gift of rigorous research, uncompromising discipline, and unabashed optimism.

James Owings had a profound influence on my entire life since he was my science teacher in grade school nearly fifty years ago. Fearlessness, risk-taking, and relentless inquisitiveness were his lessons for me.

RR: Have you changed the way in which you teach acting?

AD: Yes, I have. As a matter of fact, I no longer consider myself a teacher of acting, but rather as a practitioner of extreme performance. This evolution was substantially informed by my work with Alfred Presser at the Classical Theatre of Harlem. Alfred and I have collaborated on two projects, Derek Walcott's *Dream on Monkey Mountain* and *Caligula*. My principles of extreme performance were developed as a result of my embrace of three major treatises: *Towards a Poor Theatre* by Jerzy Grotowski, *The Theatre and Its Double* by Antonin Artaud, and *The Living Theatre: Art, Exile, and Outrage* by John Tytell.

It has been my experience that students of acting want more than anything to know how they can procure an agent, and thereby achieve stardom. I lose no time in reminding them that there are only two guarantees in this industry, and they certainly are not fame and fortune, but rejection and insecurity. If, when you are hungry, you can make a meal of rejection, and when lonely, a companion of insecurity, then you have acquired the most useful tools of your craft, because, more than anything else, acting is about service. And it is shortsighted to believe that theater is a way of life; it is a way to life. It is a means, not an end, a journey, not a destination—a vehicle for understanding your authentic self and for living the legend that you have written for yourself.

I prefer to answer questions such as: What is the purpose of my life? What are the immutable laws of the universe? How can I be of best service to the most people? How can I quiet my mind so that I might hear my inner voice? What does it mean to reveal one's god self?

RR: Why should an actor study the craft of acting?

AD: Every person, not just those pursuing an acting career, should study the craft of acting in order to appreciate the differences between direct and indirect living. When we live indirectly, we lead a very shallow life, one tyrannized by our rational minds, which constantly tell us we can't, we mustn't, we're not good enough; whereas direct living is a much more visceral approach to life, telling us the opposite: We can; we must; we deserve; we have merit; we are worthy. Life is not cerebral. When we feel shame, love, guilt, envy, hate, anger, rage, joy, reconciliation, the catalyst for those emotions is not in the rational mind, but in the viscera. I teach individuals to get out of their heads and into their guts.

Forty years as a professional actor have provided me a wealth of hands-on opportunities to experiment with systems of exercises and methodology best suited to the notion of extreme performance. My teaching technique is greatly informed by Tom O'Horgan, who in 1969 cast me in the Chicago production of *Hair*, my first professional employment. I spent the early seventies honing my craft with Stuart Gordon and Chicago's Organic Theater Company. Upon coming to New York, I was invited by Ellen Stewart into the world of La Mama, E.T.C. These three giants of experimental theater taught me to embrace crisis. That's the most effective way of exposing both your limits and your capabilities. And this is what I attempt to bring to my relationships with students—an appreciation for the brief moment we have between the two portals that describe life—birth and death. I teach my students to live with responsible abandonment.

The preponderance of my in-class exercises is based on animal work. Because when you look at an animal, many of them don't make a move until they are sure they can have what they want, especially predatory animals. And we are predators. Look at the big cats. They wait, they wait, and then they pounce on their prey. Or, when all else fails, they'll run it down. But it has to be within their reach. Humans have no such limits. If what we desire is not within our reach, we'll devise a way of getting it. Robert Browning: "Oh, that a man's reach should exceed his grasp, or what's a heaven for?" That's what I want to see in my students' commitment to their work.

RR: Do you stress the importance of voice/speech and body work of the actor's instrument?

AD: These elements are essential, if by voice/speech you mean the ability to master the language and an awareness of the many resonators in an individual's anatomy. To be able to effectively convey emotion with timbre and placement of voice speaks volumes about inner discipline. And to possess sufficient stamina to physically support the emotional and mental makeup of a character testifies to the actor's outer discipline. Without both virtues the actor will not be taken seriously, so breathe deeply and proceed gently.

RR: How should an actor begin to work on a role?

AD: Always begin with the question "What do I want?" What the character does will be dictated by the answer to that question. Until that question is answered, do not make a move, regardless of how subtle or nuanced. Stillness and silence are gold in an actor's toolkit. Often more can be communicated by not moving, by not speaking than by being animated and loquacious. If a character moves unnecessarily or too frequently, he/she runs the risk of appearing mundane. On the other hand, if a character is silent or still, he/she puts the audience on notice that when he/she does move or speak, attention must be paid.

RR: Do you place an emphasis on the actor understanding the playwright and the world of the play?

AD: I love language. I love vocabulary. I think words are beautiful. One of the more beautiful words I use is "exegesis." It's borrowed from Bible scholarship, meaning to analyze scripture, but it has been borrowed by dramatic literature. For me, it means to make a deep, thorough, exhaustive analysis of the text. When you do that, you realize the world of the play, the intent of the playwright. The information you glean doesn't always apply to the interpersonal relationships of the characters. But it's always valuable to have the information because every character, no matter how prosaic, is informed by some kind of esoteric knowledge.

RR: How valuable is your unique presence to the work that is actually occurring in the classroom?

AD: Indispensable. Without my presence the work doesn't get done. My unique perspective ensures that I am not heading just another training program, another assembly line for an industry, which unfortunately promulgates the attitude that actors are interchangeable and instantly replaceable. And many of us buy into that way of thinking. My presence is a challenge to do better, to achieve more, to not settle for anything other than excellence, to practice tolerance, acceptance, and inclusion.

Actors deal with the volatile world of desire, and desire has no preference for color, race, creed, gender, nationality, religion, sexual persuasion, disability, age. I want that which reinforces our humanity. What do you want? Once you decide, go about getting it.

I heartily believe that I have made a valuable contribution to the health and continuity of American theater. It is part of my artistic mission to increase the Afrocentric canon of dramatic and musical literature. I have been blessed with opportunities to create characters that have in turn opened doors for other actors of color.

JILL MELANIE WIRTH

Jill Melanie Wirth (formerly Jill Kilter) is an actress, singer, and playwright of one-person, one-act "remedies." She has performed in theater, film, television, concerts, commercials, and voice-overs in Chicago, Los Angeles, New York, and London.

RR: What drew you to work/study with André De Shields and how long were you with him?

JMW: I was directed by André in two productions (*Lempel* by Lonnie Carter and *Lonnie Carter's Greatest Hits*), as well as in two staged readings (*Ira* by Donald Grady and *The Gospel According to Paul* by Michael Dinwiddie) between 1996 and 2000. Also, during that same time Andre invited me to participate in his Black History Month celebrations, for which I wrote and performed three one-person one-acts. So I knew him as an inspiring producer and an "extreme" director.

André's direction in the productions and readings took me to a performance place that I had never experienced before. It had the mind/body/spirit connection. I felt André guided me to become the embodiment of the material . . . it was performance art. André then coached me on musical material from 2001 to 2005. André brilliantly intuits the perfect way to present song and text, always considering the demands of the audience and the material, as well as the abilities of the performer.

RR: What were you hoping to discover about yourself and the craft?

JMW: I knew André as an exciting, innovative performer, and I knew from the *Lempel* audition that working under his direction would be a very unique experience. At the callback there was no "table," and no pictures and resumes in sight. Everyone arrived at Lonnie's home at the same time and we were all in the living room. André gave us material and we worked on it together; it was very much like a rehearsal. After a couple of hours we were served food, and then it was very much like a party.

When I started working with André as a coach, what I expected at our initial coaching session was to block a musical number for musical theater auditions. André began by saying, "If you were on the radio, I would change stations." We concentrated on breathing support to get the best sound. That session inspired me to go back to work with a voice teacher and rethink my approach to singing. That was our first coaching session. He worked with me about a dozen times over the next five years. We called it the "André De Shields Finishing School—Everybody gets in, nobody gets out." I would bring in material that I considered to be performance level, completely rehearsed, and André infused it with form and added finishing touches. It was up to me to fill it in.

RR: How would you describe what you learned as an actor?

JMW: During our sessions together, André would say things that I consider to be pearls of wisdom; I call them André De Shields-isms. Such as: "Burn down the house! Take no prisoners! Start the working process slowly and in a relaxed manner. Don't be in a hurry. One movement leads to the next. Don't ask questions; you already know everything you need to know. There's no such a thing as 'I can't' or 'I don't care.' Make a choice with every cell of your body."

He'd say, "When you make an entrance, what do you want to convey with your walking on? *Be* the coming or going event." I also learned to focus and specifically sculpt my material, and that I must direct myself using my intuition.

"Get out of your comfort zone, get out of your head and into your gut," he'd say. "When perched capriciously on the precipice of the abyss, jump! Take the leap! One of two things will happen. You'll either sprout wings and fly, or the net will be there to catch you. Your effort may not succeed, but it is impossible to fail. The only way to fail is not to jump."

The most profound lesson I've taken away is to allow my intuition to guide actions, so that the greater forces of the universe may be permitted to inhabit the character and embody the material.

RR: How have you been able to apply what you learned in your work?

JMW: It's pretty much in everything theatrical I do: plays, musicals, and my one-person, one-act "remedies." Working with André has made me a better performer. When I truly apply what he encourages, I am working toward a mind/body/spirit connection, and my hope is that the audience experiences a deeper multidimensional performance. I knew I had graduated from the André De Shields Finishing School when I performed material for him and he said, "You don't need me. You can do this on your own. Let's go get something to eat."

STEPHEN MCKINLEY HENDERSON

Mr. Henderson is a member of the LAByrinth Theater Company and The Actors Center and is a Fox Fellow. His Broadway credits include August Wilson's *King Hedley II* and the revival of *Ma Rainey's Black Bottom*. He was also a member of the award-winning ensemble of Mr. Wilson's *Jitney* (Olivier Award). Mr. Henderson played Pontius Pilate in *The Last Days of Judas Iscariot*, directed by Phillip Seymour Hoffman (Public Theater). He is a tenured member of the State University of New York at Buffalo and a former chair of that school's Department of Theatre and Dance.

RR: Who has been most influential in how you teach?

SH: Michael Kahn, Marion Seldes, Harold Scott, William Esper, and Lloyd Richards are the major influences among an army of others who patiently endured me as a student.

When I worked with Michael and Marion, I had no intention of ever teaching acting. I met them both in 1968 when the Juilliard Drama Division was formed. In retrospect, I realize that both of them were major influences on my "taste" as an actor and teacher. Michael's critical eye was most discerning. Marion made you feel that you were exactly where you should be at this time in your growth. The ability to see and dissect the work clearly and also inspire tireless examination is something to which I aspire due to their examples.

I never actually studied acting with Harold Scott, but his rehearsals were master classes. The table work exploring the text is so important, and no one is a better guide through the world of the play than Harold. His work on style, particularly what he refers to as "characterizing the language," gives accessibility and clarity to the classics. Bill Esper introduced me to the work of Sanford Meisner. His unrelenting adherence to actual contact with oneself and one's fellow actors found me at a time when I was in the most need of resurrecting my early love for the craft of acting.

Due to Harold Scott's urging, I took a summer session with Bill in the early nineties. It was the turning point in my life as an actor. I believe it prepared me for my work on the plays of August Wilson with Marion McClinton.

Israel Hicks, the noted director, and J. Michael Miller of The Actors Center led me to work on a Fox Fellowship with Lloyd Richards. Now I am as fulfilled through teaching as I am through acting. That is Lloyd's doing. I now have something that will sustain me for years to come as I pursue the unattainable goal of his example.

It is Lloyd who has most influenced me as a theater person in whatever contribution I am attempting to make.

RR: Have you changed the way in which you teach acting?

SH: Absolutely. Before I tried to get it right. Now I try to get it true.

I want the student to connect to the material, not simply perform it. Not trying to replicate something, but to come in contact with something, discover how it resonates within you.

RR: Why should an actor study the craft of acting?

SH: To be an actor in the largest sense leads you outside your comfort zone. There is a philosophical dimension to the craft. At the first Congress of Actors and Acting Teachers held in 2006, a student wrote in his essay, "Actors are professional human beings." By that I take him to mean that we have trained ourselves to reveal or expose facets of human behavior and motivation. This would require mental and physical preparation. Some teachers, because of their own exceptional attributes, have made a concentrated study of physical theater and lead the student to flexibility, strength, and endurance. Text analysis, phonetics, period dance—all factor into a lifetime of examination and reexamination. Mask work is probably the origin of performance training, and we should all experience that form of expression. All the rituals that led to the language-based art we now practice should be touched upon.

My primary motivation to teach is contained in G.B. Shaw's quote: "Acting is the art of self-revelation." It is that self-revelation that I embrace as a teacher. Character development is not limited to roles. Our personal character is also being developed. We have arrived on the shoulders of the giants who preceded us. It is only right that we should be versed in the steps that led us to our contemporary theater. It's important to see how long we've been trying to have a dialogue about the nature of being human, about how we've been grappling with the same issues as the ancients. Drama says to us: You're not alone, we're all human, and we share great legacies.

My work with Michael Kahn convinced me that silent improvisation is an essential first step in actor training. Bill Esper made me a believer in the foundation exercises of Sanford Meisner. The repetition and independent activity demand true contact and specific use of language while playing an action. As you move into language and character work, improvisations related to specific circumstances in the text are useful. Lloyd often brought everything into focus through paraphrasing. Communication doesn't occur when words are exchanged; communication occurs when meaning is exchanged.

RR: Do you stress the importance of voice/speech and body work of the actor's instrument?

SH: I believe in theater training. If an actor wants to be versatile enough to make a living on the stage for several decades, he has got to master these skills. Physical theater, mime, musical theater—all require discipline and training. The level of craft you attain is in your hands; the level of career you attain often is not. You must measure your success by your craft, not by your career.

RR: How should an actor begin to work on a role?

SH: I will share a way of working with you, but only you can decide if it is of value. I think you should look at the work as a whole first with no singular perspective in mind, if possible. Then look at the function or responsibilities of your character within the arc of the work. Finally, you should put your focus on how every element in the world of the play is experienced from your (the character's) perspective. The director's guidance and your experience of the world taking shape around you should bring you ever closer to the character's experience.

RR: How valuable is your unique presence to the work that is actually occurring in the classroom?

SH: I've got to believe my presence is important. And I say this humbly. I know that when I was in class with Lloyd [Richards], I knew I was in the presence of his entire life in the theater. Only the work can convince you that you're on the right path. The teachers I've had were genuinely there to help me encounter the truth in the work, and that's where I am, and why.

CHRISTOPHER ROBERTS

Mr. Roberts received his MFA at Brooklyn College in 1997, after which he began working as an actor and a teacher. In 2006 he founded SteppingStone Theatre Company, inspired by his time working with Steppenwolf Theatre Company. His first full-length play, *Reflections of a Heart*, was co-produced by SSTC and The Actors Center in New York City, directed by his friend and mentor Stephen McKinley Henderson.

RR: What drew you to study with Stephen McKinley Henderson and how long did you study with him?

CR: I met Stephen in 1991 during my freshman year at the State University of Buffalo. Stephen had a reputation of being the kind of teacher you wanted to study with. I was kind of scared. I came from high school; I did musical theater. It was the first time I was asked to do a dramatic monologue from a play.

When I auditioned for Stephen, I used something by Pablo Neruda. It was totally wrong. Stephen said to me, "Chris, stick around." I did. He was the only African-American teacher in the theater department, and what drew me to him was his spirit. The following year I was able to get into his class; it was highly competitive to get in. I was able to take his basic acting class.

RR: What were you hoping to discover about yourself and the craft?

CR: He was the person you wanted to study with because of his passion for the craft. He would let you have it if you came in with excuses. When I told him I was legally blind, he told me, "You'll have a story that's unique." And that's always followed me. Subsequently, through the exercises we did in class, he introduced me to how to live moment to moment. He put it in a human sense. Stephen made me understand the foundation of "one person interacting off another person." That was his gift as a teacher.

I grew up in a rough part of Brooklyn; my brother is in jail. It could have gone either way for me. We both had the same influences. Only through the higher power, and the people around me, was I was able to latch on to something else. For me, that was the performing arts, that was the theater.

When I went to Buffalo and studied with Stephen, I discovered that the theater is a viable way of life. I had thought I'd go into engineering, but by the end of Stephen's class, I knew I didn't want to do anything else. When I returned to

Brooklyn, I was able to apply what I had learned to my own life. I could sense the very things he had taught us about in class. Things my sister would say and do in her life—how she lived moment to moment. It allowed me to discover a lot more nuances in life.

RR: How would you describe what you learned as an actor?

CR: I had classes for three years, and in 1996, when I graduated, I did some more workshops with him, and I also assistant-directed for him. I learned that I had a great capacity to show my humanity through the craft. I have a lot of friends who are lawyers and doctors, and they are trained to keep their vulnerable side hidden. I know that Stephen taught me it's all right to be vulnerable. That there's strength in that. That there's a craft to be learned. That it's all right to show your vulnerability and to be secure in it. I was the only black student in his class. I felt people didn't know what to make of me. But Stephen said, "Don't worry, let them deal with it. They have to be confronted with your humanity. There's nothing else to be said."

Preconceptions can be shattered. It's about not being afraid to show who you are.

RR: How have you been able to apply what you learned in your work?

CR: I teach acting at the Henry Street Settlement in lower Manhattan. I teach about twenty kids, about six to seventeen years of age. I go into high schools to bring theater to them, teaching the students the basics and fundamentals I learned as an actor from Stephen.

Most recently I was teaching in Spanish Harlem, and there was one kid in particular whom I spent a lot of time with. I had all the students write their own short plays, or short poems. And this kid wrote something really special. His brother had gone off to war and he was scared. He was very frightened. So he shared what he wrote with me. The only problem was, he was a tough guy and you didn't mess with him. I asked him if he would share what he had written with everyone in class. He said, "I can't do that. People will look at me differently." I told him, "They'll look at you and appreciate you differently. This is a story you have to tell. You'll comfort others by having those similar feelings."

After a week of coaxing, he eventually saw it differently. He was a damn good actor, too. This boy came out and read what he had written to the class and it was amazing. We had thought of him one way and he shattered it with his humanity, and that is straight from Stephen. He taught me that it's all about doing it honestly and truthfully. That's the concept I literally live by—no matter where I go, what I do. You have to show your humanity, because it's who you are. To be present in yourself. Not too many people do it—it's sad.

Being blind, you're out there with a stick, testing the ground. As soon as you find solid ground, you're willing to walk ahead. You feel a bump, you stop, you might retreat, you might hold back. It takes a certain amount of bravery to go ahead. You don't know what people will say, but it's worth the travel.

ANNE JACKSON

On Broadway, she has appeared in *Summer and Smoke* (Tony nomination); *Oh Men, Oh Women* (Tony nomination); *Middle of the Night* (Tony nomination); *Lost in Yonkers*; *Major Barbara*; *Rhinoceros*; *LUV*; *Promenade All*; *Waltz of the Toreadors*; and *Twice around the Park*. Off-Broadway: *Nest of the Wood Grouse* (Public Theater), *Café Crown* (Public Theater), *This Property Is Condemned*, *Awake and Sing*, *Tennessee Williams Remembered*, *Down the Garden Path*, *The Madwoman of Chaillot*, and *Mr. Peter's Connection* (Signature Theatre). In London: *The Typist and the Tiger*, *Twice around the Park*. Her film work includes: *So Young and Bad*, *Lovers & Other Strangers*, *The Secret Life of an American Wife*, *The Shining*, *Folks*, and *Man of the Century*. On television she has been seen in: *84 Charing Cross Road*; *Saturday,*

Sunday and Monday; Golda (with Ingrid Bergman); *Baby M; The Rescuers; Law & Order;* and *Inside The Actors Studio.* Ms. Jackson was in Eva Le Gallienne's production of *The Cherry Orchard,* a member of the American Repertory Theatre Company, and a charter member of The Actors Studio.

RR: Who has been most influential in how you teach?

AJ: There wasn't one person; it was a series of steps of learning. The very first influence was an English teacher, Ms. Edwards, in junior high school, who asked me to do a monologue from *Anne of Green Gables.* I had to imagine riding in a carriage and re-create being out in the fresh air. That kind of "sense memory" came naturally to me.

While I was still in high school, I would go to a class at The New School with Herbert Berghof. Early on he gave me a part to read. In the directions it said, "The character bursts into tears." I went to him and told him, "I can't play this."

"Why not?"

"It says this and I'm a comedienne." (I didn't know how to do it; it frightened me.)

He looked at me for a long moment and said, "Oh, I see." He took a pen, crossed out the stage direction, and gave it back to me. That stayed with me. It taught me a very important lesson: Don't anticipate; go moment to moment. He told me I should study full-time and helped get me into the Neighborhood Playhouse on a scholarship.

Sandy Meisner. I was all of eighteen years of age when I got to the Neighborhood Playhouse. Sandy was my first introduction to learning how to act. I thought I could act, but I'd get into trouble because I didn't know what to do. What Sandy really was saying was *listen.* The actor sometimes forgets to, but you can take what you need from your partner.

Very soon I was chosen to perform in *The Cherry Orchard* with Eva Le Gallienne in Margaret Webster's company, the American Repertory Theatre. I learned a lot from that production. Every night, on cue, Eva Le Gallienne would burst into tears; it amazed me.

I worked with Lee Strasberg in his private classes, even before The Actors Studio was founded. I learned about clichés in acting from Lee; he called one's attention to them. He'd ask me, "Why do you look up to think?" That kind of specificity was very important for me. I did a lot of scene work with him.

At one point, when I was doing a scene as Cleopatra, I took the beaded necklace I was wearing and began throwing the beads in every direction, even toward Lee at his feet. I ended the scene and walked out. When I came back, he said, "That was all right." I had surprised him with my imperiousness. I had found Cleopatra's force. It was magical; I knew I had succeeded in what I needed to do.

Elia Kazan. Gadge [Elia Kazan's nickname] used psychological ways to get you going. He'd create an atmosphere of freedom, which was very good to work in.

I also found a lot from Josh Logan. He'd give line readings of the part—but they were helpful, concise, and real to me.

RR: Have you changed the way in which you teach acting?

AJ: A year before Herbert died, he told me I should teach. "I'd like you to try it," he said to me. "If you know to act, you know how to teach." That got through to me, so I thought I could do it. Gradually, I stuck with it.

I respected Uta as a great teacher; she was practically a kind of living force. What she taught got through to the students, and that inspired me. So yes, I've grown as an actress/teacher, and so has my work with the students.

RR: Do you stress the importance of voice/speech and body work of the actor's instrument?

AJ: When I was a young actor I had classes with Martha Graham. I was afraid of her but I loved doing the contractions. The contractions came in handy when I was doing my first film. I had to look through a glass panel at an actress who was holding a baby and the camera has me turn away from the window and burst into tears. I thought to myself: How can I do that? They were shooting it in a close-up. So using the contraction that I had learned from Martha Graham, I stood close against the wall, and slowly allowed my body to move down the wall to the floor and put my hands up to my eyes and started to cry. It came out of the physical behavior and it brought on the emotion. For the actor, it's terribly important to do this kind of work on yourself. It's important to move well.

It's also of vital importance for an actor to speak "the speech I pray you, trippingly on the tongue." My father was Yugoslavian, my mother spoke with a slight Irish brogue. I had hard r's, which I had to learn to get rid of.

I have my students do poetry in class because it gives a sense of language to the student, an emotional expression and joy. They become intoxicated with the language. I want them to have the joy of using poetic language.

RR: How should an actor begin to work on a role?

AJ: First you read the whole play, and get a feeling of what's going on. When I worked with Josh Logan, he told me, "Try and never a leave a pause between when someone speaks and your character speaks. You should be ready to respond."

I worry about actors today. An actor may say, "If I can rent and watch the movie, why do I have to read the play?" I tell them, "It's about how you respond directly to what you read, what it means to you." Within each new play is a new human being an actor can create.

Actors have to have a sense of the influence the writing has on them—to just listen and instinctively hear the play.

When I did *The Cherry Orchard*, I remember sitting in the garden scene with Eva Le Gallienne, with the sense of night coming on, the moon rising, and I'd say my lines as if it's going from dusk into night, and in one line you look up and you see the night . . . it was sheer poetry.

RR: How important is imagination in the actor's work?

AJ: For those of us who were lucky enough to have seen Laurette Taylor in *The Glass Menagerie*, Marlon [Brando] as Stanley in *A Streetcar Named Desire*, or Geraldine Page, Jason Robards, or Kim Stanley onstage—these are outstanding actors who knew how to use their imagination. We remember their expressions in those moments when their imagination released them to go those heights. How painful Jason made O'Neill's *Hughie* in the lobby talking to the night clerk. There was such a sense of loneliness.

And to see performances such as Judith Anderson as Medea, Christopher Plummer as Iago, and then Zoe Caldwell as Medea. To see what they went through, with such integrity, such spontaneity, imagination. They brought you into their world of experience. They knew how to hypnotize an audience—to be one with the author. Julie [Harris] as Joan in *The Lark*—it went beyond tears for me.

What we got to know about was a human being. They owned the part they played. Great acting is living inside the other heart, and these actors were able to bring you into their pain. The playwright brings them to that, and then they bring that to the audience. And that's the joy of acting.

RR: How valuable is your unique presence to the work that is actually occurring in the classroom?

AJ: I learn from them as much as they do from me. I teach acting because it keeps me on my toes. I also learn what not to do.

Acting is about wanting to know what you can do to improve yourself. That's where I take them—a step further.

CHRIS CHIN

> Mr. Chin's theater appearances include Song Liling in *M. Butterfly* (Monterey Mainstage), the world premiere of Tennessee Williams's *The Day on Which a Man Dies* (White Barn Theatre), *In Perpetuity throughout the Universe* (Wellfleet Harbor Actors Theater), *The Manchurian Candidate* with Carrie Snodgrass (West Coast Ensemble), and *Exit the Dragon*, produced by Ming-Na Wen (Berkeley Repertory Theatre). His television includes Dr. Chet Metananda on *One Life to Live* and Larry on *Saved by the Bell*.

RR: What drew you to study with Anne Jackson?

CC: I've been studying with Anne on and off for six years. I went to HB Studio because of what it represents—it was founded by Uta Hagen. What drew me to study with Anne was her no-nonsense approach to the work while being nurturing. I wanted someone who would tell me like it is. I've learned from Anne how to work for truthfulness.

RR: What were you hoping to discover about yourself and the craft?

CC: I hoped to learn about those things that weren't working. Anne is very observant and teaches life lessons in class. I had spent years working in California and I really wanted to get back to focusing on the work; that's what's really important to me as an artist. Anne comes to the work from that perspective.

RR: How would you describe what you learned as an actor?

CC: The most important thing is learning to trust myself when I make a choice. Anne makes you make up your mind to trust yourself. It seems so easy and basic, but it's not. Anne says, "Have the modesty to believe in yourself." She says it often. I'm still working on it.

Acting is an ongoing process for me. She lets me bring in whatever scenes I want to. I tend to work on complex characters; I'm drawn toward them—characters I wouldn't normally be cast as. It's great having that freedom—to work on what inspires me. Sometimes in class she'll critique perhaps four or six scenes; other times she'll spend time on only three scenes because she wants to spend more time on a particular scene. She has amazing insight, and the ideas she offers plant little seeds in my head.

RR: How have you been able to apply what you learned in your work?

CC: One of the most important things she talks about is, "What makes this day different from any other?" and "the moment before." I take that into my auditions and it really helps me in doing the work.

Last season I did *The Rack*, a play about a stockbroker. When the play begins, he's just about to kill himself. Now, I had been working on Hamlet in class, so I was able to use a lot of what Anne had worked on with me in class. Hamlet covers every single emotion, and working on the role is an ongoing challenge. What Anne said about Hamlet's soliloquies I was able to apply to my role in *The Rack*.

I think the biggest thing is about trusting myself; it always comes back to that. Anne drives that point home a lot. It's about basically getting me out of my own way.

AUSTIN PENDLETON

Austin Pendleton is an actor, playwright, director, and teacher of acting. He has appeared on Broadway in *The Diary of Anne Frank*; as Motel, the tailor, in the original production of *Fiddler on the Roof*; *Doubles*; Mike Nichols's revival of *The Little Foxes*; and *Grand Hotel*. He has acted extensively Off- and Off-Off-Broadway, playing title roles in *Hamlet, Richard III, Richard II,* and *Uncle Vanya,* and in regional theaters, as King Lear (Boston's New Repertory Theatre), Vladmir in *Waiting for Godot,* and the Marquis de Sade in *Quills*. As a playwright, his plays include: *Orson's Shadow* (Barrow Street Theatre), *Uncle Bob* (Mint Theater Company, Soho Playhouse), and *Booth* (York Theatre, starring Frank Langella.) He has directed four Broadway shows: *Shelter, The Runner Stumbles, The Little Foxes* (with Elizabeth Taylor), and *Spoils of War* (with Kate Nelligan), which among them garnered eight Tony nominations. He has also directed Off-Broadway and at many regional theaters, beginning with the Williamstown Theatre Festival, where he apprenticed and worked for many years. He is a twenty-year member of the ensemble at Chicago's Steppenwolf Theatre, where he worked on *Love Song* as a director, and *The Sunset Limited* as an actor. He has also acted in about seventy movies, and his television experience includes *Homicide, Oz, Law & Order, Miami Vice, Frazier*, and many others. He teaches acting at the HB Studio in New York City.

RR: Who has been most influential in how you teach?

AP: Uta Hagen and Herbert Berghof and Robert Lewis.

Recently, a playwright I was working with put it into perspective, the way in which Uta approached acting. He said it was like a scientist staring into a microscope and examining what she saw, which is a very good way of putting how she worked. Uta dealt with acting as if it were a very specific set of dynamics, and it's articulated in her two books, especially her second book, *A Challenge for the Actor*. Herbert was more a visionary and articulated what it meant to be a visionary.

Bobby Lewis essentially taught what Uta taught. He had a set of exercises I still use every day. Bobby would say things you'd remember forever: "If acting was crying, my Aunt Rivka would have been Duse!" What it means is that actors get hung up by measuring their emotional truth by how much they cry. Crying is a byproduct; it's not an indicator of acting talent.

RR: Have you changed the way in which you teach acting?

AP: Probably, but gradually over time. Sometimes I've been accused by my students of being accessibly gentle, but I feel you can do a lot of damage if actors are spoken to too bluntly. It's a call you have to make as a teacher. Am I just going to point out what they need to look at in their work? I decide by each individual actor.

RR: Why should an actor study the craft of acting?

AP: Because even very gifted actors can become blocked up, and have to get on the right path. They need a place to work. I do believe that if you go too long without acting, it can get rusty. In my whole life, I really could only point to one actor who didn't do intensive study—George C. Scott. He just knew how to do it. George had an instinct; he could release his talent.

I get too anxious if I go too long without acting. I understand the need to do it. Actors who are talented can get into a rut and develop bad habits. They need to reinvigorate themselves and shake everything loose.

Sometimes I ask my students to use a technique that Bobby Lewis used. He encouraged me, early in the work, to take the time and look at the other actor when I talked. I find it sets people free. I teach that early on in the work. I have also used Uta's exercises.

RR: Do you stress the importance of voice/speech and body work of the actor's instrument?

AP: A lot. I don't teach these things, but we have teachers here at HB Studio. Actors have to work on their voice and speech no matter what. The voice affects everything. I tell that to my students three or four times a class. In terms of the body, I refer them to other teachers. I keep after them; I expect to see improvements in class from their working with these other teachers. In my class, there are students from other countries; some of them are wildly talented, but sometimes I can't understand what they're saying, so I encourage them to work on their speech to be able to do the work so we can understand them.

RR: How should an actor begin to work on a role?

AP: I always say first: Forget the emotional work. Find out everything about the life of the play. It's in the script. If the play refers to different things from your own world, then you have to explore them.

What are the relationships in the play? Can you substitute a relationship of your own—will that help you? You have to learn what the obstacles are. How does the character react to situations? The work must then become emotionally specific, rather than just playing an emotion with a general idea of a person. If you live under the control of the czar, that's specific. That's entirely different from how you live in our society. It's not like the relationship you have with your Uncle Morty if you're living at home. How did the czar treat specific people? These kinds of questions help you play the play. A blanket generalization will make your work very confusing.

RR: How valuable is your unique presence to the work that is actually occurring in the classroom or theater?

AP: Probably any teacher I've studied with has had a very specific energy, and that becomes the channel through which the student receives what's there to receive. I'm there to teach them to act, and you know you're making an impact on the private areas of their life—there's no way to avoid it. An acting teacher has to allow those students before him or her to be as open as possible in expressing themselves.

MOLLY REGAN

Molly Regan has appeared on Broadway in *Stepping Out* and *The Crucible* and Off-Broadway in *Booth; Say Goodnight, Gracie;* and *The Seagull*. Since 1985 she has been a member of the Steppenwolf ensemble in Chicago, where she acts, teaches, and directs. At Steppenwolf, Ms. Regan directed *Pacific*, and her appearances include *Love Song, Maria Arndt, David Copperfield, The Glass Menagerie, Another Time* (Jeff Award), *Three Sisters, Aunt Dan and Lemon, Miss Julie,* and *Cat on a Hot Tin Roof*. She spent nine seasons at the Williamstown Theatre Festival and has worked at the McCarter Theatre, Hartford Stage, and Virginia Stage Company. Her film and television work includes *The Emperor's Club, Pollock, Bullets over Broadway, New York Stories, The Sopranos,* and *Law & Order*. Ms. Regan has appeared as soprano soloist in symphony orchestra performances of Handel's *Messiah* and Fauré's *Requiem*.

RR: What drew you to study with Austin Pendleton and how long did you study with him?

MR: I was drawn to him by his reputation. A friend of mine recommended his technique and scene study class. Coincidentally, I had just seen him in the movie *The Front Page* and had wondered who that terrific actor was hiding in the desk. So when I found out that he taught, I signed up for his class.

I studied with Austin for three years, and I feel I have never stopped. I'm on the phone with him often when I'm working. I've discussed many roles with him; I really consider him my mentor.

RR: What were you hoping to discover about yourself and your craft?

MR: I was looking for a solid technique. I had gone through a famous Midwestern university which had a renowned theater department. I had several different acting teachers there. We'd do exercises or a scene and we'd get feedback that was all appropriate and intelligent, but I felt it was a rather haphazard approach, and I wasn't getting the underpinnings of a technique—something I could use and take with me wherever I went. That's what I got in Austin's class.

And what surprised me most, and only later did I realize this, was that Austin had taught me a lot about how to think as a person as well as an actor. I realize now that I didn't know how to think, how to analyze; I didn't have the ability to look at something and really understand it, not just respond to it emotionally. I wanted the tools to solve problems that I couldn't solve instinctually. Austin has the capability to analyze material in a way that is extraordinarily insightful, original, and specific. He would make a seemingly small observation about circumstance or character that would open up worlds of behavior for the actor. It made me aspire to think that way myself.

Besides being an actor, Austin is also a director and playwright, so he brings a deeper understanding of all the elements of the craft. The combination of all that is extremely rare in a teacher, but it is only useful if he or she has the ability to communicate it as well. Austin respects every student, and when you fail you feel the failure is an opportunity to learn and not a humiliation in front of your classmates.

RR: How would you describe what you learned as an actor?

MR: Basically, I would say that I've been empowered. I have a pretty set routine of approaching a role now: I read the play about ten times and then I start taking notes, gleaning as much purely factual information about the characters and circumstances as I can. I also try to make sure I understand what the play is about, trying to find what my character's place is in it. Then I take everything I know in my head and turn it into behavior.

Austin taught Uta Hagen's object exercises, which I find to be pure gold and use in every single role I do. They are an enormous help in gaining the free imagination grounded with specificity that I need to find in that behavior. I would say Austin disciplined my intellect and freed my imagination with great insight, support, and patience.

RR: How have you been able to apply what you learned in your work?

MR: For the most part, I've learned to solve my own problems, which is what we want to do as actors. In film, and especially television, there's rarely any time to rehearse, and many of the directors are technicians, so I've learned how to take care of myself.

MARIAN SELDES

The daughter of noted author Gilbert Seldes, Marian Seldes began her studies at the Neighborhood Playhouse under the tutelage of Sanford Meisner and Martha Graham. On Broadway she appeared opposite Judith Anderson in *Medea*, followed by *Tower Beyond Tragedy, The High Ground, That Lady, Ondine, Crime & Punishment, The Chalk Garden, A Gift of Time, The Milk Train Doesn't Stop Here Anymore, Tiny Alice, Father's Day* (Tony nomination, Drama Desk Award), *A Delicate Balance* (Tony Award), *Equus, The Merchant, Ivanov* (Drama Desk nomination), and her Guinness World Records performance in *Deathtrap*, which lasted from 1978 until late 1982, without her ever missing a single performance. Off-Broadway: *Tongue of a Bird, Diff'rent, The Ginger Man* (OBIE), *Mercy Street, Isadora Duncan* (OBIE), *Painting Churches, Richard II, Richard III, Gertrude Stein & a Companion, A Bright Room Called Day, Another Time, The Boys from Syracuse* (Encores!), *Dedication or The Stuff of Dreams* (Drama Desk nomination), *Three Tall Women*. Also, at the Williamstown Theatre Festival in *The Royal Family, Dead End*, and *The Matchmaker*. Ms. Seldes began acting in television in 1952 and has appeared in over eighty different series appearances and in such films as *Mona Lisa Smile* and *The Haunting*, as well as in 179 episodes of CBS' Radio Mystery Theater. She has recorded works by Willa Cather, penned a novel, *Time Together*, and her autobiography, *The Bright Lights: A Theatre Life*, as well as articles in the *New York Times*'s Arts & Leisure, Book Review, and Travel sections, plus *Victoria* and *American Theatre* magazines. Ms. Seldes was inducted into the Theatre Hall of Fame in 1996. She taught at The Juilliard School from 1967 until 1991, and in 2002 began teaching at Fordham University.

RR: Who has been most influential in how you teach?

MS: All the teachers I have worked with have influenced the way I teach. Beginning at the Dalton School in New York, and then at the Neighborhood Playhouse. Guthrie McClintic, the famous director, suggested I study there. The work with Sanford Meisner and Martha Graham at the Playhouse was and still is invaluable to me.

My father was a great influence. He was a theater critic, a writer, and all through my early life, until I was on my own, I went to the theater with my family.

And of course, Garson Kanin—I learned from everything he said and wrote and directed.

And John Gielgud. I did three plays with him. His nobility, his sensitivity were unparalleled and I loved him dearly. He directed Robinson Jeffer's *Medea* with Judith Anderson. She was an inspiration to me.

And John Houseman. He chose me to join the Drama Division faculty at Juilliard, where I taught for over twenty years. My students taught me.

I have changed and developed with every decade I have lived. My experiences—in my life and work—inform my teaching.

My whole reason for being an actress has been the written word. What I'm interested in is for the actor to explore the text. To learn how to read a play.

To never stop listening, looking, waking up to new discoveries in his own life. To learn how to use himself. To respond to the other actors.

RR: Why should an actor study the craft of acting?

MS: I was serious about becoming a fine teacher. For a long time I did not admit it. I held teaching in too high a regard to think that I could do it, and among theater people there are endless conversations about how acting can be taught. But an actor needs to sensitize his mind and body as well as his talent. If you are passionate about having a career in the theater and you are given a chance to learn about technique and begin to learn the literature of the theater and its history, it will enrich your life.

RR: Do you place an emphasis on the actor understanding the playwright and the world of the play?

MS: Yes, learn all you can about the playwright and his times.

Every year at Juilliard I directed a Shakespeare play. In the second year, the students would also do a Russian play. I also directed Williams, Wilder, Inge, Hellman, Ibsen, García Lorca. By working on these kinds of plays we learn about history, human behavior. I tell them to go to the theater, to museums, look at paintings and sculpture. Listen to the music of the period.

It is also important to have an understanding of the other actor's world, as well as your own, a perception in the play not only in relation to your part but to the whole enterprise. A caring that is beyond what is written in the script or staged by the director. If this caring does not exist, the space we have come to fill remains empty. The play cannot live.

Martha Graham said, "The unique must be fulfilled." It has to do with transformation, the use of the self. It's like a birth.

RR: How important is imagination in the actor's work?

MS: An actor's imagination is his greatest strength, and his most cherished secret. It's a rare gift to watch a complete actor, to see him transform into another human being right in front of your eyes.

RR: How valuable is your unique presence to the work that is actually occurring in the classroom or theater?

MS: As with so many of these questions I feel it is my students, not I, who can answer them. I know that when Sanford Meisner or Martha Graham was in the room, the world widened for all of us—every time, every day. They changed our lives.

I want to prepare the actor to look for what is real in themselves. That is why one studies. It is what has kept the theater going for over a thousand years.

PATTI LUPONE

Ms. LuPone began her career as a founding member of John Houseman's The Acting Company. Her New York appearances include the revival of *Sweeney Todd* (Tony Award and Drama Desk nominations), *the Demon Barber of Fleet Street* (Tony Award nomination, Drama Desk Award), *Accidental Death of an*

Anarchist, Pal Joey (Encores!), *Anything Goes*, (Drama Desk Award, Tony nomination), *The Old Neighborhood, Evita* (Tony and Drama Desk Awards), *The Robber Bridegroom* (Tony and Drama Desk nominations), and *Patti LuPone on Broadway* (Outer Critics Circle Award). In London, she created the role of Fantine in *Les Misérables* (Olivier Award) and created the role of Norma Desmond in *Sunset Boulevard* (Olivier nomination) and Maria Callas in *Master Class*. Regionally, she starred in *Regina* (Kennedy Center) and *Passion*. Her television work includes *Life Goes On* and *LBJ*. Her latest solo CD, *The Lady with the Torch*, is based on her sold-out Carnegie Hall concert.

RR: What drew you to study with Marian Seldes and how long did you study with her?

PL: When I was at Juilliard, Marian was one of the teachers I had during the four years I was there. I think she started with us in the second year.

RR: What were you hoping to discover about yourself and the craft?

PL: I was just a young, vulnerable, desirous student, not formally trained. I had acted as a child, dancing, singing. I knew I'd end up doing musicals on the Broadway stage. There were various teachers along the way who directed me in a musical or in a play.

My formal training started with the acting I did at Juilliard. It wasn't about me; it was getting a technique. It was about maintaining a career. The fact that I was accepted into Juilliard was a huge surprise to me. It was there that I fell in love with plays and classical works.

RR: How would you describe what you had learned as an actor?

PL: Theatrical armor. A technique—it was about playability—the acceptance of an ability to solve any technical problems on- as well as offstage. I still struggle to understand the intention of a playwright. I was given a solid technique and it allowed me to be able to move within a period or a style in the theater, and adjust to different stages. It could be a ninety-nine-seat house or a five-hundred-seat house.

RR: How have you been able to apply what you learned in your work?

PL: You have to work to apply the craft, to hone the craft; it reveals itself. Every time I go out onstage I have the opportunity to forget it and know it will be there for me. The actor has to trust it. The more I act, the easier it becomes. The technique has grounded me. The problems are solved faster. It's about allowing less personal ego to get in the way, about getting it on and accomplishing the task, and being in an ensemble.

Marian directed me five times at Juilliard; she saw something in me. She protected me and nurtured me. That's what she gave me, and she simply did what she does best. She was incredibly well versed in plays, in books. She gave her knowledge to us and she guided me with what I brought in and buoyed it. I was making discoveries as she directed me; that was new to me.

First thing we did together was *The Jewish Wife*. That's when I broke free; it started in that first play. I knew that I could be directed and I was directed very well by Marian. I could understand and interpret, and when I came to work on Broadway it was with excitement, exuberance. I knew I wouldn't fail, I thought.

She gave me the book *The Craft of Comedy*. It's a most valuable book about the discovery of comedy in a play and the different styles and qualities of comedy.

I thank all of my teachers for the techniques they gave me. It is insurance for a long life in the theater.

PART III
DIRECTORS WHO TEACH ACTING

PHOTO BY MEGAN WANLASS SZALLA

Siti Theatre Company actors

ANNE BOGART

Anne Bogart is the artistic director of SITI Company, which she founded with Japanese director Tadashi Suzuki in 1992. She is the recipient of two OBIE Awards, a Bessie Award, a Guggenheim Fellowship, and a Rockefeller Fellowship and is a professor at Columbia University, where she runs the graduate directing program. Her recent works with SITI include *Death and the Ploughman; A Midsummer Night's Dream; La Dispute; Score; bobrauschenbergamerica; Room; War of the Worlds; Cabin Pressure; The Radio Play; Alice's*

Adventures; Culture of Desire; Bob; Going, Going, Gone; Small Lives/Big Dreams; The Medium; Noel Coward's *Hayfever* and *Private Lives;* August Strindberg's *Miss Julie;* and Charles Mee's *Orestes.* Her other recent productions include *Machinal* (Arena Stage), *Nicholas and Alexandra* (Los Angeles Opera), *Marina: A Captive Spirit* (American Opera Projects), and *Lilith* and *Seven Deadly Sins* (New York City Opera). She is the author of a book of essays entitled *A Director Prepares: Seven Essays on Art and Theater.*

RR: Who has been most influential in how you teach?

AB: Mary Overlie because she introduced me to her magnificent Viewpoints.
Aileen Passoff, who introduced the idea of composition.
Rick Zink because of his rigor and physicality.

RR: Have you changed the way in which you teach acting?

AB: I certainly hope so. I think I've gone from more choreographic principles to an investigation of what is necessary for an actor to do in order to organize energy and imagination.

I stole all the exercises I use while moving around the world and looking at what other people were doing in rehearsal and performance. I'm always trying out new ideas based on things I see or hear about or read. I imitate and then try to innovate from that inspiration.

RR: Why should an actor study the craft of acting?

AB: I don't really think that you need to study for film, but for theater it is a lifetime study. The length of training in a conservatory or grad or undergrad situation does not suffice. Much like a musician or painter or any other kind of artist, one needs to study and train and constantly stay in touch with developments.

Each actor needs to find his own way to begin. Study, free-associate, study, try something out, study, let unconscious movement happen while you sleep, study, be bold, make a choice, and study again.

RR: How important is imagination in the actor's work?

AB: Twenty percent.

RR: How valuable is your unique presence to the work that is actually occurring in the classroom?

AB: I hope to become part of the theater's DNA. Selfishly, though, I cannot direct without teaching. I like what surgeons in the medical arena say: Do one, teach one, study one. That feels like a good ratio to me.

Anyone who is highly present and pays attention with the most discriminating use of his or her faculties is helpful in the classroom or rehearsal hall or theater.

But what's important is to avoid teaching any kind of methodology vis-à-vis the artistic process. It is vital to allow the students to find their own sensibilities and crises.

SAHEEM ALI

Saheem Ali is a native of Kenya, currently studying at Columbia University under Anne Bogart and Brian Kulick.

RR: What drew you to study with Anne Bogart and how long did you study with her?

SA: I had worked at a couple of theaters after my undergraduate studies at Northeastern in Boston. And then I worked with the director Dominique Serrand at Theatre de la Jeune Lune in Minneapolis, and I mentioned to him that I was thinking of going to grad school. He was familiar with Anne's work, that she was at Columbia University—so I applied and interviewed with her in New York City. I was drawn to her personality, her openness, her warmth, her love for the theater, her passion. I read her book, *A Director Prepares*; it's an amazing book. The way she thinks of the theater makes sense to me. After I was accepted into the three-year program at Columbia, I began studying with her. I'm also her assistant.

RR: What were you hoping to discover?

SA: For me, it was an opportunity to be in a lab, to explore what interests me. I didn't know what kind of theater I wanted to make, so I expected her to help me figure out what interested me in basic theater craft. Anne became a mentor for me, a real sounding board.

I really admire Anne as both as an artist and a teacher. She's an incredible human being. When you're with her she gives you 100 percent of her attention. There are few people who give so much.

RR: How would you describe what you've learned?

SA: I was really attracted to Viewpoints. It has to do with an awareness of life onstage as it relates to time and space, the choices an actor makes relative to other people onstage—where you are, how you move, how you interact. It's an incredible ensemble-building tool and it gives actors an awareness of what they're transmitting onstage. Instead of not being a mindful presence onstage, Viewpoints makes the actor completely aware.

It helped me look at what exists in a play, in a scene—and thereby helped me to be more clear about what I want to create. It's also given me a language that I can use to speak to the actors I work with.

RR: How have you been able to apply what you learned in your work?

SA: I'm working on a new project adapted from Gabriel García Márquez's novel, *One Hundred Years of Solitude*. Anne is very big on collaboration, the work between the actor and the director. So what I've tried to do is take the rudimentary tools I've learned and use them in working with the actors in my cast.

Together we've explored *One Hundred Years of Solitude*, and in working together, we've developed a common vocabulary. So that when I use the word "tempo," the actors have a kinetic response and we're able to collaborate together.

What Anne created at Columbia in her first year is that all the actors, the directors, the designers, the dramaturges—are all working together in different combinations every week to create new pieces of theater. It's made it clear to me how valuable Viewpoints is—as a very useful collaborative tool.

ZELDA FICHANDLER

Zelda Fichandler was the co-founder and producing artistic director of Arena Stage in Washington, D.C., and its primary artistic force from 1950 to 1991. She is considered a parent of the regional theater in America. Ms. Fichandler's concern for the development of young actors led her, in 1984, to take on the role of chair of the Graduate Acting Program and master teacher of acting at New York University's Tisch School of the Arts, a position that she continues to fill. From 1991 through 1994, she also served as the artistic director of The Acting Company. She directed many of Arena's productions, including *Mrs. Klein, Uncle Vanya, Three Sisters, Death of a Salesman, An Enemy of the People, Six Characters in Search of an Author,* and *A Doll's House,* as well as the American premieres of *Duck Hunting, The Ascent of Mt. Fuji,* and *Screenplay.* In 2006, she returned to Arena to direct *Awake and Sing!* Arena Stage was the first American theater company—sponsored by the State Department—to tour what was then the Soviet Union. She directed *Inherit the Wind,* which played in Moscow and St. Petersburg in 1973, *After the Fall* (Hong Kong Arts Festival), and *The Crucible* (Jerusalem's Israel Festival). *The Great White Hope, Indians, Moonchildren, Pueblo, A History of the American Film, The Madness of God, Raisin,* and *K2* all started at Arena Stage and moved onto Broadway. Ms. Fichandler has received the National Medal of Arts, Commonwealth Award, Brandeis University's Creative Arts Award, The Acting Company's John Houseman Award, Margo Jones Award, Washingtonian of the Year Award, and the Stage Directors and Choreographer's George Abbott Award. She received the Tony Award in 1976, and she was inducted into the Theatre Hall of Fame, the first artistic leader outside of New York to receive this honor.

RR: Who has been most influential in how you teach?

ZF: Stanislavsky, Michel Chekhov, other directors including Liviu Ciulei and Alan Schneider, other actors, my children and grandchildren, awareness of my own behavior, other teachers in the school, my constant observation of daily life outside the classroom have enriched my teaching process. I also teach through the eye of a director—how to integrate the artful with the natural, shaping behavior into form, allowing form to influence behavior, to achieve a sense of the whole. One has to stay constantly awake to keep alive one's capacity for empathy—the ability to see the world from someone else's point of view. One who teaches has a large responsibility to keep expanding one's awareness.

RR: Have you changed the way in which you teach acting?

ZF: What I teach is more about who I am and what I've come to know about human behavior in my work and in my life. I teach actors through a series of études, or studies of certain aspects of human behavior, which then, being experienced and recognized in class, are transferable to the stage. A half-hour presentation of one's own psychobiography, shown through any artful means of the theater, can reveal to the actor and the class what a character is made of—it's called the "Universe Project."

The students do études on the life that lives in familiar objects; through free association, the object takes one into forgotten areas of memory and wantings. One etude is about the nature of conflict and the ambivalence that lives within every living moment. One about the imagination—how out of the simplest nothing, something can emerge. About speech rooted in the body, not in the vocal cords. These études find a logical sequence. The students use their discoveries through them in other classes, in productions, to come together as a company as they realize what is wonderfully unique in each of them, how we are all alike as members of the same species.

I believe—I hope—that over the years my classes have become more useful in releasing the self of the actor from inhibition and fear (the two great enemies of creativity), toward an appreciation, a respect, for what is special in them and is theirs alone and not duplicated in anyone else.

The ability to play is our healthiest and highest human capacity—a signpost of a healthy ego and a symbol of our released creativity. So I keep looking for ways to make play possible, so everyone's teaching becomes deeper and more effective.

I directed a production of *Awake and Sing!* in Washington, D.C., and was thrilled to see how much I had learned from Joanna Merlin's class in psychological gesture, an aspect of Michael Chekhov's work. My directing, my teaching, have achieved greater clarity over the years at NYU and, at the same time, an easier, less self-conscious spontaneity.

One of the applicants for NYU's Graduate Acting Program wrote in her statement of purpose something very simple that struck me: "I enter another reality and another character, but it's still me, it's always just me!" So while I already knew that and believe I understand it, her statement opened the door in a new way. We keep learning what we already know, only we now know it differently. The process of learning is a spiral spring: we learn, we forget, we learn again more deeply.

RR: Why should an actor study the craft of acting?

ZF: For a few rare people, acting is entirely intuitive and they needn't take it all apart. There's "Ann"—she's been endowed with a responsive body, a relaxed and open voice with great range and color; her imagination is free, brave, associative; she identifies with character easily, almost in a sweep of thought, through clues in the text, or perhaps because the character reminds her of her Aunt Martha, and she and Aunt Martha and their psychological and physical characteristics meld easily. And if there's no Aunt Martha, Ann can look around and find a model in a painting, or in a restaurant or a film or from her rich imagination. She is naïve, with an intuitive sense of truth; the text opens itself to her like a flower and she believes in it instantly. If her character is embarrassed onstage, her physiology responds and she actually blushes! Her will is strong; she makes bold choices and incorporates the unexpected with delight; she can sing like a bird, pick up choreography, whisper and be heard in the balcony; she is kind to all the craftspeople who serve her; she takes direction graciously but also contributes to the process of rehearsal with insights and ideas.

Ann has already ingested the noblest aspiration of the theatrical art and sees the theater as our final form of public communion on the subject of what it means to be human.

But then there are all the not-Anns who need to study the craft. Acting isn't this or that, it is this *and* that—an indissoluble connection of *what* with *how*, content emerging in form and inseparable from it, one not itself without the other.

RR: Do you stress the importance of voice/speech and body work of the actor's instrument?

ZF: We don't have a body, we *are* our body. We say that the eyes are a mirror of the soul, and on the telephone we can hear the mood of that person and a lot about the kind of person he is if we listen closely with our inner ear. A psychiatrist will tell you that what the patient actually says is not as important as his tone of voice or how he sits in his chair. Watch a scene in an airport between two people who speak a foreign language—watch their faces and bodies and hands and listen to their voices and see if you can tell what the scene is about.

From life, we learn the primary importance of voice and body work in the training of character actors.

The actor's voice and body *are* his instrument—his inquiring mind, his imagination, and his visceral desires. These are what he has to give to his character, in the way the particular character needs them, so they must be supple, flexible, variable, not stuck in place in the actor's habitual body/mind. Our program is physically based, following nature's program for all of us.

RR: How should an actor begin to work on a role?

ZF: Hugo Weaving as Judge Brack made this fantastic original gesture in Sydney Theatre Company's production of *Hedda Gabler* at BAM. With his shoe, he flipped Hedda's skirt aside, somewhat playfully, but not really playfully—possessively, in a gesture of ownership or one-upmanship. Several of the Sydney company came to speak to our students, and the student who had recently played Judge Brack in our own production of *Hedda* asked him how that gesture came about. Weaving replied that it had come late in the playing of the piece, out of its own will. What a wonderful example of what the actor hopes for—to enter into the life of a character so deeply that the character has acquired his own, somewhat independent life, and can even surprise the creator with it!

The actor's ultimate goal is to discover the route to this state of being, so the performance never feels stale, and new signals of life keep arising during the run of the play. The route has to be laid out via conscious means, since the unconscious eludes direct access. Appropriate and specific feelings for a moment can't be tapped by just willing them, but through the understanding and experiencing of actions, relationships, wantings, obstacles to be overcome, through props and costumes and the memories of the actor/character.

The actor begins this journey slowly, in a spirit of curiosity, with the simplest of things. As Chekhov would say, "a subject for a short story."

One opens up a script to find out what the story is, where it's taking place, at what point in the playwright's life it was written, what the cultural circumstances are, who the characters are and their relationships to each other, the tone of the play, the song of the language, and so on.

The play has to be read again and again, with a quiet curiosity, letting it come to you as much as going after it. Then comes the archeological dig to discover its birth and heritage, details of its culture, the furniture, music, and customs that define the world of the play. The character's clothes, his walk, his voice, his memories, his past, his dreams for the future, his moment-to-moment thoughts and behavior. Finally, the reactions of the audience tells the actor how they feel about you and what you do. Even a moustache, a beard, or a pair of tight shoes can start the actor on his journey. Or what you keep in the top drawer of the stage desk, which no one knows about except you.

The process is ultimately mysterious, magical, having to do with an act of possession. It is all a form of play. I'll never stop being overwhelmed by the power of the actor to teach us who we are.

RR: How important is imagination in the actor's work?

ZF: Imagination is released by knowledge, not repressed by it. That's why research into the specific culture of a period can be so helpful, or watching how someone in the supermarket actually concentrates on picking tomatoes from a basket or how he behaves when he's late and can't find the keys or how anger is often the mask for hurt, or how Nora is encased by shoes with their high laces and a corset that affects her breathing—how these specific bits of information can release the imagination and allow it to expand, attaching itself to situations and issues of larger and larger possibility. The imaginary life is but another realm of "ordinary" living, and there are many ways to knock on its door.

Reality is very specific—the smallest detail can trigger the largest image in our consciousness.

With imagination we make the world—invent flight, human society, laws, means of destruction, and art.

RR: How valuable is your unique presence to the work that is actually occurring in the classroom?

ZF: We are creatures of nature. Surely artists are. If you're asking me: Do I have my nose in everything? Do all aspects of a theater or a school attract my attention? Do I make myself known—teach, if you will—in an encounter in the hall or at a staff meeting as well as in a classroom? Can I sometimes help an actor, a director or designer, or an entire audience get over the resistances into self-recognition, delight, play, and a spirit of learning something new? The answer is yes. But at the same time, I'm listening and learning.

Actors know far more than they know they know. They've been evolving for millions of years, and the most profound information is already in their bodies for the finding. If you can give them that awareness, that trust in themselves, in their instinctual life, you've taught the first lesson and the most important one.

I do hope I have been able to touch some lives, who will touch other lives, who will touch other lives.

ADAM DANNHEISER

Mr. Dannheiser appeared on Broadway in *Proof, The Tempest,* and *Twelfth Night.* Off-Broadway, he has performed at the Public Theater/NYSF in four of Shakespeare's plays. He toured America in *Contact,* for which he received an Ovation Award nomination. Mr. Dannheiser has worked in several regional houses, including Arena Stage, Yale Rep, and American Repertory Theatre. He has also appeared in several films and television shows.

RR: What drew you to study with Zelda Fichandler and how long did you study with her?

AD: I didn't know it was my path. I had an influential teacher in my undergraduate training who turned me in the direction of studying at New York University. I was unknowledgeable about the program, though. Zelda was the first person I auditioned for. I immediately connected with her; she was so warm. She has a great curiosity about her students. She's so willing to follow you where you want to go in the work.

RR: What were you hoping to discover about yourself and the craft?

AD: I wanted to be a theater actor; I was interested in the classics but I felt woefully underprepared. I was twenty-one when I entered the program. I had a lot to learn about myself as an artist.

RR: How would you describe what you learned as an actor?

AD: I think I gained a real confidence coming out of the program.

RR: How have you been able to apply what you learned in your work?

AD: It was such a joy revisiting her after ten years since I graduated. I worked with her on the production of *Awake and Sing!* at Arena Stage, in February 2006. As a teacher, as a director, Zelda instills such a sense of anything being possible in acting. She wants you to use your imagination to create real, genuine characterizations. To fearlessly immerse yourself in the world of the play. In rehearsal, she would sit back some moments and laugh with abandon and be weeping the next—she craves emotional truth and responds in kind. That's the biggest thing I took away from my time with her—that the imagination is endless when you're approaching a role. She creates a safe environment, which gives you the freedom to explore. It proved to be a very fulfilling journey.

GERALD FREEDMAN

Presently Mr. Freedman is the dean of drama at the North Carolina School of the Arts. He has directed many plays on and Off-Broadway including: *Hair*, *The Gay Life*, *A Time for Singing*, *The Robber Bridegroom*, *The Grand Tour*, *West Side Story* (revival, co-directed with Jerome Robbins), *The Creation of the World and Other Business*, *The Au Pair Man*, *Mrs. Warren's Profession* (Lincoln Center), *The Crucible*, *King Lear* (Roundabout Theatre Company), and *Colette*. Regionally he has directed at the Shakespeare Theater of Washington, Alley Theatre, Yale Rep, and the Old Globe. He served as leading director of the New York Shakespeare Festival (1960 to 1971), the last four years as artistic director; co-artistic director of The Acting Company (1974 to 1977); artistic director of the American Shakespeare Festival (1978 to 1979); and as the artistic director of the Great Lakes Theater Festival (1985 to 1997). He is a member of Kennedy Center Fund for New American Plays. His include College of Fellows of the American Theatre, member; Hal Holbrook Award; Cleveland Arts Prize Special Citation; four Northern Ohio LIVE Awards; three Cleveland Critics Circle Awards; and an OBIE Award. Mr. Freedman has also taught at Yale and Juilliard.

RR: Who has been most influential in how you teach?

GF: Alvina Kraus—she was my first acting teacher and mentor at Northwestern University—and Bobby Lewis.

When I took classes with Alvina, I didn't know anything! As far as I can tell, she was self-taught. She had observed great acting and had worked out what she taught on her own. I'm still teaching some of the techniques she taught. You can look at her influence in the work of Penny Fuller, Tony Roberts, Richard Benjamin, and Paula Prentiss.

Bobby Lewis codified it for me.

What I teach is an American eclectic style, based on Stanislavsky. There have also been other great influences: Harold Clurman was very influential, as was Uta Hagen, Stella Adler, and Lee Strasberg. I was an early member of The Actors Studio, and having been there influenced what I do. They all represented different facets of the Stanislavsky System. It's the same thing, except with different emphases. At the same time, I was doing Broadway musicals and working at the New York Shakespeare Festival. It all influences the way I teach acting.

RR: Have you changed the way in which you teach acting?

GF: I didn't teach acting early on; I was a director. I taught my method of direction; my work was very collaborative with the actor. The actor is my basic material and I have to understand his process to help turn that into the material for the play. My thrust is the play.

How can I use the actor's resources to make the play live? I would direct *School for Scandal* in much the same way I direct Shakespeare and not different from the way I approach a contemporary play. I often quote [John] Gielgud's well-known adage: "Style is knowing what play you're in." Style comes from the author's language and the given circumstances.

RR: Why should an actor study the craft of acting?

GF: You used the key word: "craft." If a person calls himself an actor, and if someone hires you, you've earned the title. But without craft you can't get anywhere. You're at a disadvantage. Having the tools with which to operate, the actor is able to come at the work with a craft. Conservatories of acting weren't necessary seventy or eighty years ago and beyond. There was a network of stock companies where the young actor could work and learn from watching, from being onstage. That's always the best way. But that system disintegrated and professional training programs have taken its place.

The North Carolina School of the Arts is basically a four-year program. It's what I know an actor needs to compete. If you come out of this program, having worked with me, the actors have the tools to begin to work. It still takes many more years to master the tools. Four years of conservatory training isn't enough. The program does include speech and movement and singing. I maintain that these disciplines are each a very important part of acting training. I teach a certain way, a process.

RR: Do you place an emphasis on the actor understanding the playwright and the world of the play?

GF: Yes, the world of the play, but only if helps move you to action. I try to get the actor out of his mind and into his body. Acting is doing, meeting the obstacle. Too often it stays in the mind. An actor can't play a mood. The given circumstances ground the actor, and that includes understanding the period, the clothing the character wears, the cultural influences. Just saying the words will not do it. Understanding all the sources is part of developing your own process of how to work.

RR: How important is imagination in the actor's work?

GF: There's no substitute for belief in the given circumstances. Imaginary play without craft doesn't count for much, and craft without imagination doesn't make a play come alive. I can respond to your talent when you bring it to me. Then I can teach you skill that will help you access it. But that talent is still the mystery, and a glorious mystery, whatever it is.

RR: How valuable is your unique presence to the work that is actually occurring in the classroom?

GF: I'm afraid it's very important. I have a lot of passion when I teach. I think that has a lot of influence in impressing the student with the importance that I lay on skills and truthful acting. I have a dogged critical eye. I give actors a considerable amount of latitude in working out their roles. They have to be willing to communicate and believe. I try and reinforce the work. In a sense, it's my pulpit; I'm actually espousing values and point of view about the essence, about the passion and commitment that art demands. About what comes from the author. If the actor is charged with interpreting the writers, that's a great challenge, and the actor has to match that passion.

I was fortunate to have been able to work with Jerome Robbins as well, who had worked with George Abbott, so I have a lot to share because I was close to the source.

WILLIAM HURT

Mr. Hurt was a member of the Circle Repertory Company. His stage appearances include *My Life* **(OBIE),** *Hamlet, Childe Byron,* **and** *Richard II.* **His film appearances include** *Kiss of the Spider Woman* **(Oscar, best actor),** *Altered States, Eyewitness, Body Heat, The Big Chill, Gorky Park, Children of a Lesser God* **(Oscar nomination),** *Broadcast News* **(Oscar nomination),** *The Accidental Tourist* **(Oscar nomination),** *Michael, I Love You to Death, Alice, Jane Eyre, Lost in Space, A.I. Artificial Intelligence, Dune* **(Sci-Fi Channel miniseries),** *The Village, The King, A History of Violence* **(Oscar nomination),** *The Legend of Sasquatch, Battleground, Nightmares and Dreamscapes,* **and** *Syriana.*

RR: What drew you to study with Gerald Freedman and how long did you study with him?

WH: I was a student at The Juilliard School in 1974 under John Houseman, struggling hard to comprehend some acting terms. It was arduous work. Gerald was a member of the Juilliard teaching staff and was casting a student production he was to direct of the Jacobean drama *The Duchess of Malfi.*

RR: What were you hoping to discover about yourself and the craft?

WH: During the work, he made possible what became for me, at a pivotal moment, the single most important discovery any teacher has ever given me in my life. Two contributions, actually.

The first came during the auditions, when I was attempting to acquire the role of Ferdinand. My audition, selfish and anxiety-ridden, went poorly. But Gerry suggested I help a schoolmate with her audition for the Duchess. We worked on and acted a scene. I realized that in the act of helping her, I had become freed. Gerald was instrumental in helping me see this point of view.

Later, during the first rehearsal, he demonstrated the audacity and generosity I have never seen surpassed in training programs. He did not go the usual way of those school productions, directing its energies toward impressing others with his own talents as a director. Instead, he had the completely unusual and remarkable courage to put the play at our service as theater students. In this quest, he asked, in the pause after the first read-through, "How many people at this table feel they know what an 'action' is?"

Now, we were acting students, putting in many fourteen-hour days, working hard, sacrificing much, and the term "action" is a common one in the training environment. After a somewhat bewildered communal moment, many hands furtively went up in the affirmative.

I saw one of the great opportunities of my life. It had been a matter of great suffering, embarrassment, and frustration to me for a number of years by that time, that after untold hours of exploration, I had no idea whatsoever in the world what an action was—as Stanislavsky, or Michael Chekhov, or Alvina Kraus (all great teachers) meant it to be understood and discovered by students of theater. And it was not for an absence of looking, but from what I thought was an absence of talent on my part. Yet when I was completely frank with myself, I was pretty sure there wasn't anyone else in the school, or maybe in the state, or few even in the country, or perhaps in the world, who really, finally, completely, fully understood that much about this apparently simple but terribly, thrillingly elusive material. Actions are about doing, and what I saw was a lot of people acting like they were doing. Including myself.

I found that Gerald's question to us was asked with real weight. He had thought about it, and he meant it deeply. And it answered my own terribly long-suffered hope that someone would really, truly, sacrifice an appearance of success to help us uncover a great truth.

So I said what I thought. To my still unutterable relief, he did not mock me or naysay my opinion about our ongoing hoaxing of ourselves. Gerald was there to encourage our every tremulous effort to actually extend out over the gangplank, to take the leap into honest artistic risk.

It came to a very sharp point of his telling us that if during the actual performance we found ourselves doubting our own veracity as artists in authentically "playing an action," that we were, in fact, obligated to take stock of that fact and do whatever was necessary, including risking humiliation, to go and find that experience somehow. He meant what he said and I took him, finally, at his word.

In a scene in the second act, with Mandy Patinkin playing Bosola, I was able to calm my mind enough to realize that I was not doing my job. I was not acting, was not playing an action, and knew it, no matter how much work I had done toward that goal! So . . . I stopped, and only found the courage to do that, finally, if briefly, there in front of the terrifying audience of students, teachers, agents, even critics, because I knew Gerald Freedman would back me up, would stand up for me as an acting student trying with all his might to overcome the fear of failure to actually reach for the fearless act.

The pause lengthened as my cue came and went without a response from me. I stood staring at my fellow actor for a while, then looked down at my feet, trying to remember all the notes I had made about actions in the scene, all those laborious but somehow irrelevant hours of intellectual correctness without the audacity to give the ideas . . . life. Actions do that; they are the most important devices of liberation. People started throwing me my line. I stood there. Mandy actually gave me the line onstage, but I didn't say it. Then it started arriving from a number of directions, from the wings . . . I was mute. Finally, someone took the bull by the horns, and urgently spoke the words loudly in full voice from the wings. And, because of Gerald Freedman, I turned and said, shaking very hard, "I know the line. I just don't know how to . . . act."

And there was a pause while I stood there, suddenly free to do my work, instead of anxiously accommodating the expectations of others. In those few seconds, my thoughts, protected by Gerald's commitment, were permitted to go to the honest, and the profound experience of simplicity. I became calmer, found the name of the action I had affixed to that area of the script, considered it, and, very simply, abandoned myself to it on the line. A thousand bricks, as they say, lifted off my shoulders.

RR: How would you describe what you learned?

WH: Well, in that moment, I experienced the single most important event in the course of my artistic discoveries. I didn't act the action as simply and fully again for almost a year, but it was a real beginning, and represented an absolutely phenomenal gift to me from him. His contribution was made completely unselfishly in support of a student discovering his courage. It is what we all seek and so very rarely receive. We are all fallible; all of us tremble. But I know for myself that the kind of wise, courageous support I received from this noble man touched my life with his generosity.

RR: How have you been able to apply what you learned in your work?

WH: I can only say that after forty years of effort, after seventy stage productions and eighty films, I am still being fueled by his fearless, compassionate protection of my right and duty as an artist to seek the truth, not the show, in that time we had together.

How to describe something so elusive as the remarkable spirit of the unprepossessing teacher to the passionate student? I date the beginning of whatever I have done that is courageous to his support in that time. I received from Gerald, and from a few others, all the fuel that has made whatever goodness I have contributed possible.

MICHAEL KAHN

Michael Kahn is the Artistic Director of the Shakespeare Theatre Company in Washington, D.C., and the Richard Rodgers Director of the Drama Division of the Juilliard School, where he has been a leading member of the faculty since its founding in 1968. He is also the founder of the Academy for Classical Acting at The George Washington University. His Broadway and Off-Broadway directing includes: *Showboat* (Tony Award nomination), *War and American Hurrah, Funnyhouse of a Negro, The Rimers of Eldritch, Whodunnit,*

The Death of Bessie Smith, Hedda Gabler, the acclaimed revival of *Cat on a Hot Tin Roof* with Elizabeth Ashley, *Othello,* and *The Night of the Tribades.* His production of *The Oedipus* Plays was performed at the Athens Festival in Greece. Mr. Kahn's regional credits include *Camino Real* (Cincinnati Playhouse in the Park); *Old Times* and *The Tooth of Crime* (Goodman Theatre); *Antony and Cleopatra* with Diana Sands; (Los Angeles' Free Shakespeare in Barnsdall Park); *Long Day's Journey into Night* (Boston's Shubert Theatre with José Ferrer, Kate Reid, and Len Cariou); *'Tis Pity She's a Whore* (American Repertory Theatre); *The Duchess of Malfi* (Guthrie Theater); and *Otabenga* (world premiere, Virginia's Signature Theatre). As artistic director of the American Shakespeare Theatre in Stratford, Connecticut, he directed over twenty productions, including *The Merchant of Venice* with Morris Carnovsky, *Mourning Becomes Electra* with Sada Thompson and Jane Alexander, and *Cat on a Hot Tin Roof* with Elizabeth Ashley. He was the producing director of the McCarter Theatre in Princeton, New Jersey, created the Chautauqua Institution, was the artistic director of The Acting Company (1978 to 1988), and taught at New York University Graduate School of the Arts, the Circle in the Square Theatre School, and Princeton University. His students include: William Hurt, Laura Linney, Harvey Keitel, Val Kilmer, Kevin Kline, Patti LuPone, Kelly McGillis, Christopher Reeve, and Robin Williams. Mr. Kahn's production of *Love's Labour's Lost* was performed in the Royal Shakespeare Company's Complete Works Festival in Stratford-upon-Avon.

RR: Who has been most influential in how you teach?

MK: Michael Howard was one of my teachers at the High School of Performing Arts. And when I left, when I went to college, I continued studying in Michael's private class. I think that Michael, without question, is the most influential person on how I myself worked as an actor, and therefore teach. I also found Lee Strasberg helpful. He was incisive about acting problems. But I also learned from watching Lee that one of the dangers of teaching can be that you feel you have to be omniscient, that you have to show the students that you have the answer to every question. I learned from Lee, negatively, that if I really don't know the answer to that yet, I'll try to find it out for you. In terms of relaxation, given circumstances, moment to moment, Michael was certainly the most influential teacher I had.

RR: Have you changed the way in which you teach acting?

MK: My teaching and my directing have gone hand in hand in my career and they have influenced each other. As a director I bring a real working knowledge of the actor's instrument and acting problems and how to solve them.

The major part of my teaching has been at Juilliard. I taught acting classes for twenty-two years, following Michel Saint-Denis's exercises. His ideas had a direct influence on me. Now, many years later, I teach what I believe is a combination of a lot of practical knowledge.

RR: Why should an actor study the craft of acting?

MK: I think if an actor wants a career for a lifetime, he needs to have a technique to fall back on, when neither youth nor inspiration is present. Acting is a craft and there are tools for that craft. If you want to be able to do a wide range of material or you want to play characters who are not always like yourself, then training is essential.

The Juilliard curriculum was created by Michel Saint-Denis, bringing in many of the ideas that he had, based on his training at his classes at Strasbourg and at the Old Vic. And, we, the faculty and myself, including John Houseman, have continually adapted it, and evolved it for an American style of acting and for modern theater, as it evolves itself for contemporary theater.

It's very important for the actor to have the ability to transform himself into a character. To discover what the character wants and then discover what happens in the rehearsal process. To listen, and to not plan everything.

RR: Do you place an emphasis on the actor understanding the playwright and the world of the play?

MK: Yes. If we choose to do a play, it is our job as actors and directors to understand and bring to life that playwright's vision. If we're not interested in that, we should do another play.

The actor has to understand what's behind the play. If you're doing a play by Ibsen, you have to understand the world of Ibsen, how they lived, how they loved, everything they did. If you're doing August Wilson or Chekhov, you ignore them at your peril. And with Shakespeare you have to know what the issues are about. I'm not a historian, but I need to know about the country in Russia when I'm doing Chekhov.

RR: How important is imagination in the actor's work?

MK: Imagination is essential to the process of acting, of creating something from something else. Of creating a world that's not yours. Of being something you are not. Of living another life. Of having a different physicality. What we can imagine, we can do. What we cannot imagine, I don't believe we can act. If I can't imagine what someone else's life is like, I can't play it. If I can't imagine an animal, I can't be it. If I can't imagine why I might have to act in this style, I can't do it. It can't all be from my own personal experience. If I only act from my own personal experience, I limit myself hugely.

My own personal experience will inform that ways I look at things. And if I can't imagine other circumstances, other emotions, other relationships, my acting will be so limited that I can only play myself.

RR: How valuable is your unique presence to the work that is actually occurring in the classroom?

MK: It's a very personal thing. It's a leap of faith for a student to trust you, and not all teachers are the right teacher for the every student and vice versa. I don't believe I have a specific method.

I find when students have too much respect for you, they can abdicate their own responsibility and expect you to do the work, to be an oracle. I work hard for that not to be the case by being as honest and as human, and as humorous, in addition as being as clear, as I know how to be. I expect them to rise to their greatest potential because they expect to be actors.

This is a difficult profession, and if you're not willing to challenge yourself, I wonder whether this is what you should be doing.

The theater is an ephemeral art and all of our work is ephemeral. Of course, we hope our work has some meaning somewhere, and I take some pleasure in seeing my students grow and enter and work in the profession. I'm always challenged by my students. I try to live in the moment. I'm not always successful but I try.

LAURA LINNEY

Laura Linney is the recipient of two Tony Award nominations, two Academy Award nominations, and two Emmy Awards. She has appeared in numerous Broadway productions, including *Six Degrees of Separation*, *Honour*, *The Crucible*, and *Sight Unseen*. Her many film and television appearances include *Primal Fear*, *Absolute Power*, *The Truman Show*, *The Life of David Gale*, *The Laramie Project*, *Mystic River*, *P.S.*, *Kinsey*, *The Exorcism of Emily Rose*, *You Can Count On Me*, *Jindabyne*, *Man of the Year*, *The Nanny Diaries*, *Tales of the City*, *More Tales of the City*, and *Further Tales of the City*.

RR: What drew you to study with Michael Kahn and how long did you study with him?

LL: I was lucky enough to attend Juilliard, and Michael was head of the acting program while I was there. I studied with him for two years. We were only suppose to have class with him for one year . . . but my class squeezed him for an extra year, so I was lucky to have gotten some extra time with him.

RR: What were you hoping to discover about yourself and the craft?

LL: I wanted to learn . . . how to demystify it all, I guess. I wanted to learn how to go beyond just instinct. I wanted to learn how to listen to the plays more. How to let the material tell you what to do. And Michael was a legend at Juilliard. We all were so excited to finally make it to his class. He is wickedly funny. My first scene for him was the "gentleman caller" scene from *Glass Menagerie,* which I did very badly. And Michael let me know in no uncertain terms that I had a long way to go to do that scene any justice at all. And he was right.

RR: When you left the class, how would you describe what you learned as an actor?

LL: I'm still learning from Michael's class. One of the many great things he taught me was not to skip steps. Not to get ahead of myself. Which relates to everything, from text analysis to active thought to blocking to physical action. Whenever I am stuck or frustrated with work, regardless of the medium, the first thing I ask myself is: What have I missed? And I will slowly track through the scene or the act or the sequence and ask myself "Why?" until every why has been answered. He taught me how to personalize everything without getting in my own way and how to make the choices that will feed the story first.

RR: How have you been able to apply what you learned in your work?

LL: I have this fantastic diary that I kept while I was at Juilliard, which is filled with notes and observations and comments. I lug it around with me everywhere and still refer to it. Great teaching is timeless. Great advice can be applied to so many different situations. And it is always the basics that always helps the most: Make strong choices, don't be afraid, listen, trust the play, serve the play, be specific, behavior is always more interesting than text.

THEODORE MANN

Theodore Mann co-founded Circle in the Square Theatre with José Quintero in 1951. He has presented over two hundred productions, including Tennessee Williams's *Summer and Smoke* with Geraldine Page, which is recognized today as being responsible for the birth of the Off-Broadway theater movement. He also produced *The Iceman Cometh*, the American premiere of *Long Day's Journey into Night*, and *The Balcony*. Mr. Mann founded the Circle in the Square Theatre School in 1961. He directed *Mourning Becomes Electra* with Colleen Dewhurst; *The Iceman Cometh* with James Earl Jones; *A Moon for the Misbegotten* with Salome Jens; *Ah, Wilderness!* with Geraldine Fitzgerald; *The Glass Menagerie* with Maureen Stapleton and Rip Torn; *The Night of the Iguana* with Jane Alexander; *John and Abigail* with Salome Jens; *Pal Joey, Romeo and Juliet, The Boys in Autumn* with George C. Scott and John Cullum; *Where's Charley?* with Raul Julia; and *Awake and Sing!* He also directed New York City Opera's *The Turn of the Screw, La Bohemia* for The Juilliard School, and *The Night of the Iguana* for Moscow's Maly Theatre. Mr. Mann received the 1999 Tao House Award from the Eugene O'Neill Foundation for his distinguished career in theater and for championing the works of O'Neill.

RR: Who has been most influential in how you teach?

TM: When I teach, I do it from the experience of directing actors. When I directed Al Pacino in a workshop of *Hughie,* I saw how he used his skills for depth and train of thought and focus. With George C. Scott, he said that his creativity was at its height for only the first three hours of rehearsal. Anything after that you're treading water. When I was working on *Boys of Autumn* with George and John Cullum, we'd rehearse for three hours, go away, have these ideas during the night, come back, and rehearse again, and the work would be absolutely truthful.

As far as I know, George never studied outside of college. He was a natural, but he worked like a Method actor. In *Boys of Autumn*, there was a scene where he recalls a lady he was in love with, and his eyes would fill up every single night during performance. He had the technique to do it. It was a genuine experience he went through. After the show closed, I asked him what he used to create that moment. He told me that there had been a young woman in his early life.

I have learned to say less to the actor. To allow them the space to create.

RR: Why should an actor study the craft of acting?

TM: Everything an actor learns is a building block to a complete performance. I'm like a gardener, allowing the actor's work to take shape. The violet needs water, the tulip needs soil, the rose needs sunlight. Without training you can't do eight performances a week and be consistent.

When we started the Circle in the Square Theatre School, I wanted to have an institution rather than disparate classes, to train the actor not only in acting, but in singing, dance, scene study, Shakespeare, combat, mask, mime, movement/clown work, text work, Alexander work, and voice and speech.

RR: How should an actor begin to work on a role?

TM: I think along the lines of Uta Hagen's approach. An actor should study everything he can about the character's time, to know the environment he comes out of, to create a whole life for this human being. You start with seeing the person waking up in the morning. What does he or she do? How does he get dressed, his toiletries, etc.? It's a life you're creating, not your own life.

When Colleen Dewhurst played Christine in *Mourning Becomes Electra*, she worked this way. When the first scene of the play began, she had to convey to the audience the realization that even though her husband was coming home from the Civil War, she no longer loved him; in fact she was in love with another man. This was all conveyed without words. You can't do this kind of work unless you create that kind of life offstage.

RR: How important is imagination in the actor's work?

TM: It's what an actor needs to make the character a human being. It allows the actor to create his or her interpretation. It's an enormous part of the actor's contribution to the role. The audience has to believe they are seeing a real person onstage. There is, of course, research, but then the actor fills in the gaps with his imagination.

You, Ronald, studied with Harold Clurman. As well as you knew him in class, there were still gaps in your knowledge of him that had to be filled by your imagination to allow you to live onstage as this human being.

I've written a fifteen-minute play, *G.C.*, which is George C. Scott's initials. The play is about my experiences working with George. One of the characters is called Ted Mann. I knew exactly what he was thinking. I didn't have to do any of the "detective work" with the character. However, if another actor plays the role, then he'd have to understand the motivations of Ted Mann, and he would have to develop this character through his imagination.

RR: How valuable is your unique presence to the work that is actually occurring in the classroom?

TM: It's a slow creative process on a show for three to four weeks; while in a classroom, it's a much longer period of study. Little by little the actor learns. I put my hands on carefully, gently, not pushing. Like a piece of sculpture, they become solidified. Of course, I need the cooperation of the actor willing to go in that direction in order to achieve the living person.

I have learned that what you do is to share your real life experiences. Every time I work with an actor or a student, I'm growing. It's very enriching.

SALOME JENS

Salome Jens appeared on Broadway in *Far Country, The Disenchanted, A Patriot for Me, A Lie of the Mind*; Off-Broadway in *The Bald Soprano,* José Quintero's production of *The Balcony; Desire under the Elms;* and *A Moon for the Misbegotten* (Chicago Critics Award); and at New Jersey Repertory Company as Sarah Bernhardt in *Memoir*. A charter member of Elia Kazan's Lincoln Center company, she starred in *After the Fall*, *Tartuffe*, *But for Whom Charlie*, *Mary Stuart*, and *Ride Across Lake Constance*; at the Stratford Shakespeare Festival, Connecticut, in *A Winter's Tale*, and *Anthony and Cleopatra*. Her television and film work includes *Tomorrow's Child*, *The Grace Kelly Story*, *Star Trek: Deep Space Nine*, *Just Between Friends*, *Clan of the Cave Bear*, and *I'm Losing You*. For the past six years she has been a visiting associate professor at UCLA's theater department.

RR: When did you work with Theodore Mann and how long were you with him?

SJ: I was directed by Ted in *A Moon for the Misbegotten* in 1962. I played one of the leads in the play; it was a very successful production. It was the first production done of the play where the New York critics finally realized that this was one of the major plays of [Eugene] O'Neill. It was before the famous production with Jason Robards and Colleen Dewhurst on Broadway. We ran at Circle in the Square for about four or five weeks and then toured it around the country.

I was also directed by Ted in *John and Abigail*, which is about John and Abigail Adams. We did it at Washington, D.C.'s, Ford's Theatre; it was very successful.

RR: What were you hoping to discover about yourself and the craft?

SJ: I had been in *The Balcony*, which José Quintero had directed at Circle in the Square, so I had already been familiar with Ted as a director. He produced *The Balcony*, and we ran for two years; it was a huge success. I also replaced Colleen [Dewhurst] in *Desire under the Elms* at Circle. I knew we were doing quality plays.

Ted has absolute taste when it comes to what the theater should be doing. I knew I was involved in a worthy journey, and to take it with Ted was very special. We lived with the play's problems every day and worked at solving them. It was hard work; Ted is a perfectionist. He wants what you do it well; our rehearsals were very intense.

RR: How would you describe what you learned?

SJ: How to work with Ted Mann. He made incredible demands on you, but it was wonderful to fulfill them; I learned a lot. After a run-through, he'd give us notes, then we'd do another run-through—then there were more notes. By the end of the day I was exhausted. But it was a real collaboration; we learned together. Ted allowed me the space to find my way—I, as the actress; he, as the director. And I learned how great a play *A Moon for the Misbegotten* was.

RR: How have you been able to apply what you learned in your work?

SJ: Working on *John and Abigail* in Washington, we visited the Adams's house and saw where they were born. Ted made sure we were fully inspired as to who they were. Their letters to each other also inspired me. We had a lovely thing that had never happened before for me—the director and the cast researched together in a true and real way.

Through the research I realized how extraordinary and divinely inspired those who went through the Revolution were. I could feel the sense of the adversity against them, getting through the winters, the epidemics—they were warriors. Abigail Adams was extraordinary—taking care of the farm, their children. They worked as a team, neither more important than the other. I felt such an enormous sense of their love.

From working with Ted, I felt that I could handle the big roles. And it added to my becoming a member of The Actors Studio. I had a craft to fulfill the play and to truly do something together that was important.

LLOYD RICHARDS

Lloyd Richards was represented on Broadway as the director of *Seven Guitars*, his sixth collaboration with playwright August Wilson. Mr. Richards received Tony nominations as best director for three of these plays and received the Tony Award for *Fences* in 1987. The CBS production of *The Piano Lesson* received eight Emmy nominations, including one for outstanding individual achievement in directing for Mr. Richards. His other TV directing credits include *Roots: The Next Generation* and American Playhouse's *Medal of Honor Rag.* He began as a drama instructor at New York University School of the Arts and Hunter College. Later, he became director of the National Playwrights Conference at the Eugene O'Neill Theater Center, dean of the prestigious Yale School of Drama, and artistic director of the Yale Repertory Theatre. It was in these capacities that Mr. Richards influenced the careers of many playwrights and actors. He was a professor emeritus at the Yale School of Drama and taught at The Actors Center in New York City. Mr. Richards was inducted into the Theatre Hall of Fame and received the National Medal of Arts.

RR: Who has been most influential in how you teach?

LR: I studied with Paul Mann. He was an excellent basic teacher. He had directed me in an Off-Broadway show. He liked the way I worked as an actor. So he said, "Come and study with me." Paul's work sprang from the Stanislavsky System. The way he worked was in contention with the Strasberg Method. Strasberg, Stella Adler—they all interpreted Stanislavsky a little differently.

When he permitted me to teach, I taught the basics that I had learned with Paul. I did everything for him; I was his assistant. Other actors would ask me whom I studied with, so I'd bring them to Paul. I didn't have a class of my own. Sidney Poitier and Cecily Tyson were in my group.

RR: Have you changed the way in which you teach acting?

LR: The way I teach hasn't changed, no, not consciously. You learn and grow or you don't. I haven't attempted to teach another way. But I'm sure it has evolved, probably in my interpretation of the work. As any of my students will tell you, I do my own thing.

RR: Why should an actor study the craft of acting?

LR: For the same reason students study the craft of music or carpentry: to be more proficient in your skills. It's good to have someone looking over your shoulder and say, "What about it?" It keeps you on course.

When I teach, I begin with basic exercises at the beginning, and then I move into scene work. I ask myself: What does this young actor need to know in order to fulfill what he's projecting? What tools does he need? We work on them, putting it all together.

RR: Do you stress the importance of voice/speech and body work of the actor's instrument?

LR: Those are the tools. To the extent you're limited with them, you're limited as an actor. I point this out to my students. Sometimes I have very pointedly. Sometimes it depends on where they are in terms of what the next step is—in relationship to what they're working on, and in relationship to the work.

RR: How should an actor begin to work on a role?

LR: By reading the play. Discovering what you understand about the part. What the character is going through. What he or she wants and why. Every character is doing something in relationship to the different characters.

There are certain things I expect to see from the actor: how the character has been affected by the time, by the clothes he or she is wearing. All the things he hears. Actors have to take the time to research their character. What's the music their character listens to? What does he hear in the street, in his life? The visual things he encounters in his daily life, the attitudes of the day. These things all affect how you stand and move. They all become informative in the life of the character. You'll play yourself unless you find the character. Of course, you can use yourself to find the impulses of the character. But it's vital to know what one responds to, all the things we do in the nature of response, how one uses one's senses, and the will to do what you have to do. Actors who have strong personalities sometimes find it impossible to let go. Which, in turn, makes the experience less theater and more of an event because those who are coming want to see the personality, and not necessarily a character.

When I originally cast *A Raisin in the Sun,* it was not an easy play to cast. I don't know how we did it. I must have seen over six hundred people for that play. It wasn't easy to put it together, but we had Sidney Poitier. One thing that occurred, and it was brought to my attention, was the creation of an ensemble in the work. And that is what theater is to me. When I was recognized for that, I considered that a very valuable and special recognition.

RR: Do you place an emphasis on the actor understanding the playwright and the world of the play?

LR: Of course, if something comes up that informs the work, it can become very important. I remember Lorraine [Hansberry] on the very first day of *Raisin,* talking about the history of all the characters in the play to me before we began. It was something I had gone over with Lorraine. So I put it together, and when I was finished speaking, at the break, she came to me and told me it wasn't exactly the history of the people as she had seen it, but it was very close. I felt I was thinking as she was thinking.

There's no question that the things in the history of the characters affect their behavior: where they come from, what they had been before the play begins, what has brought them to this point.

RR: How valuable is your unique presence to the work that is actually occurring in the classroom?

LR: It does make a difference. I know that to be so because I'm told that by my students. I think who I am and what I share with them gives them a wider body of experience, things they can understand. What I'm doing as a teacher is I'm constantly looking for a way to "turn the light on" for them, seeking something that is evident when the light finally does go on. A student can say "I understand," but when he truly understands, you can see it when it happens.

Whatever I'm teaching has been going on for a long time; we've all been here already. It's wonderful to see these talented human beings giving themselves over to this very special art.

SIDNEY POITIER

Sidney Poitier appeared in the original production of Lorraine Hansberry's *A Raisin in the Sun* on Broadway, directed by Lloyd Richards, in 1959, and in its Hollywood adaptation. His other films include *Blackboard Jungle, Something of Value* (the first actor of African descent to win a prestigious international film award at the Venice Film Festival), *The Slender Thread, In the Heat of the Night* (the first actor of African descent to win an Academy Award for best actor), *The Defiant Ones, Lillies of the Field, Guess Who's Coming to Dinner, Sneakers,* and *Cry, the Beloved Country.* He appeared in the television docudrama *Mandela and de Klerk* and as Supreme Court Justice Thurgood Marshall in *Separate but Equal.* Knighted by Queen Elizabeth II in 1974, he also received the SAG Life Achievement Award and the Academy of Motion Picture Arts and Sciences Honorary Award for lifetime achievement. He has also served as non-resident Bahamian ambassador to Japan since April 1997 and to the United Nations Educational, Scientific, and Cultural Organization (UNESCO). Mr. Poitier authored *This Life* and *The Measure of a Man: A Spiritual Autobiography.*

RR: What drew you to study with Lloyd Richards and how long did you study with him?

SP: It was Paul Mann and Lloyd Richards together, and it was because they were together. They were both teaching at the Paul Mann Actors Workshop.

RR: What were you hoping to discover about yourself and the craft?

SP: I was actually interested in becoming a member of The Actors Studio, but I was turned down; I was glad to find someplace else to work. I had heard of the Paul Mann Actors Workshop and they both greeted me graciously and warmly when I met with them. They invited me to join them, and were very friendly toward me.

They both were about something that was important to acting, that is, *reflective.* And it threw a certain texture of life onto what I did as an actor. So that the audience was watching life onstage. That was how they spoke about it.

RR: How would you describe what you had learned?

SP: I didn't understand the Stanislavsky System at that time. And what they were doing was trying to create a full actor. So that the actor can find the life behind the words, so that he can express the life of the character completely. This was very exciting for me.

RR: How were you able to apply what you learned when you began performing?

SP: It's always a question of what the life is behind the words. Understanding that gave me the ability to behave, to move about as the character in the life of the play, as this human being. It made a great difference in my work.

And when you look at Lloyd's contribution—where he came from, the work he did in the theatrical community, the work he did on Broadway—he leaves this generation and all generations to come that much richer. There is no question of the deep legacy he has left us. And it has to do with what he was so intent on— creating a *full* actor, and knowing the difference between yourself as the actor and as the character.

LARRY SACHAROW

Mr. Sacharow directed Edward Albee's Pulitzer Prize–winning play *Three Tall Women* (Lucille Lortel Award, Outer Critics Circle Award nomination), as well as *Five of Us* (OBIE award), *Beckett/Albee* (Century Center for the Performing Arts), *Dylan's Line* (McCarter Theatre), *The Golem* (Manhattan Ensemble Theatre), and *The Beard* (La Mama, E.T.C. E.T.C.). He received the Last Frontier Directing Award for lifetime achievement from the Edward Albee Last Frontier Theatre Conference. Mr. Sacharow conceived and directed *The Road Home, Stories of Children of War*, touring nationally, and at Moscow's Taganka. His play, *The Concept*, performed by recovering drug addicts from Daytop Village, played three years Off-Broadway, at the White House, and toured under the auspices of the U.S. State Dept. to the Moscow Art Theatre. Founding Artistic Director of River Arts Repertory in Woodstock, N.Y., he produced two International Festivals at River Arts Summer Festival Theatre in Woodstock, N.Y. He was the Chair of the Theatre Dept. at Fordham University at Lincoln Center, and taught at The Actors Studio, Michael Howard Studio, NYU Graduate Acting, University of Tokyo, Shanghai University & Arts Akademi in India. Mr. Sacharow was working on a stage adaptation of the novel *Mount Analogue* by Rene Daumal, and writing a book: *Modern Theatre/Ancient Sources*, at the time of his death.

RR: Who has been most influential in how you teach?

LS: Jerzy Grotowski, in two different phases of his own development. When the Polish Lab Theatre came to New York City in the late 1960s, they introduced a physical approach to acting that opened up new possibilities for performance and training. Grotowski gave several talks and many of us working in the downtown theater were influenced by his work and ideas in the book, *Towards a Poor Theatre*.

I had the great fortune to connect with him again in the ten years before he died. This last phase of his work was conducted in Pontedera, Italy and involved work with ancient songs and the impact of the songs on the energy of the actor singing. During several trips to Pontedera, and many meetings with Grotowski during this time, I began to internalize an approach to teaching that was inspired by his research. I developed an understanding about the energy in the body, and how that could be worked with to create character. Inspired by this to find a way to work with energy in the body through psychological and physical expression, I began to develop exercises for the actor that would bring character and story telling more vividly into the physical work of the actor in performance.

I also studied with Lee Strasberg in the Directors Unit at The Actors Studio when I was a young director and got a lot out of it from a philosophical and artistic point of view.

RR: Have you changed the way in which you teach acting?

LS: Absolutely. When I first began, what I taught grew out of what I did in the late 1960s and early 1970s. The productions I did during that period influenced my teaching. I had gone on a trip to Europe where I spent two weeks with the Berliner Ensemble, watching the original productions that Brecht had worked on with the actors. I saw Helene Wiegel in *Coriolanus*—it was an enlightening experience. I also traveled to Damascus and met with the Whirling Dervishes.

RR: Why should an actor study the craft of acting?

LS: We expose them to Artaud, Grotowski, and performance art in the first semester, and they create their own solo performance pieces based on personal experiences. There is also a lot of physical work, including yoga and tai chi. I want them to understand ritual theater and expand their vocabulary of what is possible in performance.

RR: Do you stress the importance of voice/speech and body work of the actor's instrument?

LS: I stress a lot of physical work in our training, including yoga, tai chi, and Butoh. Movement work that is about energy and imagination that releases emotion. It gives young actors a kind of plasticity, allowing them to be fluid in their movement. We want them to connect inner life, imagination, and energy to the outer movement of the body. Voice work is also very important.

RR: How should an actor begin to work on a role?

LS: The very first thing an actor should do is enter the imaginary reality of the role. Read all there is to find out about the character, the universe of the play. Look at pictures of the environment. I encourage imaginary expression, letting yourself in your dreams to begin living the imaginary life of the text. As an actor reads the script, images come up as you need them. And you ask: What do they mean? You begin to make connections to the physical life of the character using these images inspired by the text.

STEPHANIE DIMAGGIO

Ms. DiMaggio graduated with honors from the theater department at Fordham University at Lincoln Center. She is currently pursuing her MFA at the NYU/Tisch Graduate Acting Program, class of 2008. Her work has been seen on television and with numerous New York City theaters, as well as regionally with the Williamstown Theatre Festival.

RR: What were you hoping to discover about yourself and the craft?

SD: He was my first real acting teacher; I never studied formally. I did some plays in high school and knew I wanted to study theater.

Larry believed the best classroom is life. In my first acting class, we didn't use any conventional scenes; the entire semester was spent playing theater games and doing psycho-physical exercises. Larry's most admirable quality was that he doesn't separate acting from theater. For him, it was about the art form, the process—never the result.

The more he could get us to be imaginative and creative without judgment, the more it served us.

RR: How would you describe what you learned?

SD: I learned to approach the work for the sake of the work and for what I, as a person, can gain from it, and not to approach it with the end result in mind. That it's about my ability to be open, to be willing to be creative and to push my own body and imagination. That way, the process will be more fulfilling than anything than I ever hoped for other than just thinking "career-wise."

RR: How have you been able to apply what you learned in your work?

SD: When I'm working, if there are things that need to be solved, I look at how many different ways I can approach it. Never ruling anything out along the way and knowing that my body knows the answer. If I can tune into what my body is telling me, it will lead me—then my work will be ten times as exciting.

Larry instilled a sense of wonder in me—always making me aware that there are so many possibilities, to look beyond and broaden my horizon, to look to the ancient sources. It's all there, if I'm just wiling to look beyond.

MEL SHAPIRO

Mel Shapiro is head of the Theater Department at UCLA. A director and play-wright, he was one of the founding members of New York University's Tisch School of the Arts and the head of drama at Carnegie Mellon University. His directing includes the Broadway production of *Two Gentleman of Verona* (Tony and New York Drama Critics Awards); a revival of *Stop the World—I Want to Get Off* with Sammy Davis, Jr.; *Bosoms and Neglect*, the original Off-Broadway production of *The House of Blue Leaves* (New York Drama Critics

Award); and Vaclav Havel's *The Increased Difficulty of Concentration* for Lincoln Center Repertory Theatre (OBIE). Mr. Shapiro is also the author of *The Director's Companion* and *An Actor Performs*.

RR: Who has been most influential in how you teach?

MS: When I was young, I observed many teachers, but I don't know that I emulate any of them; I certainly learned how not to teach. There were those who sort of directed the student, and that's not really teaching acting; there were those who directed by indirection and who were so oblique and obscure as to make a mystery of the whole thing because no one actually understood them; there were those who were fervently dogmatic and whose way was the only way. I've been told I teach more or less by the Socratic method, which is a lot of asking questions, challenging the student to dig more deeply, and to explore more than one side of the moment—to come up with the unexpected answer.

I'm always changing the way I teach. Every five years or so I think I've discovered a better way. This is because I have many questions about myself as a teacher. I keep saying acting is a self-taught art. Then a student says, "If it's self-taught, why am I here?" The truth of the matter is, I can illustrate what an objective is, what an action is, we can do endless exercises, but the actor has to teach himself how to make this a working technique.

But the way one teaches cannot be divorced from the times one is teaching in. Times change, students change. Today students need education more than they need "art" as some lofty thing disconnected from the world we're living in.

They need to read books and newspapers, online news sources about world events—to get actively involved in causes—to think about coping with what's been left to them. I believe in the activist/artist/educator/entertainer—that's where my teaching is today. I find that's where many young people want to be.

RR: Why should an actor study the craft of acting?

MS: Skills come slowly and only with great dedication. Studying acting is a form of apprenticeship. But one must study where there are opportunities for performing. Otherwise, it's like trying to learn how to swim from a book.

RR: Do you stress the importance of voice/speech and body work of the actor's instrument?

MS: When you go to a reading, what are you doing? You're reading. You have to know how to shape a line, phrase it, time it, feel it, give it range and color, and articulate it in any kind of accent or dialect; then you stand a good chance of getting a job, because you are telling the story.

Body work is as important for stamina, flexibility, and strength. Skills in combat, gymnastics, mime, and mask work are essential. A good characterization is expressed by voice, body, and mind.

RR: How should an actor begin to work on a role?

MS: I wrote a book on this. Start by working on the play, not your role. What's the play about? How does this character fit in? Start with the large, then collect the details. And don't be frightened if you're confused about the play, the process, how to start, etc. Everyone is.

RR: Do you place an emphasis on the actor understanding the playwright and the world of the play?

MS: If you have a role in *Threepenny Opera*, ask: When did Brecht and Weill write this? What were the times like then? What issues were they addressing? What was *The Beggar's Opera*, and what's the difference between the two? How is the world similar from John Gay to Brecht to now? How are all three periods relevant? What about poverty, crime, social injustice, con men, and corrupt police? What is all this stuff about alienation? Why are these characters so angry? Do I know people like this? Can I find them? Am I an entertainer or a political mouthpiece or both? And the music, what is the style? How does it make me feel? And this translation, what are the others like? On and on . . . the actor begins with questions, ends up with his own answers. The whole journey is an act of self-education done by researching the facts and marrying your imagination with the author's.

RR: How important is imagination in the actor's work?

MS: Imagination is everything. Without it, without the crying need to utilize and express it, without the extreme degree one has to transform it into playing another person and putting that person on the stage in a completely fictional and unreal setting, there is no actor. Even when the actor is accessing his own life's memories to get to certain emotions, it can't be done without imagination, which becomes a bridge from some internal source to its expression.

RR: How valuable is your unique presence to the work that is actually occurring in the classroom?

MS: I enjoy the collaboration, but the real work happens when I've become invisible and they are doing it: pure ephemera—which is why I love the theater.

LAURA SAN GIACOMO

Laura San Giacomo made her film debut in *sex, lies and videotape* (Palme d'Or Grand Prix, Cannes Film Festival; she also received the New Generation Award from the L.A. Film Critics Association and a Golden Globe nomination) She portrayed Maya Gallo in NBC's *Just Shoot Me* (Golden Globe nomination). Her other film and television work includes *Once Around, Pretty Woman, Under Suspicion, Quigley Down Under, Suicide Kings, A House on the Hill, Sister Mary Explains It All,* and *The Stand.* Off-Broadway and regionally she appeared in *Beirut, Italian American Reconciliation, Wrong Turn at Lungfish, Three Sisters* (McCarter Theatre), *Romeo and Juliet,* and *Crimes of the Heart.*

RR: What drew you to study with Mel Shapiro and how long did you study with him?

LSG: Mel was the head of the drama department at Carnegie Mellon during my first year. I had him as a teacher during my junior and senior year. In my senior year he directed me in *The Greeks.* It was a nine-hour adaptation of all of the Greek plays in modern poetry and prose. It was a fantastic experience. We did it in three nights during the week and then we did all three sections together on the weekend.

RR: What were you hoping to discover about yourself and the craft?

LSG: I was really happy to be able to study acting. I had done a year of liberal arts before I came there. Everyone knew about Mel because of his famous production of *Two Gentlemen of Verona* in Central Park in New York City in the 1970s. There was a very exciting buzz when Mel came. He tipped the whole department on its head and did the most amazing things. He brought in two teachers from Peru, and several of his actor friends were always coming to work with us to teach, direct, and do workshops. It was a very eclectic, vibrant atmosphere.

We were always doing independent projects all the time, in every available space, or in the hall. We'd produce a production at eleven P.M. and work on it for a month. It was an enormously creative outlet for everyone—it took guts, drive, and creativity.

Every day the program started at eight A.M. We'd work all day long and then as part of a tech crew till eleven P.M., then continue rehearsing after that or prepare for class. It was total immersion; the atmosphere created required a great work ethic and stamina. For me personally, it was an idyllic situation.

Mel had tremendous energy and innovation, and we'd pick up on it. We were really proud to be a part of this "new wave." Mel's first productions on the main stage were two shows in rep. We nicknamed the pair of shows "The Pig," because it was such a huge undertaking—two shows at the same time, two casts, two costume crews, two lighting crews, two set crews. Mel jacked it through the roof. It was an all-around amazing, energizing experience.

RR: How would you describe what you learned?

LSG: One thing Mel talked about was, "What's the human event?" I played Iphigenia in *The Greeks,* and he made it clear to me what the human event meant. That she's going through a tragic situation and she accepts it, even while everyone around her is freaking out about it. Certainly when you're nineteen, you experience some major shifts in your life, but nothing like what's going on in *The Greeks.*

Mel was impassioned about us understanding what was happening to the people in the play so we could make the leap as young actors. He stretched us and would draw us into the history of the play so we had a context to grab onto. Mel always emphasized the passion—to do something when you're onstage. To grab the moment and make a damn choice, even if it's wrong.

During rehearsals there was a moment when things weren't going very well, and Mel got up and talked to us. He was giving us "that lecture." It's when everything hasn't quite come full circle, and you're totally off base. So we were getting that lecture and there was a trapdoor open onstage. And Mel was backing up as he was talking and we all screamed for him to stop. He turned around and looked. He then told us, "I've got to tell you all a story." And he laughed, and it broke the "authority figure" director.

"There's a very famous story about a director," he said, "And he had lost the love of his cast and the crew. And as he was speaking to them, they let him back up and he fell in. So I know you really love me because you saved my life!"

That was the kind of relationship we had with him. He was a rock, an authority figure, but you could joke with him, he was accessible. He endeared himself to all of us.

RR: How have you been able to apply what you learned in your work?

LSG: The biggest thing for me is always making the strongest choice I can. It's all about the human event. As a young actor I'd get great feedback from my auditions because I always made strong choices, even if it wasn't what they were looking for.

I've been on the other side of the table in casting a project, and when someone walks in and the room changes, it's an amazing thing. But you can't *make* a room change. You have to be authentic. Because at the end of the day, all you've got is yourself.

I always work to know what the human event is, what it means, and then bring myself as close as I can to it. To be true to myself.

ARTHUR STORCH

Arthur Storch has acted, directed, produced, and taught in a career spanning forty-five years. He has directed Al Pacino in *The Local Stigmatic*, John Savage in *Of Mice and Men*, Geraldine Page in *Clarence*, Alvin Ailey in *Talking to You*, Shelley Winters in *Under the Weather*, Anne Jackson and Eli Wallach in *The Typist and the Tiger*, Hume Cronyn in *Promenade All*, Joanne Woodward in *Hay Fever*, Jack Lemmon in *Tribute*, Alan Alda and Diana

Sands in *The Owl and the Pussycat*, Alan King in *The Impossible Years*, and a national tour with Rudolph Nureyev in *The King and I*. In 1974, Mr. Storch founded Syracuse Stage, where, as producing artistic director, he directed thirty plays ranging from Shakespeare to Beckett, and supervised the production of more than one hundred others. During the same period, 1974 to 1992, he was chairman of Syracuse University's Drama Department. He received the Mayor's Achievement Award and Syracuse University named the Arthur Storch Theatre in his honor.

RR: Who has been most influential in how you teach?

AS: There's no question—Lee Strasberg. I was an actor at The Actors Studio in the early 1960s. I asked Lee for permission to observe the Directors Unit. I don't know what compelled me to ask, but he gave me permission and I watched. After a couple of weeks I thought I'd like to try directing. Lee said, "What makes you think you're a director?"

"Maybe not," I said, "but we'll find out." Well, I found I loved directing and started working on projects. Later, I directed *Talking to You* by William Saroyan, and after the usual trial and tribulation, it was a hit, and overnight I was a recognized director. Stella Adler saw the production, liked its improvisational quality, and invited me to teach for her.

I read everything about directing I could get my hands on. However, I don't believe a director can be created through study, though study is important. It's a calling. You have it or you don't. Lee, Stella, Sandy Meisner, Bobby Lewis, and, of course, Harold Clurman were influential in my work. I was mesmerized by Harold when he spoke. Among many things, I learned techniques to evoke from actors "honest behavior." Yet a director has to have an "eye." I am not talking about a results-oriented approach; rather, how to work with the actor, not by rote, but with respect and the desire to help the actor toward truth—theatrical truth.

RR: Have you changed the way in which you teach acting?

AS: Yes. When I started, there was much intellectual discussion of the play, the character, etc. I have gone through this with directors when I was an actor. In fact, many of them weren't helpful. They confused or irritated me. Intellectual point-making could even be destructive. I now deemphasize intellectual discussion. I pride myself on knowing how to help actors touch their creativity and insight solving the problem of the character.

RR: Why should an actor study the craft of acting?

AS: It's a shortcut. If he works enough, an actor will find his way—hopefully. A good teacher can shorten the process—a creative shortcut.

I am a great believer in the actor becoming self-sufficient. He should have an arsenal of techniques—aside from talent—to solve the problems of character and situation. He should not rely on the director to solve his acting problems.

RR: Do you stress the importance of voice/speech and body work of the actor's instrument?

AS: When I created the Drama Department at Syracuse University, voice, speech, and dance were part of the four-year program. However, in contemporary theater, with its emphasis on naturalism, those abilities are rarely called for and are neglected.

Bobby Lewis, in his production of *My Heart in the Highlands*, which he did for The Group Theatre, had a strong emphasis on voice, speech, and body movement to create a specific style rooted in theatrical truth. I believe times are a-turning. We will see more plays calling for voice and speech.

RR: How should an actor begin to work on a role?

AS: The moment a student actor reads a role, all the television and films he has seen influence him, and he gets conventional ideas and images. In the early readings and rehearsals, the actor must not press too hard for results. A performance level is not required immediately. When the actor tracks too quickly, he is like a trolley car caught on those tracks. Start easily; let intuitions and ideas come. "Float like a butterfly" in the early stages. A human being is a myriad of possibilities. Too often the actor plays too few colors. In life, expressiveness is infinite.

RR: How important is imagination in the actor's work?

AS: To play a king or a killer, a leap of imagination is absolutely necessary. One way to make the leap is to believe that there are traces of all human experience inside us. Even if we can't find it consciously, imagination comes into play. How is character created? Through imagination, intellect, and technique. When you were a child, you knew nothing about technique—you were a king, a murderer, a queen; imagination was the impulse into the character and the situation. The desire to act, that initial impulse, started with imagination.

RR: Do you place an emphasis on the actor understanding the playwright and the world of the play?

AS: Not as much as I did when I first started directing. Of course, I do not neglect it entirely, but I work more with the actor, creating the character, the personal relationships, and the circumstances. I suppose in an ideal world it would be possible to have the actor know everything. But I've learned how to help the actor create a reality rooted in a sense of truth. I tell them, "The audience doesn't know what's going on in your mind." I keep in mind the dichotomy between Lee's work and

Stella's. Stella emphasized working in the given circumstances with your imagination, while Lee's emphasis was to touch the emotional and psychological button within yourself. The actor has to make up the subtext and give a sense of reality; it takes confidence and freedom to do that. The actor should be aware of and use all approaches.

RR: How valuable is your unique presence to the work that is actually occurring in the classroom?

AS: While I'm in class, I feel I'm with comrades who are as devoted as I am. I am not trying to impress those I teach. I believe we're in this together. I'm not a guru. I'm there to share and help them create. But I make no effort to prove myself. I respect them for what they have chosen to do. I try to show them the way—the roads. I'm a "book of knowledge" about the theater, and I hope to inspire them to write new chapters.

I believe I have inspired actors and directors to the discipline and joy of creativity. I established a theater in Syracuse, which not only entertained an audience, but moved them and asked them new questions of self and society. I take pride that students of mine have created theater companies of quality.

JAY RUSSELL

Jay Russell appeared on Broadway in *The Play What I Wrote*, directed by Kenneth Branagh. Off-Broadway, he was seen in the revival of *The Normal Heart* (Public Theater); *Private Jokes, Public Places*; *The Green Heart* (Manhattan Theatre Club); and at the Pearl Theatre. He toured as Lumiere in *Beauty and the Beast* (national tour), in *Applause*, and in *Fully Committed* (Vienna's English Theatre, Austria). His regional work includes leading roles at Cincinnati Playhouse, Repertory Theatre of St. Louis, Actors Theatre of Louisville, Berkshire Theatre Festival, Utah Shakespearean Festival, and Syracuse Stage. Mr. Russell's television work includes *The Sopranos, Law & Order, Spin City*, and *The Jamie Kennedy Experiment*.

RR: What drew you to study with Arthur Storch and how long did you study with him?

JR: When I was in high school, I received a large color postcard from Syracuse University with a picture of Arthur and a quote in large letters, which read "Act Now!" I had applied to other schools, but my gut told me that Arthur's extensive experience as a director and teacher made Syracuse the right school for me.

Every Wednesday afternoon the entire theater department gathered to watch Arthur critique student scene work. He moderated the lab in a way that it was very similar to The Actors Studio. After each scene was presented, the actors had the chance to speak about the choices they had made regarding their work. Then, students and faculty responded with questions and comments. This all culminated with Arthur's critique of the work. I sat and watched every Wednesday for three years, learning a great deal, and participated as an actor a number of times. In my senior year I was fortunate to be accepted into Arthur's Advanced Scene Study class, which was an amazing experience. After graduation, I worked with him again, when he cast me in productions at Syracuse Stage and the Berkshire Theatre Festival.

RR: What were you hoping to discover about yourself and the craft?

JR: I feel I changed as an actor from day one and throughout the four years, thanks in great part to Arthur, as well as many of the faculty, and from my life experiences. The work in Arthur's class in my senior year was definitely the most intense and personal.

I wanted to learn and grow and become a better actor and figure out what I wanted to do next. I was pretty sure I didn't want to go to graduate school. After four years, I really felt ready to work. I hoped to have a chance to do leading roles, and I did.

RR: How would you describe what you learned?

JR: The way Arthur taught and discussed the work in lab as well as in scene study class taught me early on how to ask questions. This really helped develop the way that I work to this day. I like to do a good deal of research and ask a lot of questions, not only of the director and the playwright, but also of myself. Arthur and the other teachers at Syracuse taught us a wide range of skills: voice and speech, movement, sense memory, personalization, text work, and more, which have all become "tools on my belt." I learned what my strengths and weaknesses were, as well as what type of material came easily to me and what material was more difficult.

Actually, Arthur was quite intimidating; he was really a force. Years later, when I came to know him, I found that he is, in fact, quite a gentle person, with an incredible sense of humor.

I've had the great opportunity to coach and teach young actors at various regional theaters (including Syracuse Stage). I love passing on what Arthur taught me.

He said, "Talent is not nearly as important as being *ready to work*. Without tools and the passion to work, you can't get very far."

RR: How have you been able to apply what you learned in your work?

JR: For me, the tools I learned from Arthur, and the other faculty at SU, helped form this tool belt that I have at my disposal with every new job. Often you're thrust into rehearsals with actors and directors who have completely different training, or even no training at all. Sometimes it's a great fit; sometimes it is more of a struggle. The training I received at Syracuse gave me the tools to do my best work in any scenario.

I still hear Arthur's voice in my ear when I'm working on a role. He taught me to be courageous, to take risks in order to be the best actor I can be.

SUGGESTED READING LIST

Adler, Stella. *The Art of Acting*. Edited by Howard Kissel. New York: Applause Theatre & Cinema Book Publishers, 2000.

Adler, Stella. *The Technique of Acting*. With a Foreword by Marlon Brando. New York: Bantam Books, 1988.

Adler, Stella and Barry Paris. *Stella Adler on Ibsen, Strindberg, and Chekhov*. New York: Vintage Books, 2000.

Artaud, Antonin. *The Theatre and Its Double*. Translated by Mary Caroline Richards. New York: Grove Press, 1958.

Ball, William. *A Sense of Direction*. New York: Drama Book Publishers, 1984.

Bartow, Arthur, ed. *Training of the American Actor*. New York: Theatre Communications Group, 2006.

Benedetti, Robert. *The Actor at Work*. Englewood Cliffs, NJ: Prentice-Hall, 1976.

Boal, Augusto. *Games for Actors and Non-Actors*. London: Routledge, 1992.

Bogart, Anne. *A Director Prepares: Seven Essays on Art and Theater*. London: Routledge, 2001.

Boleslavsky, Richard. *Acting: The First Six Lessons*. London: Routledge, 1970.

Brestoff, Richard and Deborah Stevenson. *The Great Acting Teachers and Their Methods*. Lyme, NH: Smith & Kraus, 1995.

Brook, Peter. *The Empty Space*. New York: Touchstone, 1968.

Brook, Peter. *The Open Door*. New York: Random House, 2005.

Bruder, Melissa with Lee Michael Cohn, Madeline Olnek, Nathaniel Pollack, Robert Previto and Scott Zigler. *A Practical Handbook for the Actor*. New York: Random House, 1986.

Cameron, Julia. *The Artist's Way*. New York: Most Tarcher/Putnam Books, 1992.

Carnovsky, Morris with Peter Sander. *The Actor's Eye*. With a Foreword by John Houseman. New York: Performing Arts Journal Publications, 1994.

Chekhov, Michael. *To the Actor on the Technique of Acting*. With a Foreword by Yul Brynner. New York: Harper & Row, 1953.

Chinoy, Helen Krich and Toby Cole, eds. *Actors on Acting*. New York: Crown, 1947.

Chubbuck, Ivana. *The Power of the Actor*. New York: Gotham Books, 2004.

Cohen, Susan Grace. *Bridging the Gap: Student to Professional Actor*. New York: Stage Coach Books, 1994.

Clurman, Harold. *On Directing*, New York: Macmillian, 1972.

Clurman, Harold. *The Collected Works of Harold Clurman*. New York: Applause Theatre & Cinema Book Publishers, 1994.

Clurman, Harold. *The Fervent Years*. New York: Knopf, 1945.

Donnellan, Declan. *The Actor and the Target*. New York: Theatre Communications Group, 2002.

Garfield, David. *The Actors Studio: A Player's Place*. With a Preface by Ellen Burstyn. New York: Macmillian Collier Books, 1984.

Grotowski, Jerzy. *Towards a Poor Theatre*. Edited by Eugenio Barba. London: Methuen, 1976.

Hagen, Uta. *A Challenge to the Actor*. New York: Charles Scribner's Sons, 1991.

Hull, S. Loraine. *Strasberg's Method*. Los Angeles: Hull-Smithers Publishing, 2004.

Katselas, Milton. *Dreams into Action*. Los Angeles: Katselas Productions, 1997.

Kazan, Elia. *A Life*. New York: Knopf, 1980.

Kovens, Ed. *The Method Manual*. New York: Kovens Productions, 2006.

Lewis, Robert. *Advice to the Players*. New York: Stein and Day, 1980.

Lewis, Robert. *Method—or Madness?* New York: Samuel French, 1950.

Linklater, Kristin. *Freeing the Natural Voice*. Rev. ed. New York: Drama Publishers, 2006.

Lloyd, Benjamin. *The Actor's Way*. New York: Allworth Press, 2005.

Meisner, Sanford and Dennis Longwell. *Sanford Meisner on Acting*. New York: Random House, 1987.

Merlin, Joanna. *Auditioning: An Actor-Friendly Guide*. New York: Vintage Books, 2001.

Miller, Arthur. *Timebends*. New York: Grove Press, 1987.

Moore, Sonia. *Training an Actor: The Stanislavsky System in Class*. New York: Penguin Books, 1979.

Morris, Eric. *Being & Doing: A Workbook for Actors*. Los Angeles: Ermor Enterprises, 1998.

Morris, Eric. *Irreverent Acting*. Los Angeles: Ermor Enterprises, 1985.

Morris, Eric with Joan Hotchkiss and Jack Nicholson. *No Acting Please*. Los Angeles: Ermor Enterprises, 1977.

Moss, Larry. *The Intent to Live*. New York: Bantam Books, 2005.

Potter, Nicole. *Movement for Actors*. New York: Allworth Press, 2002.

Richards, Thomas. *At Work with Grotowski on Physical Actions*. London: Routledge, 1995.

Rilke, Rainer Maria. *Letters to a Young Poet*. Translated by M. D. Herter Norton. New York: W.W. Norton, 1996.

Rodenberg, Patsy. *The Actor Speaks*. New York: Palgrave Macmillian, 2000.

Rotté, Joanna. *Acting with Adler*. New York: Limelight, 2000.

Rotté, Joanna. *Scene Change—A Theatre Diary: Prague, Moscow, Leningrad*. New York: Limelight, 1994.

Schreiber, Terry. *Acting: Advanced Techniques for the Actor, Director, and Teacher*. New York: Allworth Press, 2005.

Seldes, Marian. *The Bright Lights*. Boston: Houghton Mifflin, 1978.

Shapiro, Mel. *An Actor Performs.* San Diego: Harcourt Brace College Publishers, 1997.

Shapiro, Mel. *The Director's Companion.* Fort Worth, TX: Harcourt Brace College Publishers, 1988.

Shurin, Sande. *Transformational Acting: A Step Beyond.* New York: Proscenium Publishers, 2002.

Silverberg, Larry. *The Sanford Meisner Approach.* Lyme, NH: Smith and Kraus, 1994.

Smith, Wendy. *Real Life Drama: The Group Theatre and America, 1931–1940.* New York: Grove Press, 1992.

Sonnenberg, Janet. *Dreamwork for Actors.* New York: Routledge, 2003.

Spolin, Viola. *Improvisation for the Theatre.* Evanston, IL: Northwestern University Press, 1963.

Stanislavsky, Constantin. *An Actor Prepares.* London: Routledge, 1989.

Stanislavsky, Constantin. *Building a Character.* Translated by Elizabeth Reynolds Hapgood. New York: Theatre Arts Books, 1961.

Stanislavsky, Constantin. *Creating a Role.* Translated by Elizabeth Reynolds Hapgood. New York: Theatre Arts Books, 1949.

Stanislavsky, Constantin. *My Life in Art.* Translated by Elizabeth Reynolds Hapgood. New York: Theatre Arts, 1948.

Strasberg, John. *Accidentally on Purpose: Reflections on Life, Acting and the Nine Natural Laws of Creativity.* New York: Applause Theatre & Cinema Book Publishers, 1996.

Strasberg, Lee. *A Dream of Passion.* New York: Penguin Books, 1987.

Suzuki, Tadashi. *The Way of Acting.* New York: Theatre Communications Group, 1986.

Wangh, Stephen. *The Acrobat of the Heart.* New York: Vintage Books, 2000.

Wilk, John R. *The Creation of an Ensemble.* Carbondale, IL: Southern Illinois University Press, 1986.

Yakim, Moni and Muriel Broadman. *Creating a Character.* New York: Applause Theatre & Cinema Book Publishers, 1990.

RONALD RAND

An internationally acclaimed actor and playwright, Ronald Rand tours the world performing his solo play *LET IT BE ART! Harold Clurman's Life of Passion* and teaches acting workshops at international festivals, universities, and colleges.

Rand made his Off-Broadway debut in *Julius Caesar* at the Brooklyn Academy of Music with Richard Dreyfuss and George Rose. Many New York appearances followed, including Hamm in *Endgame*, directed by Joseph Chaikin; all three male roles in *Perfect Crime*; Ma Rainey's *Black Bottom*; and *The Servant of Two Masters*. Mr. Rand performed with Marian Seldes, Elizabeth Ashley, Jayne Atkinson, and Rosemary Harris, in a Scheuer Book presentation that he created and co-produced at The Jewish Museum in New York City.

Photographer: Luigi Scorcia, ©2006.

His film and television credits include *The Emperor's Club, Maid in Manhattan, In & Out, Jerky Boys, Another You, Quiz Show, Law & Order, Third Watch*, American Playhouse's *A Marriage—O'Keefe and Steiglitz* (with Jane Alexander & Christopher Plummer), *Homeless* (with Yoko Ono). Mr. Rand has also appeared in all of New York City's soap operas.

His plays have been performed and read around the world, including at Edward Albee's 2006 First Great Plains Theatre Conference; in Athens, Greece; in Tbilisi, Georgia; and Off-Broadway.

A graduate of NYU/Tisch School of the Arts, his mentors include Stella Adler, Jerzy Grotowski, Bobby Lewis, Joseph Chaikin, Richard Schechner, John Strasberg, Sabra Jones, and Harold Clurman. He also studied at London's Royal Academy of Dramatic Art.

He founded *The Soul of the American Actor* in 1995, the only art theatre newspaper in North America today.

LUIGI SCORCIA

Photographer: Luigi Scorcia, ©2006.

Luigi "Babe" Scorcia, known by some as the Kamikaze Paparazzi, is a Brooklyn-born actor, musician, impresario, and photographer. His photographs have been featured in the *Village Voice*, the *New York Post*, and many music magazines. His work has also appeared in the *Miami Herald* Night Life section, *Ocean Drive* magazine, Fort Lauderdale's *Sun Sentinel*, and Fame Night Life with photographer Patrick McMullan.

He is currently working on his second book of photographs of South Beach in the early 1990's.

His photography has been influenced by Phil Bekker, Mick Rock, and David Guggenheim.

His clients have included MTV and Bravo.

Mr. Scorcia is the official photographer for Hollywood's San Gennaro's Feast in Hollywood.

INDEX

Books from Allworth Press

Allworth Press is an imprint of Allworth Communications, Inc. Selected titles are listed below.

The Actor's Way: A Journey of Self-Discovery in Letters
by Benjamin Lloyd (paperback, 5½ × 8½, 224 pages, $16.95)

Acting—Advanced Techniques for the Actor, Director, and Teacher
by Terry Schreiber (paperback, 6 × 9, 256 pages, $19.95)

The Actor Rehearses: What to Do When and Why
by David Hlavsa (paperback, 6 × 9, 224 pages, $18.95)

Clues to Acting Shakespeare, Second Edition
by Wesley Van Tassel (paperback, 6 × 9, 288 pages, $18.95)

Acting Is a Job: Real Life Lessons about the Acting Business
by Jason Pugatch (paperback, 6 × 9, 240 pages, $19.95)

The Actor's Other Career Book: Using Your Chops to Survive and Thrive
by Lisa Mulcahy (paperback, 6 × 9, 224 pages, $19.95)

The Art of Auditioning: Techniques for Television
by Rob Decina (paperback, 6 × 9, 224 pages, $19.95)

Making It on Broadway: Actors' Tales of Climbing to the Top
by David Wiener and Jodie Langel (paperback, 6 × 9, 288 pages, $19.95)

Letters from Backstage: The Adventures of a Touring Stage Actor
by Michael Kostroff (paperback, 6 × 9, 224 pages, $16.95)

Promoting Your Acting Career: A Step-by-Step Guide to Opening the Right Doors, Second Edition
by Glenn Alterman (paperback, 6 × 9, 240 pages, $19.95)

Please write to request our free catalog. To order by credit card, call 1-800-491-2808 or send a check or money order to Allworth Press, 10 East 23rd Street, Suite 510, New York, NY 10010. Include $6 for shipping and handling for the first book ordered and $1 for each additional book. Eleven dollars plus $1 for each additional book if ordering from Canada. New York State residents must add sales tax.

To see our complete catalog on the World Wide Web, or to order online, you can find us at
www.allworth.com.